Brazilian Evangelical Missions in the Arab World

Brazilian Evangelical Missions in the Arab World

History, Culture, Practice, and Theology

Edward L. Smither

☙PICKWICK *Publications* • Eugene, Oregon

BRAZILIAN EVANGELICAL MISSIONS IN THE ARAB WORLD
History, Culture, Practice, and Theology

Copyright © 2012 Edward L. Smither. All rights reserved. Except for brief quotations in critical publications or reviews, no part of this book may be reproduced in any manner without prior written permission from the publisher. Write: Permissions, Wipf and Stock Publishers, 199 W. 8th Ave., Suite 3, Eugene, OR 97401.

Pickwick Publications
An Imprint of Wipf and Stock Publishers
199 W. 8th Ave., Suite 3
Eugene, OR 97401

www.wipfandstock.com

ISBN 13: 978-1-61097-804-0

Cataloging-in-Publication data:

Brazilian evangelical missions in the Arab world : history, culture, practice, and theology / Edward L. Smither.

xii + 272 p. ; 23 cm. —Includes bibliographical references and indexes.

ISBN 13: 978-1-61097-804-0

1. Missions—Brazil. 2. Protestant churches—Brazil. 3. Missions—Arab countries. I. Title.

BV3210 S65 2012

Manufactured in the U.S.A.

To *Brennan, Emma,* and *Eve Smither*:
You are blessed to be a blessing so that all of the families
of the earth will be blessed.

Contents

Acknowledgments | ix
Abbreviations | xi

    Introduction:
    Why Study Brazilian Evangelical Missions in the Arab World? | 1

1 From a Mission Field to a Mission-Sending Base | 19
2 Brazilian Workers in Arab Culture, Part 1 | 64
3 Brazilian Workers in Arab Culture, Part 2 | 110
4 Brazilian Approaches to Mission | 165
5 Toward a Brazilian Theology of Mission | 211

    Conclusion | 240

Appendix A:
Brazilian Transcultural Workers Survey Pool | 243
Appendix B:
Brazilian Transcultural Workers Survey Questions | 248
Appendix C:
Brazilian Mission Leaders Survey Pool | 251
Appendix D:
Brazilian Mission Leaders Survey Questions | 253

Bibliography | 255
Index | 271

Acknowledgments

THIS PROJECT WOULD HAVE not have been possible without the encouragement and help of many people, including:

- My wife Shawn for allowing me the freedom to pursue this dream and for encouraging me in the process.
- My beautiful children, Brennan, Emma, and Eve, who did their best to obey mommy while daddy was in Brazil and other places doing research.
- My research advisor, Prof. CJP (Nelus) Niemandt for his encouragement and direction.
- Dr. Jones Kaleli, my colleague in intercultural studies at Liberty University, who offered helpful feedback and fresh perspectives.
- Dr. Fred Milacci for his insights on qualitative research methods.
- Dr. Emily Heady, director of the Liberty University Graduate Writing Center, who read every word of the manuscript, offered great feedback, and continues to mentor me in writing.
- Cristina Boersma and Barbara Hubbard, Brazilian students at Liberty who read Portuguese for me and provided translations of key works. Muit obrigado!
- Bryan at the Muse Coffee Co. and Rebecca at the Good Cherry Coffee and Tea who let me office on their premises for many days for the price of a cup of coffee.
- David Ruiz of World Evangelical Alliance and COMIBAM who offered great encouragement at the beginning of the project and directed me to the right people in Brazil.

Acknowledgments

- João Mordomo and the CCI-Brasil team for hosting me in Brazil and allowing me to see their work firsthand.
- Daniel Calze for allowing me to visit with him at the PMI office in Curitiba and for a wonderful meal at a churrascaria afterward.
- Valdir Steuernagel for receiving me for a brief yet powerfully insightful visit.
- Silas and Marcia Tostes for giving up a day to show me around the valley of blessing and for sharing the vision of Missão Antioquia while navigating the chaotic São Paulo traffic.
- Robson Ramos for encouraging me in this project from very early on, for receiving me in Balneário-Camboriu and involving me in his ministry, and for becoming a dear friend in the process.
- Marcos Amado for graciously taking time to share profound insights about his journey in mission in the Arab world.
- To the team at Wipf and Stock Publishers for their help in the editorial and publication process.

Mostly, I would like to thank those who cannot be named for welcoming me, for letting me tag along as they ministered, and for allowing me to experience firsthand their stories.

Abbreviations

ABU	Aliança Bíblica Universitária (International Federation of Evangelical Students, Brazil)
AMTB	Associação de Missões Transculturais Brasileiras (Association of Transcultural Missions Agencies)
APMB	Associação de Professores de Missões no Brasil (Association of Brazilian Professors of Mission)
BAM	Business as Mission
CCI-Brasil	Crossover Communications International Brazil
CEPLA	Comisión Evangélica Pentecostal Latinoamericana (Latin American Evangelical Pentecostal Commission)
CLADE	Congreso Latinoamericano de Evangelizacion (Latin American Congress on Evangelization)
COMIBAM	Cooperacíon Misiononera Iberoameriana (Ibero American Missionary Congress)
FTL	Fraternidad Teológica Latinoamerica (Latin American Theological Fellowship)
JMM	Junta de Missões Mundiais da Convenção Batista Brasileira (global missions board, Brazilian Baptist Convention)
LAMP	Language Application Made Practical
OM	Operation Mobilization
PMI	Povos Muçulmanos International (Muslim Peoples International)
PMM	Professional Ministry Model

Introduction
Why Study Brazilian Evangelical Missions in the Arab World?

Introduction

THE EXPLOSION OF THE Christian church in the Global South in the last century has great implications for missions and missionary movements. With David Livingstone and William Carey no longer fitting the profile of the average missionary in the present global church, the so-called younger churches of the Global South have now become sending churches. At the first Latin American Missionary Congress held in Curitiba, Brazil, in 1976, the five hundred delegates affirmed: "We recognize that mission cannot be an isolated department of the life of the church, rather it is an essential part of its essence, because 'the church is a missionary church or it is no church at all.'"[1] At COMIBAM (the Ibero-American Missionary Congress) in São Paulo in 1987, Luis Bush declared, "From a mission field, Latin America has become a mission force."[2] With over five thousand transcultural missionaries presently serving in Africa, Asia, and the Middle East, among other places, the Brazilian evangelical church has emerged—along with the broader church in Latin America—as a formidable example of missions sending from the majority world. In light of this historic development, my object in this study is to tell part of the story of Brazilian evangelical missions by focusing on Brazilian efforts in the Arab-Muslim world.

---

1. Cited in Salinas, "The Great Commission in Latin America," 147.
2. Cited in Prado, "A New Way of Sending Missionaries," 52.

Since Brazilian evangelical missions efforts toward the Arab world began after 1976 and in earnest since the early 1990s, there has been little scholarly reflection on the experiences of Brazilian transcultural workers or missions organizations. While Latin American mission work in the broader Muslim world has been studied in a general manner, a dedicated scholarly work on Brazilian evangelical missions in the Arab-Muslim world has yet to be published. Hence, I am convinced that the present study will be a much-needed contribution to mission scholarship that will also have implications for mission practice as well.

Definitions

Before proceeding, it will be helpful to define some important terms that will be used throughout the study. First, I define evangelical or evangelicalism as a movement within Protestant Christianity that is minimally founded on the following presuppositions: biblicism, or the commitment to the authority of Scripture; crucicentrism, an emphasis on Christ's atoning work at the cross; conversionism, the conviction that one must be converted through saving faith because of Christ's atoning work; and activism, the resulting commitment to evangelism, missions, and Christian service.[3] As I will show in chapter 1, Brazilian evangelicalism is generally broader than that of North America or Europe and, like the rest of Latin America, the terms "evangelical" and "Protestant" are typically used synonymously.

Second, what is mission? Following the consensus of evangelical missiology, I am persuaded that Christian mission flows from the mission of God (*missio Dei*) as "God is the one who initiates and sustains mission."[4] Hence, I understand mission to be all that the church does to promote the kingdom of God, while missions is the specific work of the church and its missionaries to make disciples of all nations through evangelism, discipleship, church planting, and related ministries.[5]

Third, majority world missions refers to missions movements and efforts from the non-Western world. Sometimes called third-world, two-thirds world, or even emerging missions movements, in recent years, "majority world missions" has become the more commonly accepted expression among scholars to describe this phenomenon within the global church.

---

3. This has been best articulated in Bebbington, *Evangelicalism in Modern Britain*.
4. See Moreau et al., *Introducing World Missions*, 17.
5. Ibid.

Introduction

Fourth, though much of chapter 2 is devoted to what it means to be Brazilian, I define Brazilian as a member of an affinity bloc of the cultures that make up the country of Brazil. With some 291 ethnic or cultural groups, the Brazilian mosaic is composed of indigenous, Portuguese, African, European, and Asian peoples, as well as some cultures that resulted from the intermarrying of these peoples. While a great deal of cultural diversity exists, a degree of cultural cohesiveness can also be observed. Similarly, I define Arab as a member of the affinity bloc of Arabic-speaking peoples that reside in the twenty-two Arab states of North Africa and the Middle East.[6]

Finally, I use the terms "missionary" and "transcultural worker" interchangeably, though admittedly, the former still has a rather colonial connotation to it. As this study will show, the work of missionaries or transcultural workers is generally to engage in missions, as defined above, within another culture.

Focus of Study, Limitations, and Significance

In light of the overall aim to tell part of the Brazilian evangelical missions story by focusing on Brazilian transcultural workers and missions agencies serving in the Arab world, several major questions must be posed. First, historically, how did Brazil go from being a mission field to being a country that sends out evangelical missionaries? Second, culturally speaking, what does it mean to be a Brazilian evangelical missionary in an Arab context? That is, aware of their own "Brazilianness," how do Brazilian workers describe their adaptation to Arab culture? Third, what are the characteristic mission practices of Brazilian workers, teams, and Brazilian missions organizations? How do Brazilians describe their strengths and weaknesses in mission in the Arab world? Finally, how are Brazilians thinking theologically about mission? Also, how is this Brazilian missiology relevant to transcultural mission work in the Arab-Muslim world?

This study is also bound by certain limits. In terms of chronology, my study focuses on Brazilian evangelical missions efforts following the Curitiba meeting of 1976, although most of the development has taken place since the early 1990s. Though some background on the history of the Brazilian church and its mission efforts has been offered for the sake of context, the focus of the study begins with 1976. Second, I chose to

---

6. My paradigm for regarding Brazil and the Arab world as affinity blocs is based on the thought of Patrick Johnstone (Johnstone, "Look at the Fields," 14–17).

focus only on Brazilian evangelical missions instead of Latin American missions in general. This decision was made in order to bring focus to the study, because Brazil is unique as a Portuguese-speaking country in South America, and because Brazil is the oldest and largest Latin American missions-sending country. Third, in focusing only on evangelical churches and missions from Brazil, I do not address the transcultural efforts of Brazilian Roman Catholic missionaries. Finally, I focus the study on Brazilian missions in the Arab world. Specifically, that refers to Brazilian efforts within the twenty-two Arabic speaking countries of North Africa and the Middle East.

This study is important for at least three reasons. First, there is value in telling the story of Brazilian evangelical mission work in the Arab world so that the global church might be aware of, recognize, and appreciate the work of this emerging missions movement. Second, as the global church—including the older sending churches of North America and Europe—reflects on Brazilian efforts in mission, there will certainly be lessons that can be learned. Finally, this study offers a framework for self-reflection for Brazilian transcultural workers and mission leaders to contemplate the Brazilian experience in mission, to identify apparent strengths and weaknesses, and to move forward as an evangelical missions movement in places such as the Arab world.

Locating Myself as a Researcher

For me, this study began very personally over fifteen years ago in a North African *souk* (market). At the time, I was serving as a transcultural worker in the region and I was hosting Julio (not his real name), who was in the process of moving his family from Latin America to join our work in North Africa. While visiting the *souk* one day to buy gifts for his family, I was struck by how the shop owner largely ignored me (even though I was translating for Julio) and wanted to communicate directly with him. It was only after a half hour that he could be convinced that Julio was not North African. Standing there in the *souk* that day, I first became curious about the Latin-Arab connection, including the implications it might have for mission. Since that time, I have observed and admired the work of many Latin American and Brazilian evangelical missionaries serving in the Arab world. At times, I even found myself jealous of these friends whose "look" allowed them to blend in so well and who seemed to have far fewer barriers adapting to Arab culture than I did as a North American.

Introduction

While part of my appreciation for Brazilian transcultural workers is due to differences between my culture and theirs and how those differences impact ministry in the Arab context, I also feel a sense of commonality with them. First, in terms of faith presuppositions, I would also identify myself as an evangelical as I have generally defined it in this chapter. Second, having spent over ten years living among and ministering to Arabs, I can intimately relate to the process of language acquisition, cultural adaptation, ministering in another culture, and generally living and functioning in the Arab world. Hence, the reader should be aware of the spiritual (evangelical) and experiential (transcultural work among Arabs) perspectives that I bring to this work.

Literature Survey

Before elaborating further on the methodology employed to carry out this study, it would be helpful to survey the current literature related to our subject. In recent years, much scholarly attention has been given to the southward shift of global Christianity. The three most significant voices in the discussion have been Andrew F. Walls (*The Missionary Movement in Christian History; The Cross-Cultural Process in Christian History; Mission in the Twenty-First Century*), Phillip Jenkins (*The Next Christendom* and *The New Faces of Christianity*), and Lamin Sanneh (*Whose Religion is Christianity?, The Changing Face of Christianity, Disciples of All Nations*). Miriam Adeney has also offered a winsome look at the global church in her recent work *Kingdom Without Borders: The Untold Story of Global Christianity*. Aside from these authors' monographs, Global South issues have been addressed by Dana Robert[7] and Todd Johnson,[8] while the phenomenon has certainly been the impetus behind the recently launched *Journal of World Christianity*.

The impact of Global South Christianity on missions has been treated by numerous authors and researchers, including Mark Laing[9] and the two-thirds world church research group, which met at the Lausanne Conference in Thailand in 2004.[10] For nearly three decades, the most significant research on majority world missions was done by Lawrence

---

7. See Robert, "Shifting Southward," 50–58.
8. See Johnson and Lee, "From Western Christianity to Global Christianity," 387–92, and Johnson, "World Christian Trends, Update 2007."
9. See Laing, "The Changing Face of Mission," 165–77.
10. See Ruiz, "The Two-Thirds World Church."

Keyes (*The Last Age of Missions*) and Larry Pate (*From Every People*).[11] Also, the recently released 2009 edition of Winter and Hawthorne's *Perspectives on the World Christian Movement* contains a prominent section on majority world missions. While well-known mission scholars such as Winter, Patrick Johnstone, Bill Taylor and others offer helpful contributions,[12] the reader benefits mostly from hearing directly from non-Western mission leaders and scholars that include Beram Kumar (Asia), Timothy Olonade (Africa), Bertil Ekström (Brazil), Chul Ho Han (Korea), K. Rajendran (India), Enoch Wan (China), Berting Fernando (Philippines), Carlos Scott (Latin America), and David Ruiz (Latin America).[13] Though less scholarly and more practically oriented, Ben Naja's recent book *Releasing Workers of the Eleventh Hour* is a single volume dedicated to the issue of majority world missions.[14] Within the context of missions to the Muslim world, Greg Livingstone has also recently written an article on the vital role of Global South missionaries in this effort.[15] Similar to the Lausanne Movement, which has discussed the majority world missions and published its findings, COMIBAM has continued to hold regular conferences in Latin America since 1987, has served as a resource for missionaries from the region, and has generated much helpful data on the Latin American missions movement.[16] Finally, the subject of majority world missions was the main theme at the Evangelical Missiological Society annual meeting in 2008, and its monograph *Missions from the Majority World* was recently released.[17]

Among Latin American theologians and missiologists, much helpful scholarship has come from Peruvian theologian Samuel Escobar (*The New Global Mission; Changing Tides: Latin America & World Mission Today*), representing the influential thought of the Latin American

---

11. Aside from these individual works, Keyes and Pate have collaborated on the following relevant scholarly articles: "Emerging Missions in a Global Church," 156–61, and "Two-Thirds World Missions," 188–206.

12. See Taylor, "Global Partnership," 376; Huneycutt, "New Pioneers Leading the Way in the Final Era," 377–81; Johnstone, "Expecting a Harvest," 382–86; Johnson and Lee, "From Western Christendom to Global Christianity," 387–92; Winter, "Are We Ready for Tomorrow's Kingdom?" 393–94.

13. See Kumar, "No Longer Emerging," and "Majority World Sending," 369–76.

14. See Naja, *Releasing Workers of the Eleventh Hour*.

15. See Livingstone, "Laborers from the Global South," 51–66; Johnstone, "Look at the Fields," 6; and Liverman, "Unplowed Ground," 29.

16. See "COMIBAM" and Smith, "COMIBAM: Takeoff Toward AD 2007," 53–55.

17. See Wan and Pocock, *Missions from the Majority World*.

Theological Fellowship (FTL).¹⁸ In *Changing Tides*, Escobar has succinctly narrated the key points in Latin American mission history and begun to articulate an evangelical theology of mission from a Latino perspective. Escobar and others also contributed papers on Latin American mission theology and praxis at the Iguassu Dialogue that met in Brazil in 1999—later published as *Global Missiology for the Twenty-First Century*.¹⁹ Regarding sending Latin American missionaries in general to the Arab world, Pedro Carrasco offered a brief study in 1994,²⁰ while Federico Bertuzzi edited the short work *Latinos en El Mundo Islámico* (*Latinos in the Muslim World*) in 1990.²¹

In Brazil, there is a developing literature of both a practical and scholarly nature addressing many aspects of Brazilian evangelical missions. Bertil Ekström, executive director of the World Evangelical Alliance and key participant in the Lausanne Movement, has authored numerous strategic, practical, and scholarly works.²² Valdir Steuernegal, a missiologist in the Lutheran tradition, minister at large for World Vision, and also an active participant in Lausanne, has been a leader for the past two decades in missiological reflection.²³ The Associação de Professores de Missões no Brasil (Association of Brazilian Mission Professors) began meeting in 1983 and has published the journal *Capacitando* since the late 1990s.²⁴ Oswaldo Prado, a Presbyterian pastor and mission leader, has also published works that have charted the narrative of evangelical missions from Brazil and provided vision for the movement.²⁵ Ted Limpic, a North American missionary and researcher for COMIBAM, has generated a great deal of statistical work on missions from Brazil and Latin America.²⁶

18. See Escobar, *The New Global Mission*, *Changing Tides*, "Missions from the Margins to the Margins," 87–95, and "Missions New World Order," 48–52.

19. See Taylor, *Global Missiology for the Twenty-First Century*.

20. See Carrasco, "Training Latins for the Muslim World," 1–4.

21. This was later translated into Portuguese as Bertuzzi, *Latinos No Mundo Muçulmano*.

22. Ekström was a respondent to Brandt in Ruiz, "The Two-Thirds World Church." See also Ekström, "Brazilian Sending," 371–72, and "The Selection Process and the Issue of Attrition," 183–93. His relevant works in Portuguese include *Éspiritu de Comibam* and *Modelos Missionários Brasileiros*.

23. See Steuernagel, *Missionary Obedience and Historical Practice*, and "The Theology of Mission in Its Relation to Social Responsibility."

24. See "Associação de Professores de Missões no Brasil."

25. See Prado, "A New Way of Sending Missionaries," 48–60, and "The Brazil Model."

26. For Limpic's statistical work, see "COMIBAM."

He has also contributed a helpful article on missionary attrition among Brazilians in Bill Taylor's *Too Valuable to Lose*.[27] Also in Taylor's work, missiologist Margaretha Adiwardana has offered some helpful reflection on the pre-field training of Brazilian missionaries.[28] In a dissertation completed in 2005, Donald Finley, a longtime Baptist missionary in Brazil, proposed a contextualized model for training Brazilians in mission.[29] On the subject of tentmaking, strategist Robson Ramos advocated a tentmaking model for Brazilian missionaries in 1998,[30] while more recently, João Mordomo has advanced the Business as Mission paradigm for Brazilian cross-cultural workers.[31]

This scholarship provides an excellent point of departure for the present study. The literature suggests that the Brazilian missionary movement is young, eager, and energetic, and, with the expected twentieth and twenty-first century postcolonial backlash, it is continually struggling to find its identity. Transcultural missionary training in the Brazilian evangelical churches and theological seminaries is still in its early stages, and despite its enthusiasm and commitment, the church has not fully developed the necessary support structures needed to sustain a long-term missions movement (e.g., missionary care, financial support, "tentmaking" training).[32] Again, a scholarly work on Brazilian missions in the Arab world has yet to be published; thus, the present work should help fill some important gaps in the literature.

Method of Study

As this is a study in missiology—a discipline that relies on numerous disciplines as conversation partners—my research methodology is varied. In chapter 1, my purpose is to historically locate Brazilian evangelical missions work in the Arab world; thus, I take a historical approach that includes rigorous interaction with the literature from Brazilian, Latin American, North American, and European scholars.

---

27. See Limpic, "Brazilian Missionaries," 143–54.
28. See Adiwardana, "Formal and Non-Formal Pre-Field Training," 207–15.
29. See Finley, "Contextualized Training for Missionaries."
30. See Ramos, "Tentmaking and Missions," 47–52.
31. See Mordomo, "Unleashing the Brazilian Missionary Force," 219–39.
32. See Salinas, "The Great Commission in Latin America," 140; also Cook, "Protestant Mission and Evangelization," 49.

Introduction

After some reflection, it seemed best to approach the qualitative aspect of this study—particularly the discussions in chapters 2, 3, and 4—as a collective case study. That is, "research [that] involves the study of an issue explored through one or more cases within a bounded system (i.e., a setting, a context)."[33] In this respect, my issue is the phenomenon of Brazilian evangelical missions in the Arab-Muslim world. By pursuing a collective case study, "the one issue or concern is again selected, but the inquirer selects multiple case studies to illustrate the issue," which also results in more compelling conclusions.[34]

Creswell adds, "Case study research is a qualitative approach in which the investigator explores a bounded system (a case) or multiple bounded systems (cases) over time, through detailed, in-depth data collection involving multiple sources of information (i.e., observations, interviews, audiovisual material, and documents and reports), and reports a case description and case-based themes."[35] Thus, in this collective case study, I examine Brazilian evangelical missions in the Arab-Muslim world context from 1976 to the present. This is accomplished by listening to many voices—those of Brazilian transcultural workers and mission leaders—and also interacting with the relevant published reflections of Brazilian and Latin American missiologists and theologians. By reporting on the themes that emerged from the research questions—how Brazilians describe their cultural experience in the Arab world and how Brazilians approach mission—a general description of Brazilian evangelical missions to Arabs is offered.

Finally, in chapter 5, my aim is to summarize key aspects of Brazilian theology of mission. This is pursued primarily through a rigorous interaction with the works of Brazilian and Latin American theologians in conversation with the observed practice of Brazilian evangelical workers serving in the Arab world.

Participants

The qualitative aspect of this study has been based on the input of forty-five Brazilian transcultural workers and ten mission leaders. Before describing the methods of data collection, let us offer a brief description of

---

33. See Creswell, *Qualitative Inquiry and Research Design*, 73.
34. Ibid., 74; see also Yin, *Case Study Research*.
35. Creswell, *Qualitative Inquiry and Research Design*, 73.

the participants. I give a breakdown of the survey pool of Brazilian workers and mission leaders in tables in Appendices A and C, respectively.

In terms of ministry, forty-two of the forty-five Brazilian workers continue to serve among Arabs. Of the three that are not, two are presently serving as pastors in Brazil and are involved in missions mobilization, while the other is planting churches in North America. Thirty-six participants are serving in Arab countries, three are serving among Arabs in Brazil, while six have ministered to Arabs in both Arab countries and in Brazil. The survey pool also revealed a significant array of ministry experience: one had been serving for more than twenty years; one for fifteen to twenty years; six for ten to fifteen years; thirteen for five to ten years; fifteen for three to five years; eight for less than two years; and one that gave no indication.

Demographically, eleven participants are single women, three are single men, while there was another single participant who did not indicate his or her gender. Thirteen are married women, twelve are married men, while five other married persons responded did not indicate their gender. Of the married responders, seven married couples were interviewed together.

The ten mission leaders surveyed are involved in different aspects of missions training, mobilization, and leadership. One is the dean of a theological seminary, another is an instructor in a missions training institute, while another is a part-time instructor, missiologist, and author. One participant is a pastor and leader of a small missions organization, while another is a missions pastor and former leader of a missions agency. The remaining five participants are directors of missions agencies that send Brazilian workers to the Arab-Muslim world. Two of these leaders were also included in the sample of Brazilian transcultural workers because they were missionaries in the Arab world before assuming their present roles.

Demographically, three of the participants are North American missionaries (two men and one woman) that are involved in training and mobilizing Brazilians for transcultural mission work. The remaining seven participants are Brazilian, including four married men, one single man, and one man and one woman who did not indicate their marital status.

Data Collection

As I began to develop survey questions for the transcultural workers and mission leaders survey (see Appendices B and D, respectively), my

Introduction

research values could best be described as social constructivist. That is, the questions were "broad and general so that the participants [could] construct the meaning of a situation . . . the more open ended the questioning the better."[36] Hence, nearly every question included a comments section so that maximum understanding could be given to the "meaning that the participants hold about the problem."[37] In both the transcultural workers and mission leaders surveys, open-ended questions were developed that dealt with Brazilian cultural adaption in the Arab world, approaches to mission, and missionary life and health. The two surveys also welcomed a broader perspective on Brazilian missions from those who have gone as missionaries and from those who send and offer support. While far more data was generated that could be addressed in the study, I was able to focus on the most prominent themes that emerged.

Once the two surveys were finalized, they were uploaded into an online survey program and, to invite the maximum amount of participation, the surveys were published in both English and Portuguese.[38] Also, to protect the anonymity of Brazilian workers—most of whom are serving in contexts that do not welcome traditional Christian missions—the workers survey was encrypted and participants were sent a password to enter the site. While safeguarding their anonymity, I assigned a number to each participant in order to track and analyze their responses. While anonymity was not promised to or requested by the mission leaders, I also assigned a number to each mission leader respondent. This was especially helpful when their identity was not clear.

The workers survey was placed online in February 2009 and remained available until July 2010. Beginning in February 2009, I sent approximately forty emails to Brazilian workers via trusted intermediaries—Brazilian mission leaders and other missionaries—inviting them to participate by linking to the survey site.[39] This effort yielded only fourteen responses: nine surveys that were answered in Portuguese, two in English, and three including English and Portuguese responses.[40] I quickly learned that for

36. Ibid., 20–21.

37. Ibid., 39.

38. Valuable insights on constructing a web-based questionnaire were gleaned from Dillman et al., "Principles for Constructing Web Surveys."

39. See Creswell, *Qualitative Inquiry and Research Design*, 118–25, on building rapport with participants.

40. The Portuguese responses were translated into English by a third-party, qualified translator, Cristina Boersma (MA, Liberty University). See Appendix A: Brazilian Workers Survey Pool, respondents 1–7, 14–17, 19, 22.

reasons of security and culture, this method of surveying would not be the most productive form; so I began to prepare for three trips to the field in order to conduct interviews with those who did not respond to the online surveys, as well as to meet others and to make observations.[41] Hence, my sampling strategy moved from being convenient toward a combination or mixed strategy that was also opportunistic.[42]

In July 2009, I spent ten days in Brazil and went through the survey in interview form with seven Brazilian missionaries, six that are continuing to minister to Arabs in Brazil and one who is now serving as a missions pastor.[43] Two interviews were done in English with fluent English speakers, while the other five were done through translation. In addition to interviewing the six participants who are working with Arabs in Brazil, I was able to spend several days observing their ministries firsthand, activities that included personal witness, a community dinner, a Muslim ministry training seminar, an evangelistic Bible study, and a worship service. Finally, after returning home from Brazil, I conducted one more survey in English over Skype with one worker who was sick during the time of my visit.[44]

In October 2009, I spent one week visiting ten Brazilian workers in their ministry context in a Middle Eastern country. Because of language barriers, I met the group one day for a meal at someone's home. During this time, each worker filled out a hard copy of the survey in Portuguese. Afterward, through translation, I invited them to comment further on any thoughts that were triggered by the survey. Upon my return to the United States, the responses were translated into English by a trusted, third-party translator and they were entered into the online database.[45] In addition to these surveys, I spent one entire day with a Brazilian worker observing his sports outreach. Finally, I visited with another worker (who did not complete the survey) on site at her place of ministry: a cultural center for the handicapped.

Also in October 2009, I interviewed one former worker, who is presently serving as a church planter in the United States, during his

---

41. See Creswell, *Qualitative Inquiry and Research Design*, 129–43.

42. See Miles and Huberman's framework, cited in Creswell, *Qualitative Inquiry and Research Design*, 127.

43. See Appendix A: Brazilian Workers Survey Pool, respondents 8–13, 18.

44. Ibid., respondent 21.

45. I am indebted to Barbara Hubbard (MA, Liberty University) for her translations. See Appendix A: Brazilian Workers Survey Pool, respondents 23–32.

Introduction

participation at a conference at my university. This interview was conducted in English.[46]

In January 2010, I spent a week in another Middle Eastern country and conducted twelve interviews with Brazilian workers. Nine of the interviews (including two married couples) were done in English, while the other three (including one married couple) were done through the help of a translator.[47] The only ministry activity I observed was a mission team meeting, which included Brazilians and Arab Christians worshipping together and planning for ministry outreaches.

Like the workers survey, the mission leaders survey was placed online in February 2009 and remained available until July 2010. I sent email invitations to participate in the survey to the leaders of forty missions organizations listed in the COMIBAM network and to fifteen missiologists listed on the website of the Associação de Professores de Missões no Brasil (Association of Brazilian Mission Professors). These initiatives yielded only six responses: two answered in English, while the other four responded in Portuguese.[48] During my trip to Brazil in July 2009, I was able to meet two of these respondents (Silas Tostes and Daniel Calze), visit the headquarters of their missions organizations (Missão Antioquia and PMI Brazil, respectively), and talk with them in more depth about their efforts in the Arab-Muslim world.

The remaining four surveys with mission leaders—those that did not respond to the online survey—were done through personal interviews. During my trip to Brazil, I interviewed João Mordomo of CCI-Brasil, spent three days observing a CCI-sponsored Muslim ministry training, and visited the CCI headquaters in Curitiba. Similarly, I interviewed Robson Ramos, a missiologist who is presently involved in church planting in Southern Brazil, and spent three days observing his ministry.[49] Upon returning to the United States, I interviewed Timothy Halls of PMI USA by phone and Marcos Amado, former director of PM International, over Skype.[50] Apart from my interaction with Daniel Calze, which was facilitated by translation, each interview with the mission leaders was conducted in English. It should be noted that the mission leaders survey had an

46. See Appendix A: Brazilian Workers Survey Pool, respondent 33.
47. Ibid., respondents 34–45.
48. The Portuguese responses were translated into English by a third-party, qualified translator, Cristina Boersma (MA, Liberty University). See Appendix C: Brazilin Mission Leaders Survey Pool, respondents 1–4, 6, 8.
49. See Appendix C: Brazilian Mission Leaders Survey Pool, respondents 5, 7.
50. Ibid., respondents 9–10.

overall lower response rate because several leaders declined to participate; they indicated their grasp on Brazilian mission work in the Arab-Muslim world was not sufficient enough to comment.

In light of cultural and security concerns, I felt that it would be most ethical to refrain from recording the interviews with both Brazilian workers and mission leaders.[51] Instead, I chose to take copious notes during each interview and then entered the survey responses into the online database at the earliest opportunity.[52] The collective responses of those who responded online and through interviews, which have been analyzed in discussions throughout the work, have been stored in the online database.[53]

Data Analysis

Once the data was properly stored and translated into English, I spent several months reading and re-reading the survey responses and reflecting on my own field observations in order to classify and interpret the data.[54] Following Van Manen, my main approach in the qualitative aspect of the study was theme analysis—a means of structuring the experiences and finding meaning in them.[55] This provided a foundation to make naturalistic generalizations about Brazilian evangelical missions in the broad areas of cultural adaptation among Arabs and mission practice, and to some extent, theology of mission.[56]

Hence, the data on Brazilian cultural adaptation (chapters 2 and 3) was classified according to the eight cultural themes in question, an interaction that also included rigorous interaction with cultural and missiological literature. Similarly, the data on mission practice (chapter 4) was also classified according to the themes that emerged. This included the areas that Brazilians described as strengths and weaknesses in their mission efforts.[57] Also, the data on mission practice from chapter 4 was used

---

51. See Creswell, *Qualitative Inquiry and Research Design*, 141–42.

52. Ibid., 142–43.

53. Tables with complete survey responses are available in the appendices of my dissertation (Smither, "Brazilian Evangelical Missions in the Arab World").

54. See Creswell, *Qualitative Inquiry and Research Design*, 150–52.

55. See Van Manen, *Research Lived Experience*, 78–79.

56. See Creswell, *Qualitative Inquiry and Research Design*, 163.

57. Ibid., 148, 156–57.

Introduction

to confirm and support the theological themes from the literature that were presented in chapter 5.[58]

Validation

How has this study found "credibility" and "confirmability"?[59] Following Creswell, I have endeavored to validate my findings through four strategies. First, the accumulated and analyzed data from the Brazilian workers and mission leaders surveys offered a "thick" description of Brazilian evangelical mission work among Arabs. Also, the themes that emerged have been confirmed internally through the repeated input of many Brazilian voices.[60]

Second, validation has occurred through triangulation, a "process [that] involves corroborating evidence from different sources."[61] These multiple sources included the survey results, interview notes, corroborating cultural and missiological literature, as well as my own perspectives as a researcher with a background in transcultural mission in the Arab world.[62]

Third, some findings have found confirmation through peer review. First, as portions of this study were read as papers at conferences in 2009 and 2010, the feedback of colleagues in the discipline of missiology allowed for peer review.[63] Second, the input of a qualitative research specialist outside of missiology has also served as a welcome set of fresh eyes for this study.

---

58. In my dissertation (Smither, "Brazilian Evangelical Missions in the Arab World"), these themes were represented by sixteen tables at the end of chapters 3 and 4, which corresponded to the complete data in Appendices B and D.

59. See Creswell, *Qualitative Inquiry and Research Design*, 202–3.

60. Ibid., 209.

61. Ibid., 208.

62. Ibid., 206, 208.

63. Ibid., 208. The first paper (from chapter 1) was "North American Revivals and the Beginning of Evangelical Mission in Brazil" presented at the Liberty University Conference on Revivals and Awakenings, April 16–18, 2009, and later published as Smither, "The Impact of Evangelical Revivals on Global Mission." A second paper (from chapter 3) was "Bridging the 'Excluded Middle'" presented at the Evangelical Missiological Society Southeast Regional Meeting, Greenville, SC, March 19–20, 2010, and later published under the same title. Finally, I read (from chapter 5), "Missão Integral Applied" at the Evangelical Theological Society national meeting, Atlanta, GA, November 17, 2010.

Finally, this study has benefited from member checking.[64] At least one mission leader provided written feedback on my initial rough drafts of the study. The same manuscript was circulated to others who, at the time of writing, have not responded formally. In a less formal manner, during my later trips and interviews, several mission leaders and veteran missionaries offered some rich commentary on some of my preliminary findings, which has helped in interpreting the data.

Summary

In summary, the study has been broken down according to the following chapters. In the introduction (the present chapter), the need for and purpose of the study is laid out, a literature survey given, and the research method and procedures described.

The purpose in chapter 1 is to historically locate Brazilian evangelical missions work in the Arab world. Through rigorous interaction with the literature from Brazilian, Latin American, North American, and European scholars, this is accomplished by examining the historical narrative of how Brazil went from being a nineteenth-century mission field to a missions-sending nation in the twentieth century. In attempting to identify the characteristics of Brazilian evangelicalism, which helps explain the Brazilian church's missionary convictions, I argue that evangelical awakenings in North America served as an impetus for missions sending to Brazil in the nineteenth and twentieth centuries. The chapter concludes with a brief historical narrative of missions sending from Brazil in the twentieth century.

In chapters 2 and 3, I pose the general question, What does it mean, culturally speaking, to be a Brazilian evangelical missionary in the Arab world? Forty-five past and present Brazilian evangelical workers were invited to comment and reflect upon their own "Brazilianness" and how they have adapted in the Arab world. The perspectives of ten Brazilian mission leaders are also included. As noted, in this study, I treat Brazil as an affinity bloc of cultures in which there is clear diversity as well as some elements of cohesiveness. I approach the Arab world in the same way. Hence, the framework for discussing Brazilians in the Arab world has been to reflect upon two affinity blocs and to ask members of one group (Brazilians) to share their collective experiences living among a second group (the Arab world), specifically regarding eight aspects of culture that have clear missiological implications. They include: race, economics, time,

64. Ibid., 208.

communication, family, relationships, hospitality, and spiritual worldview. After first consulting the appropriate cultural and missiological literature and then listening to the experiences of Brazilian missionaries and mission leaders, it has become evident, culturally speaking, that Brazilians are not Arabs and that Brazilians must surely work to adapt culturally. However, it also appears that there is generally less cultural distance between the Brazilians surveyed and their Arab contexts than what is normally experienced by Western missionaries in the Arab world.

In chapter 4 I ask, practically speaking, how are Brazilian evangelicals approaching mission in the Arab-Muslim world? Valuing the collective input of many voices, I pose this question to individual Brazilians and teams, as well as to Brazilian evangelical missions organizations that work in the Arab world. While a number of themes (strategies and practices) emerged, it seems that Brazilians are especially concerned about humanitarian work and personal evangelism and would regard these areas as strengths of their movement. On the other hand, Brazilian workers and mission leaders also identified the most apparent challenges in their work among Arab-Muslims. They included: a lack of Brazilian local church support for missionaries, deficiencies in language learning, lack of financial support, and difficulties faced by Brazilian women in Arab contexts. For each apparent difficulty, I propose some solutions based largely on the input of Brazilian voices.

In chapter 5 I inquire, how do Brazilians think theologically about mission? Also, how is this Brazilian theology of mission relevant to transcultural mission work in the Arab-Muslim world? While I approach this question largely by surveying the literature from Latin American and Brazilian theologians, I also look for missiological themes in the thoughts of Brazilian evangelical workers and through observing their concrete mission practices. From this, four theological themes have emerged that are also descriptive of Brazilian missions. They include: mission is holistic (*missão integral*); mission is church-centered; authentic mission originates from "below" or from a posture of vulnerability; and one's missiology must be undergirded by an awareness of the spiritual world.

Finally, in a brief concluding chapter, I summarize the general findings of the study. While this work begins to answer some questions about Brazilian missions in the Arab world, it also raises other questions for research, which are briefly discussed.

1

From a Mission Field to a Mission-Sending Base

Introduction

The purpose of the present chapter is to historically locate the work of Brazilian evangelical missionaries in the Arab-Muslim world by exploring the narrative of how Brazil went from being a mission field—a country that has historically received missionaries—to a nation that also sends missionaries to the rest of the world. This will be accomplished primarily through consulting key historical literature from Brazilian, Latin American, North American, and European scholars. Following a very brief survey of the Portuguese conquest and subsequent Roman Catholic missions in the sixteenth century, I will narrate the rise of evangelical missions in the country beginning in the mid-nineteenth century, a movement led primarily by mainline denominations from North America. The history of this first wave of evangelical work will be followed by a discussion of the emergence of Pentecostal missions beginning in the early twentieth century. Assessing the history, methods, strategies, and values of the pioneer evangelical missionaries in Brazil will have a number of helpful outcomes. First, it will become evident that this movement was probably a consequence of evangelical awakenings, particularly those in North America and most likely the Second Great Awakening. Second, it will help to clarify Brazil's evangelical identity—one that is much more inclusive than its North American or European counterparts. This, in turn, will help to explain the character of the evangelical missions movement from Brazil—a history that will be briefly related in the closing section of the chapter.

Roman Catholic Missions and Protestant Immigrants

Following Pedro Cabral's voyage to Brazil in 1500, the Portuguese established settlements along the coastline and the city of São Paulo was established around 1553.[1] Brazil's indigenous population, referred to by the sixteenth-century Portuguese as simply "Indians," was already quite diverse well before the arrival of the European power.[2] The discovery of sugar cane in the South American colony in the late sixteenth century moved the Portuguese to begin importing a significant slave labor force from Africa in order to exploit the product.[3] This African presence, even after the liberation of millions of slaves in 1888, contributed to the country's increasingly diverse ethnic landscape. This also resulted in the development of a *mulatto* race—a mixture of Portuguese and African peoples—which now comprises around 25 percent of the Brazilian population.[4] In addition, between 1820 and 1915, the Brazilian government opened its doors to millions of immigrants—many of whom were agricultural workers—from Germany, Italy, Portugal, Spain, France, England, Switzerland, Belgium, Austria, Russia, Poland, Turkey, and the Arab countries.[5] Thus, Stephen Neill is correct in describing Brazil as a "melting pot of nations," and today around 291 ethnic groups can be counted within Brazil's territory that covers roughly one-half of the South American continent.[6]

Following Pope Alexander's decree in 1494 that the land that is now South America be divided between the Spanish and Portuguese for discovery and evangelization, Franciscan monks accompanied Cabral on his journey to Brazil in 1500. Jesuit missionaries soon followed in 1549

---

1. See Neill, *A History of Christian Missions*, 144; also León, "Invasion and Evangelization in the Sixteenth Century," 51–52.

2. See Hoornaert, "The Church in Brazil," 186–87.

3. See Dias, "Brazilian Churches in Mission," 350; Iulianelli, "Brazilian Peoples, Brazilian History," 354–56; and Levine and Crocitti, *The Brazil Reader*, 121.

4. See Iulianelli, "Brazilian Peoples, Brazilian History," 357–59; also Latourette, *A History of the Expansion of Christianity*, 5.86; and Kane, *A Concise History*, 145.

5. See Latourette, *A History of the Expansion of Christianity* 5.89; and Mendonça, "A History of Christianity in Brazil," 382.

6. See Neill, *A History of Christian Missions*, 463; also "Brazil (Joshua Project)" and Read and Ineson, *Brazil 1980*, 5–6.

From a Mission Field to a Mission-Sending Base

and Brazil's first bishop was appointed in Salvador da Bahia in 1551.[7] Despite being the official and overwhelmingly majority religion of the Brazilians for the last 500 years, Roman Catholicism does not appear to have penetrated past a superficial level for most Brazilians.[8] According to Latourette, it has been a passive faith that has had a continual colonial feel to it.[9] This seems in part due to the liberal ideas of Brazil's leaders, including some leaders in the Brazilian Catholic Church who sought to distance themselves from the Vatican.[10] Consequently, the Brazilian Constitution of 1824 offered increased religious freedom, while the inauguration of the Brazilian republic in 1889 also spawned general openness to new ideas, liberal thought, and even other expressions of Christianity.[11]

For most of the first 350 years of Brazil's existence after the arrival of the Portuguese, there was no deliberate evangelical Protestant missionary effort. While this may seem surprising, it is actually typical, for there was no observable Protestant missionary movement anywhere in the world until the latter half of the eighteenth century. Nevertheless, Protestant settlers and immigrants were present in Brazil from the mid-sixteenth century onward.

Around 1555, John Calvin sent fourteen ministers and a group of French Huguenots to establish a colony in Rio de Janeiro. While attempting to export a Genevan-style theocracy to their Brazilian settlement, the group's main evangelical concerns were correcting the errors of Roman Catholic theology. Given that, they failed to evangelize the indigenous peoples and the colony ended up being destroyed by Portuguese settlers and Jesuit missionaries. Similarly, in 1624, the Dutch invaded Salvador da Bahia and the accompanying Dutch Reformed clergy attempted to establish their own Genevan-style society. Like the Huguenots before them, the

---

7. See Neill, *A History of Christian Missions*, 121, 144; Kane, *A Concise History*, 64; Mendonça, "A History of Christianity in Brazil," 368–77; León, "Invasion and Evangelization in the Sixteenth Century," 51–52; and Braga and Grubb, *The Republic of Brazil*, 17.

8. See Saracco, "Mission and Missiology from Latin America," 358.

9. See Latourette, *A History of the Expansion of Christianity*, 5.69; also Braga and Grubb, *The Republic of Brazil*, 36.

10. See Latourette, *A History of the Expansion of Christianity*, 5.86.

11. Ibid., 120; also Braga and Grubb, *The Republic of Brazil*, 20–21; Bastian, "Protestantism in Latin America," 325–28; and Penyak and Petry, *Religion in Latin America*, 190.

Dutch colony was destroyed and the Reformed Christians were expelled in 1654.[12]

As Brazil received millions of European, Middle Eastern, Asian, and even North American immigrants during much of the nineteenth and early twentieth century, and at the same time provided religious freedom, the establishment of immigrant Protestant churches was a natural outcome.[13] In 1819, the first Anglican congregation was established in Rio de Janeiro. German immigrants also planted Lutheran churches that remained largely separate from the Brazilian population through most of the twentieth century.[14] Around 1866, a rather unlikely group of immigrants—North Americans—began to enter Brazil. These Southern confederates, whose cause had been lost in the Civil War, settled near São Paulo where they could continue to be slaveholders. Among this group were significant numbers of Baptists, Methodists, and Presbyterians. Pastors from these North American denominations were dispatched to Brazil to lead English-speaking, expatriate congregations. Though the North Americans did not move to Brazil with missional motives, their presence indirectly made North American Protestants aware of Brazil's spiritual needs. According to Anderson, some of the immigrants developed an evangelical heart for the local population, and the Baptists in particular appealed to their denomination to send missionaries.[15]

History of Evangelical Missions

The history of evangelical missions to Brazil can be traced to initial Bible Society efforts that began around 1816. In contrast to the rather lukewarm Christianity of the immigrant churches and their members' general disinterest in the Brazilian population, Guillermo Cook refers to this development as the beginning of "traditional missions" in Brazil and Latin America.[16] In this section, a brief history of evangelical mission work in

---

12. See Braga and Grubb, *The Republic of Brazil*, 18; Kane, *A Concise History*, 76; Mendonça, "A History of Christianity in Brazil," 377–79; and González, *Christianity in Latin America*, 186–88.

13. See Latourette, *A History of the Expansion of Christianity*, 5.106–107; also Braga and Grubb, *The Republic of Brazil*, 48–52; and González, *Christianity in Latin America*, 190.

14. See González, *Christianity in Latin America*, 191, 196–97.

15. See Anderson, *An Evangelical Saga*, 20–21; also González, *Christianity in Latin America*, 199–200.

16. See Cook, "Protestant Mission and Evangelization," 44.

Brazil, especially at its pioneering stages, will be given. Beginning with the Bible Societies in the early part of the nineteenth century, this survey will highlight the mission work of the mainline denominations (Methodists, Presbyterians, and Baptists), some smaller denominations, and early twentieth-century Pentecostal missions, as well as the contribution of some parachurch organizations.

Bible Societies

A practical outgrowth of the Second Great Awakening, which emphasized a renewed zeal for Scripture, the American Bible Society was formed in 1816.[17] Almost immediately, the organization began sending Portuguese Scriptures to Brazil, and the first missionary personnel on the ground were colporteurs—society representatives who labored to distribute the Scriptures.[18] By 1850, increasing numbers of colporteurs were operating throughout the country, including one who was killed in the Amazon region in 1857, and the quantity of Scripture distributed only increased.[19] Hugh Tucker, a Bible Society representative in Brazil from 1886-1900, provides helpful insights into a colporteur's experience in his work *The Bible in Brazil*: "My custom was to go, early in the morning, into the streets with as many Bibles, Testaments, and Gospels as I could carry. I usually sold out by nine or ten o'clock: then returned for breakfast, a rest and some reading. In the afternoon I would go again loaded down with Scriptures, which I generally disposed of by five o'clock."[20] Relating his work to the goal of church planting, he adds, "Both the Methodist and Episcopal missionaries and their helpers are following up the colporteurs, establishing regular services in many places and gathering in the fruits."[21]

In addition to the American Bible Society, the British and Foreign Bible Society began work in Brazil around 1820. Between 1821 and 1824, thousands of Bibles in Portuguese were distributed, and by 1889, forty-one distribution centers had been established around the country.[22] The

17. See Spickard and Cragg, *A Global History of Christians*, 276.
18. See Mendonça, "A History of Christianity in Brazil," 382; also Braga and Grubb, *The Republic of Brazil*, 48, 73–74; Latourette, *A History of the Expansion of Christianity*, 5.121; and Sinclair, "Research on Protestantism in Latin America," 111.
19. See Latourette, *A History of the Expansion of Christianity*, 5.121.
20. Cited in Penyak and Petry, *Religion in Latin America*, 196.
21. Penyak and Petry, *Religion in Latin America*, 196.
22. See Latourette, *A History of the Expansion of Christianity*, 5.109–110.

National Bible Society of Scotland also began its work in Brazil beginning in 1871. Bible distribution continued well into the twentieth century and around 1930, Erasmo Braga, a Brazilian Presbyterian leader, reported on the Sunday School Union of Brazil's "Million Testaments Campaign"—an effort to saturate the country with Bibles and Scripture portions.[23]

Methodists

In 1834, Northern Methodists in the United States made an appeal for missionaries for Brazil. Fountain Pitts and R. J. Spaulding were the first to respond and began preaching in the Rio de Janeiro area in 1835, while attempting to establish a Sunday school ministry the following year. In 1837, Daniel Kidder arrived in the country and, aside from distributing Scripture, his ministry involved making frequent contact with political leaders. It was during Kidder's ministry that Roman Catholic leaders published the first anti-Protestant literature.[24] Kidder is most remembered for collaborating with the English Presbyterian James Fletcher on their work *Brazil and the Brazilians*, a chronicle of their travels throughout the country that also made Brazil's spiritual needs known to evangelicals in North America and Europe.[25] In the 1870s, William Taylor, a well-known Methodist evangelist who had previously served in South Africa, Australia, Britain, India, and California, placed some missionaries in Brazil; however, the mission was short-lived.[26]

In 1867, Southern Methodists from the United States arrived in Southern Brazil primarily to minister to the North American immigrants. However, in 1876, J. J. Ransom went beyond his role as an expatriate pastor and began preaching in Portuguese. In 1880, another Methodist minister, J. E. Newman, befriended a certain Prudente de Moraes Barros, a prominent attorney who would eventually be elected president of the Republic. This contact surely resulted in greater favor for Protestant work within the country.[27]

---

23. See Braga and Grubb, *The Republic of Brazil*, 88.

24. See Latourette, *A History of the Expansion of Christianity*, 5.121; also Braga and Grubb, *The Republic of Brazil*, 53–54; and Mendonça, "A History of Christianity in Brazil," 382.

25. See Fletcher and Kidder, *Brazil and the Brazilians*.

26. See Latourette, *A History of the Expansion of Christianity*, 5.118.

27. Ibid., 5.122; also Braga and Grubb, *The Republic of Brazil*, 62.

In 1930, a national Brazilian Methodist Church was founded. In order to encourage indigenous leadership, the Northern Methodist Church—after nearly 100 years of ministry in the country—voted to dissolve as an official entity.[28] Despite this positive move toward national leadership, Brazilian Methodists have not experienced a great deal of growth in the twentieth century and currently have around 120,000 members.[29]

Robert Reid Kalley

A survey of Brazil's early mission history would be incomplete without mentioning Robert Reid Kalley. A Scottish Presbyterian missionary, Kalley's work is recorded independently because of its interdenominational and free church qualities. After stints on the island of Madeira (off the Atlantic coast of Portugal), Malta, Ireland, and Palestine, and after learning of Emperor Pedro II's concessions toward Protestants, Kalley and his wife settled near Rio de Janeiro in 1855. He is remembered for being the first foreign missionary to evangelize Brazilians in Portuguese and his strategies included door-to-door witnessing and Bible distribution—efforts the Roman Catholic Church opposed.[30]

In 1858, Kalley planted the Igreja Evangélica Fluminense, generally regarded as the first Protestant church in Brazil. Though Presbyterian and a Calvinist, his church plant was based more on a free church, congregational model that was presented in the local context as a "house of prayer." A second church was planted in Recife in 1873 and Kalley's efforts eventually resulted in the founding of the "Help for Brazil" mission in 1893.[31]

How was Kalley innovative in mission? Apart from his commitment to ministering in the local language from the outset, Kalley also recruited Portuguese-speaking believers from Madeira to serve in the Brazilian work. Opposed to establishing a foreign denomination in the country, Kalley's commitment to planting indigenous churches was evident when Brazilian pastor João Manuel Goncalves dos Santos was set apart to succeed

---

28. See Latourette, *A History of the Expansion of Christianity*, 7.182; also Braga and Grubb, *The Republic of Brazil*, 63.

29. See Johnstone and Mandryk, *Operation World*, 120.

30. See Anderson, *The Evangelical Saga*, 62; González, *Christianity in Latin America*, 226; Mendonça, "A History of Christianity in Brazil," 383; and Every-Clayton, "The Legacy of Robert Reid Kalley," 123, 125.

31. See Anderson, *The Evangelical Saga*, 62–63; González, *Christianity in Latin America*, 227; Latourette, *A History of the Expansion of Christianity*, 5.111; Neill, *A History of Christian Missions*, 329; and Kane, *A Concise History*, 149.

him at Recife in 1877. These values were also apparent in Kalley's worship ministry as he wrote hymns in Portuguese and encouraged worship in the heart language of the people. Finally, Kalley's ministry did not ignore social issues and he was also a vocal opponent of Brazil's slave trade.[32]

Presbyterians

Though Kalley was certainly influential, he was not the first Presbyterian missionary to enter Brazil as James Fletcher, already mentioned for his travels with Methodist Daniel Kidder, arrived in country in 1851.[33] Fletcher was followed by Ashbel Simonton, the first American Presbyterian missionary, who came to Brazil in 1859.[34] Simonton was diligent in his efforts to master Portuguese. He then did a demographic study of Rio de Janeiro and São Paulo before determining that there was an openness and need for mission work there. In 1862, the first Presbyterian congregation in the country was planted in Rio de Janeiro and a presbytery was established in 1865. In 1864, Presbyterians published the first Brazilian evangelical publication while the first theological institution was founded in 1867.

With the inauguration of the presbytery in 1865, the first Brazilian Presbyterian pastor, José Manuel da Conceição, was ordained. An ex-Catholic priest from São Paulo, Conceição had been a member of the Rio de Janeiro church prior to his ordination. As his ministry primarily consisted of travelling to his former Catholic parishes proclaiming his new faith, Conceição appeared less interested in establishing Protestant churches. Among Catholics, he became known as the "crazy" or "Protestant" father and, eventually, the American Presbyterians would distance themselves from this rather eccentric pastor.[35]

In addition to planting churches, Presbyterians were also eager to minister to social needs, especially in the area of improving education. In 1870, Mackenzie Institute was founded in São Paulo, which became one of the more influential universities in the country. While some have

---

32. See Anderson, *The Evangelical Saga*, 62–63; and Every-Clayton, "The Legacy of Robert Reid Kalley," 125.

33. See Neill, *A History of Christian Missions*, 329; also George, "Presbyterian Seeds Bear Fruit in Brazil," 136–39.

34. See "American Presbyterians in Brazil."

35. See Mendonça, "A History of Christianity in Brazil," 380–83; González, *Christianity in Latin America*, 226–27; George, "Presbyterian Seeds Bear Fruit in Brazil," 136; Braga and Grubb, *The Republic of Brazil*, 58–59; and Latourette, *A History of the Expansion of Christianity*, 5.122

criticized this approach as a mere byproduct of America's Manifest Destiny—importing a "superior" culture to Brazil more than bringing the gospel itself—others have countered that educational efforts were sincere humanitarian ministries intended to aid the work of evangelism and church planting.[36]

In 1888, the Presbyterian Church of Brazil was founded, and in 1903, following more schism and conflict, the Brazilian entity became completely self-supporting, separate, and independent from the Presbyterian Church in North America. Despite more division and splintering in the twentieth century, Brazilian Presbyterians numbered around one million in 2006.[37]

Southern Baptists

The beginning of Southern Baptist work in Brazil can actually be traced to Luther Rice, who after spending two months in Salvador da Bahia in 1813, raised the need of evangelizing Brazil and South America during a subsequent speaking tour of Baptist congregations in the United States.[38] Though the Southern Baptist Convention contemplated South American missions from its outset in 1846,[39] it was not until 1881 that William and Ann Bagby entered the country as the denomination's first missionaries.[40] Initially connected to an expatriate church, the Bagbys were soon joined by Mr. and Mrs. Z. C. Taylor and a national believer named Antonio Teixeira de Albuquerque. After surveying the country, they began preaching and distributing literature in Salvador da Bahia and successfully planted a church there in 1882. Out of this initial effort, churches were planted in Recife, Maceió, and Rio de Janeiro before 1889.

Between 1893 and 1897, Eric and Ida Nelson lived on a houseboat and evangelized villages along the Amazon basin. The Nelsons, in partnership with Solomon Ginsburg, planted a church in Belem in 1897, and then another in Manaus in 1900. Serving a total of forty-eight years in Brazil, Nelson planted churches along the Amazon between Belem and Manaus

---

36. See Arnold, "A Peek in the Baggage," 126–29; also Bevans and Schroeder, *Constants in Context*, 207–8.

37. See Latourette, *A History of the Expansion of Christianity*, 5.122; also George, "Presbyterian Seeds Bear Fruit in Brazil," 138–46.

38. See Anderson, *An Evangelical Saga*, 8-10.

39. Ibid., 64–65.

40. Ibid., 136–39.

until his death in 1939. Ginsburg, a gifted evangelist, apologist, musician, and writer, was also innovative in developing Christian literature and aided in church planting in Rio de Janeiro, São Paulo, Campos, Espírito Santo, and Minas Gerais. In 1901, a Baptist magazine and publishing house were founded.[41]

By 1907, Southern Baptists had planted eighty-three churches—twenty-six of which were led by national pastors—made up of 5000 members. Despite these encouraging signs, North American missionaries still largely directed the work. A positive step toward establishing indigenous leadership came in 1907 when the Brazilian Baptist Convention was formed at Salvador da Bahia. This new infrastructure seemed to enable some new ministries and initiatives, including a Brazilian Women's Missionary Union in 1908, which contributed to Brazil's missionary awareness; the founding of a Bible school and seminary in Rio de Janeiro the same year; new churches planted in Paraná, Paranaguá, Goiás, Maranhão, and among tribal peoples around 1910; a women's training center which began in 1917; and the establishment of schools around the country.[42]

By 1922, the Brazilian Baptist Convention had experienced rapid growth; however, the problem of paternalism on the part of North American missionaries was still apparent. In the same year, W. C. Carver, a foreign missionary who was committed to the value of national leadership, was influential in helping the Brazilian Convention come entirely under Brazilian leadership. Though conflict was not absent between the Southern Baptist Foreign Mission Board and the Brazilian Convention during the rest of the twentieth century, there was generally a better spirit of cooperation after 1959.[43]

Despite these challenges, Brazilian Baptist work was invigorated by the efforts of some gifted national pastors and missionaries. Under the ministry of L. M. Reno in the province of Vitoria, church membership grew from 488 members in 1910 to 7136 in 1936. Around 1926, Zacarías and Noemi Compelo were sent out as missionaries to Brazil's indigenous peoples, ministering between Goiás and Maranhão.[44]

In 1981, Southern Baptists celebrated 100 years of work in Brazil and reaffirmed their evangelical distinction from the Roman Catholic Church. In 2000, there were over 1.4 million members in some 4800 Brazilian

---

41. See Anderson, *An Evangelical Saga*, 142–47.
42. Ibid., 148–56.
43. See Anderson, *An Evangelical Saga*, 157–58, 162–64, 168.
44. Ibid., 159.

Baptist Convention congregations. Including other smaller Baptist denominations, there are nearly 6000 congregations with close to two million members in Brazil, making it the fourth largest Baptist country in the world, behind the United States, Nigeria, and India.[45]

Other Denominations and Missions

Aside from the Bible Societies, Methodists, Presbyterians and Baptists, there were other denominations and missions that became involved in Brazilian evangelical mission work in the latter half of the nineteenth and early twentieth century. After showing initial interest in the country as far back as 1853, American Episcopalians began work in Southern Brazil in 1889 and later set apart Lucien Kinsolving as bishop of an independent Brazilian Episcopal Church. The American Episcopalians seemed to value training and consecrating national clergy and found some success in doing so.[46]

Between 1851 and 1861, the American and Foreign Christian Union sent missionaries to Brazil, while Anglicans and Lutherans sent workers toward the end of the century.[47] In 1896, a YMCA movement for Brazil was organized and in 1922, the Salvation Army began a ministry of preaching and caring for the poor.[48]

Pentecostals

It would be impossible to discuss Protestant evangelical Christianity in Brazil or Latin America without mentioning the rise of Pentecostalism, which comprises 70 percent of Brazil's evangelicals today.[49] While significant scholarly work, particularly by sociologists, has been published on Brazilian Pentecostalism,[50] the goal of this section is to narrate briefly

---

45. Ibid., 129, 170–73; also Barrett et al., *World Christian Encyclopedia*, 135, 138.

46. See Latourette, *A History of the Expansion of Christianity*, 5.123.

47. The Anglican work was focused on the Japanese immigrant population. See Latourette *A History of the Expansion of Christianity*, 5.108, 122; and Kane, *A Concise History*, 149.

48. See Braga and Grubb, *The Republic of Brazil*, 69.

49. See Escobar, *Changing Tides*, 89; and Paul Freston, "Brazil: Church Growth," 226.

50. See Willems, *Followers of the New Faith*; Martin, *Tongues of Fire*; Stoll, *Is Latin America Turning Protestant?*; and Chestnut, *Born Again in Brazil*.

the movement's emergence in Brazil as well as to describe some of its characteristics.

In what González refers to as a "third great awakening," global Pentecostalism generally traces its roots to the Asuza Street revival that took place in Los Angeles in 1906 under the ministry of William Seymour, an African Methodist Episcopal pastor. Initially impacting the Methodist, Wesleyan, and Holiness churches, the movement also spread to Baptist churches in North America and quickly moved to Latin America and Brazil.[51]

In 1907, Luigi Francescón, an Italian immigrant living in Chicago, reported experiencing the baptism of the Holy Spirit in an Asuza Street affiliated church. Around 1909, he arrived in São Paulo where he ministered initially to Italian immigrants. Originally attached to the Presbyterian Church where he was involved in preaching, Francescón was later expelled for his Pentecostal views before founding the Congregacão Cristã no Brasil (Christian Congregation in Brazil). Primarily located in urban settings, the denomination, with its 12,000 "houses of prayer" in 4000 towns and cities and two million members, is presently the second largest Pentecostal church in the country.[52]

The Pentecostal story continued in 1910 when Gunnar Vingren and Daniel Berg, two Swedish Baptist immigrants also residing in the Chicago area, were led to Brazil.[53] González records that they were led to the country by an amazing vision:

> In the summer of 1910, in his kitchen in South Bend, one of the members of Vingren's church who has the gift of prophecy declares that God was calling Vingren to a great mission elsewhere. A few days later, the prophet told Berg essentially the same. The prophet did not know where their mission was, but he knew that the place was called Pará, and that the two were to sail from New York on November 5. Since no one knew where Pará was, Vingren and Berg went to the library and there discovered that there was a state by that name in Northern Brazil. They then traveled to New York, where they learned that there was a ship, the *Clement*, leaving New York for Pará on November 5! Without further arrangements, they bought two passages

---

51. See González, *Christianity in Latin America*, 270–71; and Martin, *Tongues of Fire*, 28–30.

52. See González, *Christianity in Latin America*, 280–81; Anderson, *An Evangelical Saga*, 605; Kane, *A Concise History*, 148; and Chestnut, *Born Again in Brazil*, 29–30.

53. See Escobar, *Changing Tides*, 77; and Chestnut, *Born Again in Brazil*, 26–29.

in steerage and arrived in Belem do Pará two weeks later, with ninety dollars between the two of them and without knowing one word of Portuguese.[54]

Vingren, who had previously served as a pastor, focused on evangelism while Berg supported the two of them as a metal worker.[55] At first, they were connected to the Baptist church in Belem do Pará but, as their Portuguese developed and their Pentecostal doctrine became apparent, they left the church along with many Baptist friends to begin the Missão da Fé Apostolíca (Mission of the Apostolic Faith).[56] In 1918, the Missão da Fé Apostolíca affiliated with the recently constituted Assemblies of God Church in North America, which resulted in the formation of a Brazilian Assemblies of God denomination. After slow beginnings, they had established churches in every state in the North and Northeast of Brazil by 1920 and in every state in the country by 1944. Since 1950, the Brazilian denomination has grown from 100,000 members to 14.4 million, making it the largest Assemblies of God communion in the world.[57]

Around 1940, another Pentecostal church, Brasil para Cristo (Brazil for Christ), began as an offshoot of the Igreja do Evangelho Quadrangular (Foursquare Church) through the ministry of Brazilian evangelist Manoel de Melo who was preaching in Pernambuco and São Paulo.[58] By 2000, the denomination—known for its attractive buildings, lavish headquarters, and savvy use of media—had a membership of 1.2 million in 4500 congregations.[59]

It should be noted that the phenomenal growth of Brazilian Pentecostalism in the twentieth century has also been accompanied by the rise of neo-Pentecostal movements or what Paul Freston calls "autonomous" and "local sects."[60] The most famous group is the Igréja Universal do Reino de Deus (Universal Church of the Kingdom of God), founded by

54. See González, *Christianity in Latin America*, 282.

55. See Escobar, *Changing Tides*, 79; and González, *Christianity in Latin America*, 281–82.

56. See Anderson, *An Evangelical Saga*, 606.

57. See González, *Christianity in Latin America*, 282–83; and Stoll, *Latin America Turning Protestant?*, 107–108.

58. See Kraft and Kraft, "Evangelical Revival vs. Social Reformation," 7. It should be noted that the Igreja Quadrangular continues to be an active Pentecostal denomination in Brazil today.

59. See Anderson, *An Evangelical Saga*, 606–7; also Read and Ineson, *Brazil 1980*, 33.

60. See Freston, "Contours in Latin American Pentecostalism," 236–37.

Bishop Edir Macedo in the 1990s.[61] With a current membership of over two million, the movement has emphasized financial prosperity and deliverance from evil spirits. At the same time, it has also been accused of financial mismanagement and blending Pentecostalism with traditional animistic beliefs such as Umbanda.[62] Though Freston has referred to the Igréja Universal as "an innovative updating of Pentecostalism's theological and liturgical possibilities," Latin American historian Carmelo Alvarez has called the group a "heretical Pentecostal movement." In 2001, the Latin American Evangelical Pentecostal Commission (CEPLA) determined it to be a dangerous neo-Pentecostal sect.[63] In short, Brazilian Pentecostals have endeavored to maintain doctrinal purity within their tradition and confront such excessive and heretical movements, one of the key reasons for the formation of the Brazilian Evangelical Association (AEVB) in 1991.[64]

Though Pentecostals presently comprise 70 percent of Brazilian evangelicals, the movement was still considered to be a sect by other Protestant denominations until the mid-twentieth century.[65] Evangelical acceptance of Pentecostals in Brazil seems to have followed the movement's affirmation at the World Conference on Evangelism in Berlin in 1966, a precursor to the Lausanne Movement.[66] Hence, Freston's assertion that Pentecostals are indeed Protestants—distinct in their emphasis on speaking in tongues and Spirit baptism—seems consistent with the general Brazilian evangelical regard for Pentecostals.[67]

Historically, a relative latecomer to the Brazilian evangelical landscape, Pentecostalism has experienced phenomenal growth in the twentieth century down to the present day. What has been its specific appeal in the Brazilian context? First, while Methodists, Presbyterians and Baptists

---

61. For more on this movement from the perspective of the church itself see "Igreja Universal de do Reino de Deus."

62. See Barrett et al., *World Christian Encyclopedia*, 137; and Anderson, *An Evangelical Saga*, 607.

63. See Freston, "Contours in Latin American Pentecostalism," 264; Alvarez in González, *Christianity in Latin America*, 295–96; Penyak and Petry, *Religion in Latin America*, 366; and Chestnut, Born Again in Brazil, *Born Again in Brazil*, 45–48.

64. See Freston, "Brazil: Church Growth," 240; see also Steuernagel, "Learning from Escobar," 129.

65. See Escobar, *Changing Tides*, 89; and Freston, "Brazil: Church Growth," 226.

66. See Escobar, *Changing Tides*, 77–78; Willems, *Followers of the New Faith*, 118–22.

67. See Freston, "Contours in Latin American Pentecostalism," 225–26.

have been successful at reaching the middle classes, Pentecostal churches have focused more on the poor.[68] As Chestnut asserts, "Brazilian Pentecostalism is a faith of the poor and disenfranchised."[69] With its founders coming from the working and lower classes, the movement has multiplied rapidly among the urban poor and those in the margins of society.[70] According to Anderson, Pentecostalism has addressed the plight of the poor and in some senses, offered a new identity and a way of escape.[71]

Second, Escobar highlights the "participatory nature" of Pentecostal worship assemblies.[72] Characterized by an intense spiritual atmosphere that may include healing, a typical service includes public testimonies and celebratory worship facilitated by guitars and tambourines, allowing the poor and illiterate the opportunity to participate actively.[73] This invitation to participate fosters a sense of community and seems to result in churches that are characterized by warmth and care.[74]

Third, also in contrast to some historic mainline denomination practices, Pentecostal churches place less emphasis on a pastor or church member's educational level.[75] Indeed, the preacher is more of a storyteller who connects with an audience of predominantly oral learners. Finally, because any believer can potentially be set apart by the Holy Spirit to serve as a spiritual leader, Pentecostals remain largely free of an ecclesiastical hierarchy.[76]

Finally, Pentecostalism seems appealing because of its emphasis on personal and moral transformation. Following a salvation experience and the baptism of the Holy Spirit, many Pentecostal Christians have testified to being delivered from drug and alcohol addiction, to renewed family

68. See Willems, *Followers of the New Faith*, 206; and Bonino, *Faces of Latin American Protestantism*, 54.

69. Chestnut, *Born Again in Brazil*, 3.

70. See Freston, "Contours in Latin American Pentecostalism," 241; Escobar, *Changing Tides*, 55; and Cook, "Protestant Mission and Evangelization," 48.

71. See Anderson, *An Evangelical Saga*, 613–14.

72. See Escobar, *Changing Tides*, 55.

73. See Sepúlveda, "The Pentecostal Movement in Latin America," 73; Mariz, "Religion and Poverty in Brazil," 79–80; Chestnut, *Born Again in Brazil*, 51–56; Escobar, *Changing Tides*, 56, 81; Martin, *Tongues of Fire*, 175–77; and Penyak and Petry, *Religion in Latin America*, 366–67.

74. See Mariz, "Religion and Poverty in Brazil," 79–80; and Escobar, *Changing Tides*, 56.

75. See Escobar, *Changing Tides*, 55; Penyak and Petry, *Religion in Latin America* 369; and Martin, *Tongues of Fire*, 66.

76. See Escobar, *Changing Tides*, 55, 81; and Anderson, *An Evangelical Saga*, 619.

bonds after rejecting sexual immorality, and to pursuing a better economic situation.[77] Perhaps Pentecostalism's moral appeal was best summarized by Presbyterian missionary and theologian John Mackay: "The Pentecostals had something to offer, something that brought a thrill to people benumbed by the drabness of their existence. Millions responded to the gospel. Their lives became transformed, and their horizons were widened; life took on dynamic significance . . . People became persons with something to live for."[78]

Parachurch Movements

Concluding the historical narrative of evangelical work in Brazil, it is important to note the presence of a number of parachurch organizations that began work in the country in the 1950s and 1960s. They included Open Doors, Word of Life, Campus Crusade for Christ, Youth for Christ, OC Ministries, World Vision, and the International Federation of Evangelical Students (IFES).[79]

Finally, though created to serve the Latin American church in general, the Latin American Theological Fellowship (FTL), founded in 1970, is an indigenous parachurch movement that has certainly encouraged missiological reflection in Brazil. Committed to a high view of Scripture and the historic doctrines of the faith, this evangelical movement has also shown concern for the poor and social issues. In some respects an evangelical response to Liberation Theology, these Latin American thinkers have influenced the Lausanne Movement to also address social problems and the needs of the poor.[80]

Summary

The rise of evangelicalism in Brazil is an amazing phenomenon as the narrative has shown. Writing in 2000, Osvaldo Prado summarizes the

---

77. See Chestnut, *Born Again in Brazil*, 56–65, 93–97; Escobar, *Changing Tides*, 56; and Cox, *Fire from Heaven*, 81.

78. Cited in Anderson, 599–600.

79. See Freston, "Brazil: Church Growth" 227–28. IFES is affiliated with Intervarsity Christian Fellowship in North America.

80. Ibid., 237; Stoll, *Is Latin American Turning Protestant?*, 131–32; Bonino, *Faces of Latin American Protestantism*, 50–51; and Bevans and Schroeder, *Constants in Context*, 261.

growth of Brazilian evangelicalism over the past 150 years: "In 1890 we numbered 143,000. In 1950: 1.7 million. In 1960: 2.8 million. In 1970: 4.8 million. In 1980: 7.9 million. And finally, at the beginning of our present decade, we numbered in excess of 17 million. If we continue to grow at this present rate, by the year 2014 we evangelicals will constitute 50 percent of the entire population of Brazil."[81] Elsewhere, Prado indicated that in 2003, Brazilian evangelicals numbered around thirty million, making it the third largest evangelical country in the world behind the United States and China.[82]

Evangelical Revivals and Evangelical Missions to Brazil[83]

As we begin to analyze the historical narrative presented, it seems that the driving forces behind evangelical missions to Brazil—particularly during the pioneering stages—were evangelical revivals, especially those in North America in the eighteenth and nineteenth centuries. Echoing thoughts from Latourette and other scholars, Escobar asserts generally that evangelical work in Brazil and Latin America "sprang out of the Pietistic revival and was shaped by it."[84]

Bevans and Schroeder refer in particular to three periods of Pietistic revivals that had missional implications.[85] The first was the Great Awakening, which occurred in Europe and North America in the early eighteenth century.[86] Though a deliberate foreign missions movement did not directly result from this awakening, Ahlstrom argues that it birthed a missionary spirit, which was most visibly observed in evangelical work among Native

---

81. See Prado, "The Brazil Model."

82. Prado, "A New Way of Sending Missionaries," 54; also Bush, "Brazil, A Sleeping Giant Awakens."

83. A modified version of this section has been published as Smither, "The Impact of Evangelical Revivals on Global Mission."

84. See Escobar, *Changing Tides,* 41; also Latourette, *A History of the Expansion of Christianity,* 6.442–48; Noll, "Evangelical Identity," 32; and Escobar, *The New Global Mission,* 50–53, 126–27.

85. Though mention has been made of González (González, *Christianity in Latin America,* 270–71) referring to the rise of Pentecostalism as the "third great awakening," this section will focus largely on the influence of eighteenth and nineteenth century revivals on evangelical work in Brazil.

86. See Bevans and Schroeder, *Constants in Context,* 209–10.

Americans.[87] Besides being a key preacher during the Great Awakening, Jonathan Edwards was instrumental in facilitating prayer for global mission while casting a general vision for it through the publication of his famous *Life of David Brainerd*.[88] In the second period—the Methodist revival—Bevans and Schroeder add that Wesley and his followers integrated evangelical preaching with social action, successfully blurring the lines between domestic and global mission.[89]

It was not until the third period of revival—the Second Great Awakening that occurred in North America in the first third of the nineteenth century—that a connection to foreign mission work becomes apparent. Chaney asserts that by 1817, missions had become a conviction for evangelicals in North America and a number of scholars agree that evangelical missions to Brazil emerged largely as a result of the Second Great Awakening in North America.[90] While acknowledging that "the origins of traditional evangelism hark back to the eighteenth-century evangelical awakening in Britain and parts of the continent," Guillermo Cook asserts "the Great Awakening in the nineteenth century propelled U.S. missionaries to Latin America."[91] Willems adds that after 1850, an evangelical missions movement characterized by the values of North American revivalism could be observed emerging in the Brazilian context.[92] Finally, Bonino offers this helpful summary: "The initiators [of Latin American evangelicalism] were missionaries—largely North American or British . . . who arrived in Latin America from the 1840 decade onward. It is remarkable to note that, despite their confessional diversity (mostly Methodists, Presbyterians, and Baptists) and origin (North American and British), all shared the same theological horizon, which can be characterized as *evangelical*."[93]

In light of Bonino's comments, it would be worthwhile to answer briefly: what were the values and characteristics of British and North

---

87. See Bosch, *Transforming Mission*, 278; Ahlstrom, *A Religious History of the American People*, 289; Kidd, "Prayer for a Saving Issue," 139; and Hall, "The Protestant Atlantic Awakenings."

88. See George, "Evangelical Revival," 48; also Hall, "The Protestant Atlantic Awakenings," 21–24.

89. See Bevans and Schroeder, *Constants in Context*, 209–210.

90. See Chaney, *The Birth of Missions in America*, 174; also Bosch, *Transforming Mission*, 279.

91. See Cook, "Protestant Mission and Evangelization," 44.

92. See Willems, *Followers of the New Faith*, 4–6.

93. See Bonino, *Faces of Latin American Protestantism*, 27.

American evangelicalism that were championed during these revivals, and that spread to Brazil and Latin America? Though articulated in a British context, David Bebbington's famous quadrilateral seems to offer the best description of evangelicals—regardless of nationality or denomination—in the eighteenth and nineteenth centuries. They include: biblicism, that is, the commitment to the authority of Scripture; crucicentrism, an emphasis on Christ's atoning work at the cross; conversionism, the conviction that one must be converted through saving faith because of Christ's atoning work; and activism, the resulting commitment to evangelism, missions, and Christian service. While Bebbington's categories were developed in his classic work *Evangelicalism in Modern Britain*, there has been recent fresh interaction with them in Haykin and Stewart's *The Advent of Evangelicalism*, and they continue to offer a helpful reference point for defining evangelicalism.[94]

Evangelical Missions and Roman Catholicism

Perhaps the most significant impact of the nineteenth century evangelical awakenings on missions in general was that they sparked a seismic paradigm shift in missional thinking. That is, Roman Catholic countries, including Brazil and Latin America, were now being considered legitimate evangelical Protestant mission fields.[95] Indeed, the relatively late start of evangelical missions in Latin America can best be explained by the fact that the majority of mainline Protestant denominations worldwide—especially Anglicans—did not regard Roman Catholics as unbelievers.[96] Even the planners of the 1910 Edinburgh global consultation on world evangelization held this view, as they did not invite Protestant missions groups working in Latin America to attend the conference.[97]

This change in thought came on the heels of the Second Great Awakening that, among other things, insisted on the need for personal conversion—a value that will be discussed in more detail shortly. This evangelical value, especially when applied to the spiritual state of Latin America, was

94. See Bebbington, *Evangelicalism in Modern Britain*; Haykin and Stewart, *The Advent of Evangelicalism*; and Noll, "Evangelical Identity," 36.

95. Hall helpfully notes (Hall, "The Protestant Atlantic Awakenings," 8) that the incipient missionary zeal of the First Great Awakening also had an anti-Catholic sentiment to it.

96. See González, *Christianity in Latin America*, 208; Kane, *A Concise History*, 147; and Saracco, "Mission and Missiology from Latin America," 359.

97. See Escobar, *Changing Tides*, 24; also Scott, "Latin American Sending," 375.

nurtured and advanced within the Student Volunteer Movement. In some respects, this movement had strong parallels with the famous Haystack prayer meeting at Williams College in 1806—a revival that led to the formation of the American Board of Commissioners for Foreign Missions (1810) and the American Bible Society (1816).[98] While the American Board was primarily focused on Asia during its early stages, there was still great interest in South America. As noted, the American Bible Society began work in Brazil in the first years of its existence.

The Student Volunteer Movement was birthed in 1886 in Mt. Herman, Massachusetts following a four-week YMCA collegiate camp led by Dwight L. Moody. Though Moody's focus was on North American missions and the camp did not have a deliberate global focus, the revivalist atmosphere nevertheless sparked a vision for global missions for which 100 students immediately volunteered. Officially constituted in 1888, the Student Volunteer Movement's watchword was "evangelization of the world in this generation," and according to Michael Parker, between 1886 and 1920, over 8700 individuals followed through on the call and went into overseas missionary service.[99]

From its very first year, the movement's leadership was concerned with evangelizing Roman Catholic Latin America. In 1886, A.T. Pierson, referring to Catholic countries in general, declared that the "priest ridden masses are weary of their thralldom."[100] By far, the most influential voice from the Student Volunteer Movement on the Latin America situation was Robert Speer, who later authored *South American Problems*.[101] Despite the Roman Catholic presence in Brazil and Latin America, Speer cited the "problems of alcoholism, sanitation, disease . . . high mortality rate . . . [and] illiteracy."[102] He added, "No land can be conceded to have a satisfactory religion where there moral conditions are as they have been shown to be in South America. If it can be proved that the conditions of any European or North American land are as they are in South America, then it will be proved also that that land needs a religious reformation."[103]

98. See Ahlstrom, *A Religious History of the American People*, 422–24; and George, "Brazil: An 'Evangelized' Giant," 104.

99. See Parker, *The Kingdom of Character*, 2–21; also Robert, "The Origin of the Student Volunteer Watchword," 146.

100. Cited in Parker, *The Kingdom of Character*, 69.

101. See Speer, *South American Problems*.

102. Cited in Parker, *The Kingdom of Character*, 116.

103. Cited in Escobar, *Changing Tides*, 25; see also Cook, "Protestant Mission and Evangelization," 44.

While discouraging direct polemical attacks on the Catholic Church, Speer initially viewed evangelical efforts in South America as a means to purify the Roman Church.[104] However, he later concluded "the only hope of reformation would seem to be separation from Rome and the formation of national churches."[105]

Speer and Pierson's thoughts resulted in concrete action as a consultation met in New York in 1913—just three years after the Edinburgh meeting—to consider evangelical mission work in Latin America. In 1916, a conference was held in Panama to discuss further strategies for Latin America, while subsequent conferences with similar goals were held in Montevideo in 1925 and Havana in 1929. Speer and others helped to form the Committee of Cooperation for Latin America, while a similar group was started to focus specifically on Brazil. Finally, in 1930, a federation of evangelical churches for Latin America was founded.[106]

In the early twentieth century, other evangelical leaders affirmed Speer's view on the need to evangelize South America. At the 1916 congress in Panama, Bishop William Cabell Brown communicated compassion for Roman Catholics as well as a conviction for biblical truth: "Suppose I were talking to a Roman Catholic. You know how kindly and considerate I would be. I would not desire to offend him or drive him away. I should rather try to speak the truth in love, and if possible, lead him to the full knowledge of the truth."[107] Responding to the criticisms of those who opposed evangelizing Catholic countries, John McKay defended the work of evangelical missionaries in the region: "Sometimes those who are interested in Christian service in South America are apt to be regarded as religious buccaneers devoting their lives to ecclesiastical piracy, but that is far from being the case. The great majority of men to whom we go will have nothing to do with religion. They took up this attitude because religion and morality had been divorced throughout the whole history of religious life in South America."[108] In 1916, Brazilian Presbyterian pastor Erasmo Braga predicted that evangelical revival would actually mark the end of "paganism" in the Latin American Catholic context.[109] This concern for evangelizing Catholics, which seems to have roots in the North

---

104. See Escobar, *Changing Tides*, 60.
105. See Speer et al., *Christian Work in South America*, 2.398.
106. See Latourette, *A History of the Expansion of Christianity*, 7.172–73.
107. Cited in Speer et al., *Christian Work in South America*, 2.398.
108. Cited in Escobar, *Changing Tides*, 26.
109. Ibid., 27; also Latourette, *A History of the Expansion of Christianity*, 5.109.

American awakenings, has continued to be valued by Brazilian and Latin American evangelicals. More recently, Báez-Camargo remarked that the "self designated 'Christian world' was also a mission field itself" because "the kingdom of God cannot be defined in terms of mere territorial accretion, but that the whole of life everywhere must be brought under the Lordship of Jesus Christ."[110]

Brazil's Evangelical Identity

While a number of scholars confidently assert that evangelical mission work to Latin America and Brazil emerged as an outcome of the Second Great Awakening in North America in the mid-nineteenth century, the correlation is at best a subtle one. That is, revivalist church leaders did not deliberately announce that global mission was the logical next step in the awakenings. Also, missionaries to Brazil in the early to mid-nineteenth century were not claiming that awakenings in their home country had driven them to the mission field. Though international students at the Mt. Hermon Conference in 1886 stood up and gave a Macedonian call of sorts, this was certainly not Moody's intention when organizing the summer retreat. Bosch, offering a theological interpretation of the increased missions emphasis, asserts that in this atmosphere of revival, it was the constraining love of Christ that began to grip North American believers: "There was among the Christians touched by the Awakening, a tremendous sense of gratitude for what they had received and an urgent desire to share with others, both at home and abroad, the blessings so freely shed upon them."[111] To be sure, it does not seem to be a coincidence that the three mainline denominations most affected by the Second Great Awakening—Methodists, Presbyterians, and Baptists—were also the first to initiate mission work in Brazil.

In a rather critical fashion, Rubem Alves has asserted that the "Pietism and revivalism brought to Brazil by the early missionaries . . . has now been taken over and made an integral part of modern Brazilian Protestantism."[112] In light of this claim and the historical narrative already presented, including the lack of clear causality between the Second Great Awakening and the advent of evangelical missions to Brazil, perhaps the

110. Cited in Escobar, *Changing Tides,* 26
111. See Bosch, *Transforming Mission,* 286.
112. Cited in Penyak and Petry, *Religion in Latin America,* 230; see also Martin, *Tongues of Fire,* 273–74.

best way to show the influence of North American revivals on evangelical missions in Brazil is to examine the identity of Brazilian evangelicalism and observe the common values between the two movements. Six areas are particularly apparent and will now be explored: a high view of Scripture, a call to genuine conversion, a visible faith, a missionary zeal, the priesthood of the believer, and a free church tendency.

A High View of Scripture

The first evangelical and revivalist value observed in Brazilian evangelicalism is the primacy of Scripture in the believer's life and in the community of faith. Again, Alves refers critically to this "type of Protestantism, which has given a central place to the reading and study of the Bible."[113] Similarly, Mendonça cites the "literalist Biblicism" of Brazilian evangelicals that he argues came from North American missionaries.[114]

It seems that this regard for Scripture—a core value of the Protestant Reformation as well as the Pietistic revivals—is what motivated the evangelical pioneers in Brazil to translate and distribute the Bible. Escobar writes, "This was a pillar of Protestant missiology, which considered Bible translation and distribution as the beginning of missionary activity that would allow for the communication of the faith and the development of indigenous churches."[115] As noted, evangelical missions work in Brazil was launched before 1820 through the work of Bible Society colporteurs, while other evangelists like Robert Reid Kalley incorporated distribution into their overall mission strategy.[116] Bible distribution continued to be a valued strategy throughout the twentieth century and is regarded as important even in the present day.[117] Commenting on its impact in the early twentieth century, Braga wrote: "There are many cases illustrating the effect of reading the Bible on individual lives as well as on the community life. This has led to definite conversions, and has been instrumental in raising up many notable workers."[118] Bonino adds that as evangelical mis-

---

113. Cited in Penyak and Petry, *Religion in Latin America*, 230.

114. See Mendonça, "A History of Christianity in Brazil," 385.

115. See Escobar, *Changing Tides*, 69; also Robert, "Shifting Southward," 56.

116. See Every-Clayton, "The Legacy of Robert Reid Kalley," 325; Escobar, "The Church in Latin America," 35; and Cook, "Protestant Mission and Evangelization," 45.

117. See Douglass, "Brazil National Strategy Group Report," 1344.

118. See Braga and Grubb, *The Republic of Brazil*, 72; see also Speer et al., *Christian Work in South America*, 2.215-38.

sion work engaged the Latin American context, a polemic against Roman Catholicism developed which also encouraged an emphasis on Scripture. He writes, "It was necessary to furnish new converts with knowledge and arguments for this conflict. That need led to a great emphasis on study of the Bible and of the basic doctrines of Protestantism."[119]

While Brazilian Pentecostalism has experienced unprecedented growth in the twentieth century, Stoll and others have criticized these evangelicals for possessing only a superficial understanding of biblical Christianity.[120] However, Mariz counters that while many Brazilians have been initially attracted to the Pentecostal church because of an intense spiritual experience, it has been the knowledge gained from a literal reading of Scripture that has kept them in the church.[121] These Christians seem to resemble those described by Philip Jenkins in his recent work *The New Faces of Christianity*, which is appropriately subtitled, *Believing the Bible in the Global South*.

Brazilian evangelicalism has certainly embraced the Pietistic value of a high view of Scripture; however, evangelical missionaries, especially in the pioneering stages largely reached out to the literate population and failed to engage with the large number of Brazilians that do not read very well or at all. In 1890, Tucker estimated that only 15 percent of the population could read, while in 1930 Braga acknowledged that only 25 percent were literate.[122] At the 1925 Montevideo Congress, W.A. Waddell criticized evangelical missions in Latin America in general for a disproportionate focus on the educated classes.[123] On the other hand, Bible and literature distribution has become more relevant through the course of the twentieth century as literacy has currently risen to 88 percent among Brazilians aged fifteen and above.[124]

---

119. See Bonino, *Faces of Latin American Protestantism*, 31.

120. See Stoll, *Is Latin America Turning Protestant?*, 173; also Cook, "The Many Faces of the Latin American Church," 276.

121. See Mariz, "Religion and Poverty in Brazil," 77–78.

122. See Tucker, *The Bible in Brazil*, 72; and Braga and Grubb, *The Republic of Brazil*, 72.

123. See Speer et al., *Christian Work in South America*, 1.138.

124. See Central Intelligence Agency ("World Fact Book: Brazil"); also Read and Ineson, *Brazil 1980*, 1.

A Call to Genuine Conversion

A second observable revivalist influence on Brazilian evangelicalism is the necessity of conversion. Rene Padilla asserts, "In this respect, the evangelical churches in Latin America prove to be, in general, heirs of the great evangelical revivals of the eighteenth and nineteenth centuries, with their emphasis on the doctrine and experience of salvation by the grace of God, through faith in Jesus Christ."[125] The emphasis on conversion can certainly be traced back to the pre-Great Awakening ministry of Samuel Torrey, who insisted that spiritual reformation began with saving faith.[126] We are also reminded that Jonathan Edwards was dismissed from his pastorate at Northampton, Massachusetts, for refusing to admit the unconverted to the Lord's Table. Ironically, Edwards spent his final years as a missionary to Native Americans.[127] Finally, the preaching of Timothy Dwight, James McGready, and Dwight L. Moody among others was also under girded by this evangelical value.[128]

As evangelical missionaries to Latin America were committed to the doctrine of conversion, Cook points out that they were also motivated by a sincere concern to rescue souls from a literal hell.[129] Convinced that "the primary task of every Christian was to witness to others and seek their conversion," public preaching and personal witness—as noted in the historical narrative—were the key forms of evangelism.[130] It is interesting to note that some Pentecostal evangelistic meetings even bore resemblance to the Methodist, Wesleyan, and Holiness camp meetings of nineteenth-century North America, which included "godly hysteria, holy dancing, and laughter."[131]

Finally, the evangelical emphasis on conversion in the Brazilian context in the nineteenth and twentieth centuries implied a personal and

---

125. See Padilla, "New Actors on the Political Scene," 90; also Willems, *Followers of the New Faith*, 6; Bonino, *Faces of Latin American Protestantism*, 28; Bevans and Schroeder, *Constants in Context*, 230; and Escobar, *The New Global Mission*, 103–104.

126. See Kidd, "Prayer for a Saving Issue," 131–32.

127. See Noll, *A History of Christianity*, 104.

128. See Hankins, *The Second Great Awakening*, 6–9.

129. See Cook, "Protestant Mission and Evangelization," 45.

130. See González, *Christianity in Latin America*, 203–4; also Arnold, "A Peek in the Baggage," 125.

131. See Martin, *Tongues of Fire*, 28, 163–64; also Bonino, *Faces of Latin American Protestantism*, 32–33; and Hankins, *The Second Great Awakening*, 7.

individual conversion.[132] This Reformation and Pietistic value was, of course, quite distinct from the previous Roman Catholic model of spreading Christendom in Brazil. Jenkins points out that the anti-evangelical publication *Os Demônios Descem Do Norte* ("The Demons Come Down from the North"), only one such publication by the Brazilian Catholic Church, indicates that the Roman Church viewed evangelicalism as merely a North American invasion.[133]

Brazilian and Latin American Protestants have also expressed concern about and criticism of individual conversion. Cook argues that North Americans, influenced by the Enlightenment values of individualism, subconsciously imposed that on a Brazilian culture that was more communal in nature.[134] Mendonça has particularly accused American Presbyterians of being too "heavenly minded" and not caring enough for the social needs of Brazilians.[135] Finally, Escobar, a leading evangelical theologian, has expressed concern that a focus on individual conversion has stifled a proper ecclesiology in which the community of faith serves as an agent of transformation in society.[136]

A Visible Faith

A third revivalist value also evident in Brazilian evangelicalism is the emphasis on a visible practice of faith.[137] According to Hoornaert, it seems that a devotional and pietistic form of Christianity, introduced by Jesuit missionaries, had existed among some Brazilian Catholics prior to the arrival of evangelical missionaries. Hence, evangelical missions from North America seemed to stoke this spirit among this Catholic segment, the members of which were also anti-clerical and anti-hierarchical.[138] Alves adds that many observers of Brazilian evangelicalism are "impressed by the extraordinary vitality of the simple piety of the average Christian. Here

---

132. See Escobar, *Changing Tides*, 41; Mendonça, "A History of Christianity in Brazil," 383–85; Willems, *Followers of the New Faith*, 9; Mariz, "Religion and Poverty in Brazil," 76–77; and Horner, *Cross and Crucifix in Mission*, 26.

133. See Jenkins, *The Next Christendom*, 179.

134. See Cook, "Protestant Mission and Evangelization," 45.

135. Mendonça is cited in Arnold, "A Peek in the Baggage," 129–30.

136. See Escobar, *Changing Tides*, 43; also Escobar, "The Church in Latin America," 28.

137. See Escobar, *Changing Tides*, 102.

138. See Hoornaert, "The Church in Brazil," 193–94.

From a Mission Field to a Mission-Sending Base

are people for whom the experience of a personal relationship with Jesus Christ is the very center of life, people who read their Bibles and pray daily."[139]

This visible faith could first be observed in what Brazilian evangelicals avoided—smoking, dancing, sexual immorality, and drinking alcohol among others.[140] In fact, a key strategy discussed at the Montevideo Congress in 1925 was the implementation of a temperance movement for Brazil and Latin America.[141] González asserts that North American evangelical missionaries preached a gospel that included temperance convictions consistent with those of the American Society for the Promotion of Temperance, which had been founded in 1826 during the Second Great Awakening.[142] The other noted areas of abstinence find parallels in nineteenth-century North American Baptist meetings that confronted drinking, sexual sin, and dishonest business dealings.[143] As the evangelical message advanced in Brazil, a conflict arose between the North American missionaries and the immigrant churches, which had no problem with many of these forbidden practices. Mendonça has thus distinguished between a "Protestantism of mission" and a "Protestantism of immigration" in the Brazilian context.[144]

In addition to what was avoided by Brazilian evangelicals, this visible faith could also be observed through a resulting moral transformation. Abstinence from sexual activity outside of marriage—a counter cultural tendency to be sure—has led to increased sexual purity for singles and married persons alike, and has resulted in more stable families, which in turn has served to strengthen evangelical congregations.[145] Finally, moral transformation can also be observed in the intellectual and economic improvement of Brazilian believers.[146]

---

139. Cited in Penyak and Petry, *Religion in Latin America*, 230.

140. See González, *Christianity in Latin America*, 204; also Willems, *Followers of the New Faith*, 45-54; and Chestnut, *Born Again in Brazil*, 59-65.

141. See Speer et al., *Christian Work in South America*, 1.406; 2.10.

142. See González, *Christianity in Latin America*, 207; also Ahlstrom, *A Religious History of the American People*, 425-27.

143. See Hankins, *The Second Great Awakening*, 15.

144. See Mendonça, "A History of Christianity in Brazil," 381.

145. See Willems, *Followers of the New Faith*, 45-54, 169-73; Chestnut, *Born Again in Brazil*, 59-65; Robert, "Shifting Southward," 56; and Cook, "Introduction," xi.

146. See Comblin, "Brazil: Base Communities," 219; and Mariz, "Religion and Poverty in Brazil," 78-79.

Brazilian Evangelical Missions in the Arab World

Such a visible and transformative faith was undergirded by a gospel that was holistic and integrative. That is, while nineteenth-century North American missionaries—influenced by evangelical revival—preached a verbal gospel that invited converts to believe in the atoning work of Christ for the forgiveness of sin, they also gave much attention to real human needs. As noted, these values had already been observed in the ministry of John Wesley and the Methodist revivals. One of the outcomes of the eighteenth-century Great Awakening in New England was new initiatives in education and higher learning: Baptists founded Brown; Presbyterians started Princeton; the Dutch Reformed founded Rutgers; and the Congregationalists began Dartmouth.[147] Ahlstrom adds that one fruit of the Second Great Awakening was increased work among the poor and handicapped.[148]

Describing the integrative approach of nineteenth century evangelicals to Brazil and Latin America, Bonino writes, "Religious awakening and social reformation (revival and reform) were seen as intimately related; the 1850 evangelists took upon themselves, along with the moral improvement of society, the cause of the abolition of slavery and the struggle against poverty."[149] While many like Kalley were vocal in their opposition to slavery and others devoted their energy to the plight of the poor, one clear evangelical contribution was the development of schools—both theological and liberal arts institutions—and hospitals.[150] At the Montevideo Congress in 1925, a mission strategy for Brazil's indigenous peoples was proposed that addressed educational, medical, and economic needs.[151] Though evangelicals have continued to be criticized by liberal Protestants for not caring enough about social needs,[152] Rev. A. G. Tallon in 1925 seems to have expressed well the prevailing nineteenth- and twentieth-century evangelical missionary conviction in Brazil: "It is a

---

147. See Noll, *A History of Christianity*, 100–101; Spickard and Cragg, *A Global History of Christians*, 265–66; and Ahlstrom, *A Religious History of the American People*, 289–90.

148. See Ahlstrom, *A Religious History of the American People*, 427–28.

149. See Bonino, *Faces of Latin American Protestantism*, 29

150. See Latourette, *A History of the Expansion of Christianity*, 5.123; Robert, "Shifting Southward," 56; Arnold, "A Peek in the Baggage," 130–33; George, "Presbyterian Seeds Bear Fruit in Brazil," 139; and Braga and Grubb, *The Republic of Brazil*, 94.

151. See Speer et al., *Christian Work in South America*, 1.190–92.

152. See Bonino, *Faces of Latin American Protestantism*, 144; also Mendonça in Arnold, "A Peek in the Baggage," 129–30; and Prado, "A New Way of Sending Missionaries," 51–52.

mistake to contrast evangelism with social service. Any social work that is worthwhile grows out of spiritual convictions. A minister needs to be zealous in laying right foundations for his people . . . twenty-eight years experience in preaching the gospel emphasizing Jesus Christ, holiness of life and the embodiment of the Master's teachings and character has not gone for naught. It has developed a people ready to do their share in community service."[153]

This emphasis on an integrated gospel has certainly become one of the most vital aspects of the Brazilian evangelical identity. Referring to the contemporary church in Brazil and Latin America, Rey asserts, "It is now normal to find next to a church, regardless of its size, a health center, a school, a soup kitchen, etc. The majority of the churches have understood that they have an integral mission and that evangelization goes hand-in-hand with social responsibility."[154] While this value can be observed in the practice of churches in general, some of the most compelling missiology on the relationship of Scripture and proclamation and social engagement continues to come from men like Escobar, Padilla, Cook, and Steuernegal—all members of the Latin American Theological Fellowship (FTL)—and their emphasis on the "whole gospel" (*evangelizacíon* or *missão integral*). This aspect of Brazilian evangelicalism will be discussed in more detail in chapter 5.

Missionary Zeal

A fourth area of continuity between North American evangelical awakenings and Brazilian evangelicalism is an emphasis on missions. Despite the cultural baggage of Manifest Destiny brought by many well-meaning nineteenth-century missionaries, this hegemony did not impede the Brazilian church from cultivating its own missionary zeal. In 1923, an expatriate mission leader traveling through the country remarked "great self-supporting churches are found in the cities, with large memberships, and doing real missionary work in their own districts."[155] Braga adds that in the early twentieth century, evangelical churches from across denominational lines were collaborating in evangelistic outreaches, university student ministry, Scripture distribution, and women's ministry. In the 1930s, Brazilians were working to reach out to the Japanese, Muslim, and

---

153. See Speer et al., *Christian Work in South America*, 1.378.
154. Cited in Penyak and Petry, *Religion in Latin America*, 360.
155. See Braga and Grubb, *The Republic of Brazil*, 83.

Jewish immigrant populations in the country.¹⁵⁶ As will be discussed more later, this missionary conviction continued to manifest itself in increased transcultural efforts both inside Brazil and around the world in the latter part of the twentieth century.

This missional emphasis is perhaps best captured by those outside of Brazilian evangelical circles. Alves writes, "The church is constantly engaged in evangelistic and mission work."¹⁵⁷ José Comblin, a Belgian Catholic missionary in the Northeast of Brazil, made this remark about Pentecostals in the region: "This may be the most decisive factor; every believer is a missionary."¹⁵⁸ Finally, Bonino, summarizing Latin American evangelical theology in general, asserted that "mission" was the "material principle" of the entire movement.¹⁵⁹

Priesthood of the Believer

Quite related to its missionary zeal, Brazilian evangelicals have also noticeably exhibited the Reformation, Pietistic, and revivalist value of the priesthood of the believer. This can be understood in at least three ways. First, regarding the Scriptures, Luther's notion of perspicuity—the idea that even the simplest person could understand the Scriptures and communicate them to others—has been at work in the rise of Brazilian evangelicalism.¹⁶⁰ Bosch notes that this biblical conviction, especially among those with premillenial eschatological views, was an energizing factor in nineteenth century missions—including those who went to evangelize Brazil.¹⁶¹ This evangelical value was also certainly behind the American and British Bible Societies' decision to print and distribute Bibles without study notes or commentaries. This was distinct from the Catholic Church's strategy of using notes to teach literate parishioners about Catholic theology which seemed to diminish the role of the biblical text itself.¹⁶²

---

156. See Braga and Grubb, *The Republic of Brazil*, 88–89, 111–13.

157. Cited in Penyak and Petry, *Religion in Latin America*, 231.

158. See Comblin, "Brazil: Base Communities," 219; also Stoll, *Is Latin American Turning Prostetant?*, 109.

159. See Bonino, *Faces of Latin American Protestantism*, ix-x; also Escobar, *Changing Tides*, 102, 134.

160. See Escobar, *Changing Tides*, 73–74; and Escobar, *The New Global Mission*, 131–32.

161. See Bosch, *Transforming Mission*, 316.

162. See González, *Christianity in Latin America*, 218.

A second way that the priesthood of the believer has been observed in Brazilian evangelicalism is through an emphasis on volunteerism. An ideal largely absent in Christian history from the time of Constantine until the Anabaptist Reform,[163] the European and North American awakenings were not only led by volunteers, but the revivals also seemed to produce more laborers. While the First Great Awakening effectively empowered lay leaders and preachers, one outcome of the Second Great Awakening was the prolific formation of voluntary missionary societies.[164] Summarizing this tendency within the context of evangelical awakenings, Bevans and Schroeder conclude, "Instead of waiting for a signal from an official church, individual Christians, often across denominational affiliations, joined societies to commit themselves to the task of world mission. Lay people as well as clergy were involved in these associations."[165] Comblin's observation that in Northeast Brazil, "every believer is a missionary" suggests a strong grassroots and volunteering tendency among Brazilian churches as well.[166] This value was certainly encouraged by Kenneth Strachan's Evangelism in Depth strategy beginning in 1959, which emphasized "total mobilization for total evangelization," and the 1969 Latin American Congress on Evangelization (CLADE I), which stressed mobilizing "the whole church for the evangelistic task."[167] Remarking that this tendency is quite second nature for Brazilians, George writes: "Many Protestant churches in Brazil feel no need to have an evangelism committee because members of the congregation actively practice evangelism with relatives, neighbors, friends, and strangers."[168] Summarizing the connection between volunteerism observed in the evangelical awakenings and that of Brazil and Latin America, Padilla asserts, "the lay ministry is one of the characteristics that show the Protestantism which has taken root in Latin America is related to the revivalists Protestantism of the eighteenth century."[169]

---

163. See Stark, "Efforts to Christianize Europe," 107.

164. See Noll, *History of Christianity*, 112, 169; Ahlstrom, *A Religious History of the American People*, 422–24; and Bosch, *Transforming Mission*, 280, 332.

165. See Bevans and Schroeder, *Constants in Context*, 210.

166. See Comblin, "Brazil: Base Communities," 219; also Robert, "Shifting Southward," 56.

167. See Saracco, "Mission and Missiology from Latin America," 361; also Penyak and Petry, *Religion in Latin America*, 360; and Willems, *Followers of the New Faith*, 6.

168. See George, "Brazil: An 'Evangelized' Giant," 105.

169. See Padilla, "New Actors on the Political Scene," 89; also Martin, *Tongues of Fire*, 273.

A final way that Brazilian evangelicalism has exhibited this evangelical conviction has been through setting apart indigenous leaders—both lay and full-time vocational ministers—at an early stage. Despite the difficult relationships at times between North American missionaries and Brazilian believers—and in some cases certain paternalism by the former—the effort to place Brazilians in leadership has been evident.[170] Braga affirms, "From the very beginning, nationals were carefully selected and made fully responsible for the work entrusted to them."[171]

While such empowerment occurred on an individual level, the larger mainline denominations—Presbyterians, Methodists, and Baptists in particular—also came under Brazilian leadership at a fairly early stage. Latourette asserts that they "became ecclesiastically independent of foreign control" which "tended to reduce their foreign character."[172] In the case of the main Pentecostal denominations, they were largely Brazilian in identity from the outset. The Assemblies of God, Brazil's largest evangelical denomination, was, of course, founded by missionaries from North America who later affiliated with the international denomination.[173] In a study of Pentecostal churches in Rio de Janeiro in 1992, Freston found that thirty-seven of the fifty-two denominations were of Brazilian origin, while nearly every church was led by a national pastor.[174]

Indeed, the Pentecostal churches—official denominations and independent churches alike—have been at the forefront of setting apart spiritual leaders, especially lay leaders, including those from poor backgrounds and with little formal education. As noted, this tendency reflects Pentecostalism's general affinity with the poor while at the same time, it reveals an ecclesiology that places more emphasis on the Holy Spirit's anointing of spiritual leaders than on a minister's formal training. Kane reports in 1980 that while the Assemblies of God had twenty official missionaries in Brazil, they also had 29,000 licensed ministers and another 27,000 lay workers

---

170. See George, "Presbyterian Seeds Bear Fruit in Brazil," 136; also Speer et al., *Christian Work in South America*, 2.257–59.

171. See Braga and Grubb, *The Republic of Brazil*, 117.

172. See Latourette, *A History of the Expansion of Christianity*, 5.123; also Stoll, *Is Latin America Turning Protestant?*, 109.

173. See González, *Christianity in Latin America*, 281; Cook, "Protestant Mission and Evangelization," 46; and Sepúlveda, "The Pentecostal Movement in Latin America," 68.

174. See Freston, "Contours in Latin American Pentecostalism," 232; also Bush, "Brazil, A Sleeping Giant Awakens."

serving in the church.¹⁷⁵ Also, in its early years, the Congregação Cristã no Brasil had no ordained or full-time vocational ministers. Hence, these two larger Pentecostal denominations have relied greatly upon bi-vocational and lay ministers.¹⁷⁶ Finally, among the exploding independent Pentecostal communities in Northeast Brazil, Comblin observes that "pastors are numerous and multiply amazingly."¹⁷⁷

Free Church

A final area of continuity between the nineteenth-century North American evangelical revivals and the church in Brazil was the proliferation of a free church model—a contrast to the Constantinian state church which had been prevalent since the fourth-century until the Anabaptist Reform. A number of scholars have argued that a free church mentality was encouraged by the First Great Awakening, and that the separation of church and state paradigm was a certain outcome.¹⁷⁸ Noll remarks that Baptist churches in particular flourished in the Southern colonies at this time because there was an alternative to the official Anglican Church.¹⁷⁹

Arguably, each of the evangelical qualities discussed—a high view of Scripture, conversion, visible faith, missionary zeal, and priesthood of the believer—fueled the notion of a free, believer's church in Europe, North America, and in Brazil. As noted, the immigrant churches in Brazil that were established prior to the first wave of evangelical missions were either official state churches (Lutheran, Anglican) or they were mainline denominations with little missionary emphasis. Not surprisingly, there was conflict between the immigrant churches and the evangelical missionaries.¹⁸⁰ North American missionaries, entering a Brazilian context that was politically and culturally fatigued with a state church model, planted free churches. Some missionaries from official church backgrounds in Europe—such as the Scottish Presbyterian Robert Reid Kalley or Anglican

---

175. See Kane, *A Concise History*, 149; also Chestnut, *Born Again in Brazil*, 30–31, 135.

176. See González, *Christianity in Latin America*, 281; also Berg and Pretiz, "Five Waves of Protestant Evangelization," 62; and Willems, *Followers of the New Faith*, 145.

177. See Comblin, "Brazil: Base Communities," 219–20.

178. See Spickard and Cragg, *A Global History of Christians*, 269–70; also Hankins, *The Second Great Awakening*, 4; and Ahlstrom, *A Religious History of the American People*, 290–94.

179. See Noll, *History of Christianity*, 99–103.

180. See González, *Christianity in Latin America*, 204–5.

workers—established churches in Brazil that were much more free church in their essence. This enduring free church value is implicit in a recent article on global missiology by Steurnegal, a Brazilian missiologist from the Lutheran tradition, who advocates "a season of 'local initiative'" where "local initiatives . . . replace centralized activities" in global mission efforts.[181]

Summarizing Brazil's Evangelical Identity

Apart from the documented paradigm shift in thinking on missions in Roman Catholic countries and Latin America that emerged within the Student Volunteer Movement, the literature related to eighteenth- and nineteenth-century evangelical awakenings does not offer a deliberate connection to mission work in Brazil. However, a careful assessment of the identity of Brazilian evangelicalism reveals some Pietistic influences that were at work during the Second Great Awakening in the decades preceding the first evangelical mission efforts to Brazil in the mid-nineteenth century. Hence, it has been argued that Brazilian evangelicalism is characterized by a high view of Scripture, a call to genuine conversion, a visible faith, a missionary zeal, the priesthood of the believer, and a free church tendency.

Freston generally places Brazilian evangelicalism within Bebbington's quadrilateral; however, he rightly concludes that the movement is slightly "larger" than its European and North American counterparts. First, Brazilian and Latin American evangelicals, led largely by the Latin American Theological Fellowship (FTL), have been committed to the "whole gospel" and ministering to social needs. While not embracing Liberation Theology on a full scale, they have taken seriously these issues raised by liberal Protestants and Catholics, and incorporated them into their missiology.[182]

Secondly, Brazilian evangelicals are generally more ecumenical in their regard for other evangelicals in contrast to North American and European evangelicals who have historically found more reason to be less inclusive.[183] Within Brazil and the Latin American context, "evangelical" and "Protestant" are understood to be the same thing. Also, with 70 percent of Brazilian evangelicals belonging to Pentecostal churches, the remaining minority of Methodists, Presbyterians, Baptists and other non-Pentecostal

---

181. See Steuernagel, "Learning from Escobar," 131.

182. See Freston, "Brazil: Church Growths," 233–38; also Ekström, "Brazilian Sending," 372.

183. See Freston, "Countours of Latin American Pentecostalism," 221.

denominations made a clear choice in the second half of the twentieth century to accept Pentecostals as evangelicals. While this does not mean that there has been an absence of theological reflection (as the evangelical response to the Igréja Universal do Reino de Deus has demonstrated), Brazilian evangelicals seem to be generally inclusive of other like-minded Christians: "theologically conservative, pietistic in spirituality, and very zealous about evangelization."[184]

Understanding how Brazil was evangelized and how the Brazilian church obtained its own evangelical identity is essential for appreciating its role as a mission-sending church. It is this latter focus that we now turn our attention.

Brazil: A Missions-Sending Nation

In summarizing his work *Christianity in Latin America,* Justo González fails to acknowledge that Latin America now sends its own missionaries to the world.[185] This omission is rather odd because González, a Cuban-American, has asserted elsewhere that "the history of the church is the history of mission."[186] In a recent article, Daniel Salinas angrily notes that while the stories of North American missionaries to Latin America have been effectively related, there has been a general failure to document the work of Latin missionaries.[187] Escobar adds that for every Latin American evangelical who has gone to the mission field as an "official" missionary—remembered by the church in its documented history—there have probably been ten others who have migrated abroad in search of work. The latter have also been involved in evangelism and church planting, yet their missionary contribution has gone unnoticed.[188] Despite the general failure to document the ministries of missionaries from Latin America, the goal of the present section is to begin to tell the stories of Brazilian evangelical transcultural workers, who make up at least half the Latin

---

184. Though Escobar's definition is focused upon Latin America in general, it is quite appropriate for Brazil. See Escobar, *Changing Tides,* 10.

185. See González, *Christianity in Latin America,* 302–10.

186. Cited in Escobar, *Changing Tides,* 4.

187. See Salinas, "The Great Commission in Latin America," 134–39.

188. Cited in Salinas, "The Great Commission in Latin America," 137. Ekström adds that there are probably hundreds of Brazilian tentmakers who have not been counted in the official statistics of Brazilian transcultural workers. See Ekström, "Missões a Partir do Brasil," 369.

American missionary force, while also highlighting the role of missionary movements from Brazil and Latin America.

A Brief Narrative of Twentieth-Century Brazilian Missions

The noted missionary zeal of Brazilian evangelicals resulted in concrete mission work among Brazil's indigenous peoples in the early twentieth century. As these efforts were discussed at length at the Montevideo Congress in 1925, it is apparent that evangelicals had already been concerned with the needs of these tribal peoples. In 1923, Presbyterians, Baptists, and Episcopalians had already set apart national missionaries to work among them. This emphasis has continued to the present day, as currently there are at least seven missions agencies in Brazil dedicated to reaching indigenous peoples,[189] and there is an increasing amount of Brazilian missiological reflection on tribal work.[190] One of the key resolutions of the Brazilian A.D. 2000 committee was to "assume a commitment to thoroughly reach the indigenous tribes of Brazil, principally through translation of the Bible into all dialects."[191] In a recent study, Ted Limpic has documented the growth and success of Brazilian missions toward tribal peoples: at present, 166 of 258 tribal peoples have some type of missionary presence; five people groups have a complete Bible translation while thirty-six others have a complete New Testament; and twenty groups have a church with a local pastor.[192]

In the early twentieth century, a relatively short period after foreign missionaries reached Brazil, Brazilian evangelicals were also contemplating global missions. From its inception in 1907, the Brazilian Baptist Convention shared this global focus, and in 1920 J. J. Oliveira was sent to Portugal where he was later joined by Antonio Mauricio. Though Oliveira later joined another missions organization, Mauricio continued the Baptist work in collaboration with Portuguese pastor Pablo Torres.[193] In the same year, João Marques de Mota was the first Brazilian Presbyterian sent

---

189. The missions agencies, listed at "COMIBAM" include Associação Evangélica Missionária Indígena; Missão Evangélica aos Indios do Brasil; Missão Evangélica da Amazônia; Missão Novas Tribos do Brasil; Missão Indígena UNIEDAS; Org da Missão Indígena da Tribo Ticuna do Alto Salimões; Missão Projeto Amazonas.

190. Three recent books on indigenous ministry include: Lidório, *Indígenas do Brasil*; Souza and Lidório, *A Questão Indígena*; and Souza, *De Todas as Tribos*.

191. See Prado, "The Brazil Model."

192. See Limpic, "As Tribos Indígenas Brasileiras."

193. See Anderson, *An Evangelical Saga*, 150, 155.

abroad as he also went to Portugal.[194] When Brazilian Presbyterians closed their Portuguese mission in 1924, Erasmo Braga and his father founded an independent mission in order to continue the work.[195] Because of the great needs within Brazil and a deliberate focus on local missions, Portugal remained the sole overseas mission field for Brazilian Baptists until 1946. However, in 1948 twelve Brazilians were sent to begin work in Bolivia, which resulted in twelve churches being planted by 1965. In the same year, the Baptists began their work in neighboring Paraguay.[196]

Ekström adds that the presence and growth of international missions agencies in Brazil beginning in the latter half of the twentieth century further encouraged the Brazilian church's missionary zeal. While these agencies were primarily committed to reaching Brazil, many approached their work with a global focus.[197] One such organization was Operation Mobilization (OM). Though they did not establish an office in Brazil until 1986, OM began recruiting Brazilian youth to serve on its ships in the late 1970s. Indeed, many Brazilians presently serving in the Arab world as well as other countries had their first exposure to global missions through OM.[198]

At the Lausanne Congress in 1974, Shedd and Landrey, giving the report on the Brazilian church, indicated that Brazilians were serving in twenty-one countries—nine of which were other countries in South America, while four were Portuguese-speaking countries. At the time, there was no record of Brazilians serving in the Arab world.[199]

Missão Antioquia

Given this brief narrative of Brazilian sending until Lausanne in 1974—keeping in mind Escobar's point that the majority of Brazilian and Latin American mission work has probably gone undocumented—the Brazilian missions movement seemed to take on unprecedented life around 1975. In the midst of a charismatic renewal in the state of Paraná in the late 1960s, two young Presbyterian pastors, Jonathan Ferreira dos Santos and Décio

---

194. See Ekström, "Uma Análise Histórica," 7–8. I am indebted to Cristina Boersma who read this work in Portuguese and provided a summary in English.
195. See Salinas, "The Great Commission in Latin America," 130.
196. See Anderson, *An Evangelical Saga,* 160, 169.
197. See Ekström, "Uma Análise Histórica," 8–10.
198. Ibid., 8.
199. See "Brazil National Strategy Group Report," 1344.

de Azevedo, founded a Bible school. Preaching, prayer, healing, miracles, and holistic ministry to the surrounding communities characterized the school's existence in this continual atmosphere of renewal. Though the school's leadership was initially resistant to the idea of global missions, American missionary Barbara Burns and others who taught at the school were instrumental in sharing a global vision. As the community began to pray for the world, the first missionaries were sent to Portuguese-speaking Mozambique in the mid-1970s. Hence, not unlike the atmosphere of revival that first moved North Americans and others to Brazil in the mid-nineteenth century, revival within Brazil also pushed Brazilians to take notice of the rest of the world.

In 1975, the school went one step farther and founded Missão Antioquia (Antioch Mission), Brazil's first interdenominational and national missions organization. Azevedo was named the mission's first president. In 1977, the mission opened a seminary and missionary training center in Paraná, which, along with the mission, moved to São Paulo in 1980.[200] Missão Antioquia currently has ninety-two Brazilian missionaries on the field in nineteen countries—four of which are serving in Arab countries in North Africa and the Middle East. According to their website, their primary areas of ministry include evangelism, discipleship, church planting, children's ministry, community development, and sports ministry, among others.[201] The mission has not only sent Brazilian workers overseas, but it has modeled a spirit of unity and partnership through initiating the Associação de Missões Transculturais Brasileiras (Association of Transcultural Missions Agencies).[202]

Curitiba Conference

In the early 1970s, Neuza Itioka, a Brazilian teacher of Japanese descent and leader of Aliança Bíblica Universitária (IFES), attended a number a number of global missions consultations, including Lausanne, which instilled in her a vision for Brazil as a mission-sending country.[203] Itioka and ABU organized the first Latin American missions conference on the campus of the University of Paraná in Curitiba in January 1976 under

200. See Burns, "Brazilian Antioch Community," 515–16; also "Missão Antioquia," and Prado, "A New Way of Sending Missionaries," 55–56.
201. See "Missão Antioquia."
202. See "Associação de Missões Transculturais Brasileiras."
203. See Ekström, "Uma Análise Histórica," 9.

the theme "Jesus Christ: Lordship, Purpose, Mission." In some respects, the conference—a "Latin Student Volunteer Movement"—was attended by 500 delegates (450 Brazilians and fifty other Latinos), though another 1500 participants had hoped to attend. The meeting, which ended up serving as a watershed for Brazilian and Latin American missions, can best be summarized through these lines in its "Declaration of Curitiba":

> We recognize that mission cannot be an isolated department of the life of the church; rather, it is an essential part of its essence because "the church is a missionary church or it is no church at all." Therefore, the mission involves every Christian in the totality of their life, substituting the wrong concept of the "professional missionary labor" with the universal priesthood of all believers. We are profoundly concerned for the lack of this missionary vision of the church within the Latin American context.[204]

Indeed, the noted Brazilian evangelical values of missionary zeal and the priesthood of the believer are clearly observed in the statement. Combined with a new, profound sense of responsibility, these values would propel the Brazilian and Latin American churches to a new level of involvement in global missions.

COMIBAM

Just a decade after the Curitiba conference, the Brazilian church joined with other Latin American evangelicals for the first meeting of COMIBAM, (the Ibero-American Missionary Congress) which met in São Paulo in 1987.[205] Generally following in the wake of the historic global mission meetings at Edinburgh (1910), Panama (1916), Berlin (1966), and Lausanne (1974), the first COMIBAM gathering was attended by 3100 delegates from every country in Latin America as well as from twenty-five other countries. The conference's main goal was to provide a "wake-up call" for the Latin American church to get involved in and take responsibility for

---

204. Cited in Salinas "The Great Commission in Latin America," 147; see also Escobar, *Changing Tides*, 157.

205. COMIBAM stands for the Cooperacíon Misiononera Iberoameriana (Ibero-American Missionary Cooperation), which generally includes the Spanish and Portuguese speaking countries of Latin America and the Iberian Peninsula. See Guarneri, "COMIBAM," vi–vii, 1.

the remaining task of global missions.[206] This sense of ownership was best expressed in the articulated resolution given at the end of the conference: "United by the fervent desire to be light to the nations, we—the participants in COMIBAM 87, trusting in the help of the Lord, in the direct and power of the Word and of the Spirit—invite all of our brothers and sisters in Ibero-America to get involved with us in the faithful completion of the mission that He has given us: 'I have made you a light for the Gentiles, that you may bring salvation to the ends of the earth' (Acts 13:47)."[207] Recognizing that the Latin American church did not have the material resources of its North American or European counterparts, Guatemalan Pastor Rudy Giron gave this charge to the delegates: "Missions from Latin America will be sacrificial. We don't have computers; we don't have dollars; but 'By My Spirit, say the Lord.'"[208] Even in the early stages of the COMIBAM network in 1987, it should be noted that 1600 Latin American missionaries had been sent out by seventy missions agencies.

COMIBAM II was held in Acapulco, Mexico in 1997 and was attended by 2000 delegates.[209] The primary focus of the second gathering was to evaluate what had happened in Latin American missions sending since 1987. Ruiz elaborates: "The focus of the evaluation was based, principally, on the missionary process. Missionary screening, training, sending and pastoral care and supervision on the field were under scrutiny."[210] In large part due to COMIBAM's influence, 3921 missionaries serving with 284 missions organizations had been sent out by 1997.[211]

COMIBAM III took place in Granada, Spain in November 2006 and was attended by 2000 participants from thirty-seven countries—twenty-five of those were Ibero-American.[212] The purpose of the meeting was to provide critical evaluation of the movement in general. As Levi DeCarvalho relates, the aim was "to improve cross-cultural service and reach a new level of maturity in our mission work."[213] In order to gain an accurate read of the movement's status, 288 Ibero-American workers from diverse nationalities (fifty were Brazilian), different denominational backgrounds,

206. See DeCarvalho, "COMIBAM III: Research Project—Phase I," 20.
207. Cited in Ruiz, "COMIBAM as a process," 9.
208. Cited in Escobar, *Changing Tides,* 159.
209. See Smith, "COMIBAM Takeoff Toward AD 2007," 53.
210. See Ruiz, "COMIBAM as a process," 10.
211. See Escobar, *Changing Tides,* 160.
212. See Londoño, "General Report," 11.
213. See DeCarvalho, "COMIBAM III: Research Project—Phase I," 20.

and varying levels of experience were invited to the conference. In all, members of the group were serving in sixty-two countries—ten of which were Arab-Muslim countries.[214] Participants were asked to offer feedback on areas such as pre-field training, financial support, cultural adaptation, communication between mission leaders and missionaries, relationships between missionaries, mental and physical health, and ministry success and failure.

Despite this serious commitment to assessing the movement, Brazilian Alex Araujo rejoiced: "At COMIBAM III . . . we saw our own Latin missionaries speaking of lessons learned . . . the Ibero-American missions movement is no longer a baby or an adolescent, but a young adult, showing signs of maturity, stability, and strength."[215] At the time of COMIBAM III, the number of Ibero-American workers had grown to 9000 serving with 400 different organizations.[216] In early 2009, Carlos Scott indicated that the number of Latin American transcultural workers had reached ten thousand.[217] Guarneri affirms that 16 percent of this total missionary force is presently serving in the 10/40 window, some of which are serving in the Arab-Muslim world.[218]

After three large conferences as well as the development of COMIBAM networks within each Latin American country, the movement's vision is "to help the Ibero-American Church to become a missionary community, able to take the gospel of Jesus Christ to all nations."[219] In general, COMIBAM is focused on five major areas: strengthening national and missionary movements, reaching unreached peoples, cultivating an Ibero-American missiology, improving leadership development, and developing global cooperation and partnerships.[220]

In light of its history, vision, and focus, what are COMIBAM's distinct values? First, as a network of networks, COMIBAM seeks to facilitate communication and partnership among pastors, training centers (biblical, theological, and missiological), and sending structures (churches and mission boards). COMIBAM's emphasis on communication with pastors

---

214. The countries include: Saudi Arabia, Algeria, Chad, Iraq, Jordan, Morocco, Western Sahara, Mauritania, and Tunisia. See DeCarvalho, "COMIBAM III: Research Project—Phase I," 20.

215. See Araujo, "Impressions of III COMIBAM," 29.

216. See Ruiz, "COMIBAM as a Viable Regional Mission Movement," 7.

217. See Scott, "Latin American Sending," 375.

218. See Guarneri, "COMIBAM," 23.

219. See Scott and Londoño, "Where is COMIBAM International Heading?"

220. See Guarneri, "COMIBAM," 22.

and churches points to the fact that Latin American missiology is distinctively church-centered—a tendency less observed in North America and Europe.[221] Second, in terms of leadership structure, Guarneri notes that one of COMIBAM's strengths is that it is far less bureaucratic than a typical denomination or mission.[222] Bertil Ekström, a Brazilian who served as the movement's director following COMIBAM II, summarized this philosophy of leadership: "COMIBAM seeks to be a facilitator and a catalyst, working to strengthen existing mission efforts in Latin America and to start new ones."[223] Third, COMIBAM's global focus has been greatly facilitated by a healthy unity between Latin American evangelicals from various denominations and theological persuasions.[224] This evangelical "ecumenism" has, of course, been noted as a key aspect of Brazilian evangelicalism. Finally, though delegates seemed to disagree over the relationship between social action and evangelism at COMIBAM II, the movement has been influenced by the Latin American Theological Fellowship's (FTL) value of the "whole gospel," which has resulted in more ministries devoted to community development and caring for human needs.[225]

Associação de Missões Transculturais Brasileiras (AMTB)

As noted, shortly after Antioch Mission was founded, the Associação de Missões Transculturais Brasileiras (Association of Transcultural Missions Agencies) began in 1976. Beginning with a small group of mission leaders and organizations in the 1970s, Ekström notes that by 2002 the AMTB included forty-six agencies.[226] The AMTB's objectives are mobilizing Brazilian evangelical churches to great mission involvement, promoting dialogue and cooperation between missions organizations, developing materials to educate the Brazilian churches in global mission, and encouraging and offering training for Brazilian missionaries.[227] Distinctively interdenominational, the AMTB deals with issues such as: the relation-

---

221. See Ruiz, "COMIBAM as a Viable Regional Mission Movement," 6–7.

222. See Guarneri, "COMIBAM," 17–18.

223. Cited in Ruiz, "COMIBAM as a process," 10.

224. See Guarneri, "COMIBAM," 5; and Ruiz, "COMIBAM as a Viable Regional Mission Movement," 5.

225. See Smith, "COMIBAM Takeoff Towards AD 2007," 54.

226. See Ekström, "Uma Análise Histórica," 19–23, 122–23. Presently, the web sites of thirty-five organizations are linked to the AMTB site.

227. See Ekström, "Uma Análise Histórica," 55.

ship between local churches and missions agencies, selecting and training missionaries, pastoral care for missionaries, fund raising, mission strategy, and the Brazilian church's missionary vision.[228] Aside from publishing books and literature on mission, and maintaining a web site that is rich in content and a vehicle for networking, the AMTB has convened five missionary congresses since 1990 in order to facilitate dialogue.[229]

PM International

The story of PM International is also unique in that it is a missions agency founded by Mexican missionary Pablo Carillo in 1984 in order to send Latin American missionaries to the Muslim world.[230] Currently, there are 120 Ibero-Americans from fourteen nationalities serving in Muslim countries and PMI has national offices in Argentina, Spain, the United States, and Brazil. The mission statement of PMI Brazil, which opened in 1998, is "to see the Brazilian evangelical church committed to the expansion of the kingdom of God among Muslims."[231] With a focus on planting indigenous churches and ministering the whole gospel among Muslims, PMI also emphasizes pre-field preparation in missiology and Islamic studies, cultivating healthy teams, member care, general supervision, and assisting missionaries to gain entry into creative access nations.[232]

Missão Horizontes

In 1992, Brazilian pastor David Bothelo connected with the Welsh-based mission World Horizons and eventually a vision was birthed to send Brazilians and Latin Americans to the 10/40 Window. In 1998, the newly constituted Missão Horizontes initiated the Sahel Project in which sixteen Brazilians, after some training in Brazil and Paraguay, were sent to Niger in West Africa. A ministry characterized by voluntary poverty and communal living, it was at that time the largest group of Brazilian missionaries sent out in the history of Brazilian mission sending.[233]

228. Ibid., 57–112.
229. Ibid., 85.
230. See Miller, "Mission-Minded Latinos," 70.
231. English translation by Cristina Boersma from "PMI Brasil: Latinos ao Mundo Muçulmano."
232. See "PMI USA."
233. See Bothelo, "The Principles, Practice and Plan."

Brazilian Evangelical Missions in the Arab World

In 1999, Bothelo and Horizontes mobilized a second outreach called the Radical Project, which was comprised of ninety-six laborers. Though mostly made up of Brazilians, participants also came from three other countries. While generally more Pentecostal, the group included workers from sixteen different denominations. After making a five-year commitment, participants spent the first year in training in Brazil, the second year in cross-cultural ministry training in Argentina or Paraguay, and part of the third year in Wales learning English. In the final two and a half years of the project, they dispersed to various 10/40 window countries for ministry—including some Arab-Muslim contexts. Like the Sahel Project, the Radical Project championed poverty and communal living, yet it also went further emphasizing thorough cross-cultural training as well as focused ministry on the field.[234]

Eventually, Bothelo's Missão Horizontes split with the British-based World Horizons office. Nevertheless, these initiatives proved to be great strides forward for Brazillian evangelical missions among unreached peoples and, at present, Brazilians from the Sahel and Radical Projects continue to serve in the Arab world.

Current Status of Brazilian Evangelical Missions

In a recent work, Mark Noll notes, "Today more Christian workers from Brazil are active in cross-cultural ministry outside their homelands than from Britain or Canada."[235] Citing the growth of Brazilian evangelical missions in the last four decades, Ekström writes, "The number of evangelical missionaries from Brazil has increased significantly since the 1970s. There were 595 missionaries in 1972; 791 missionaries in 1980; 2040 missionaries in 1988; 2755 missionaries in 1992; and 4754 missionaries in 2000. Today, Brazilian missionaries are working on every continent."[236] By 2006, these transcultural workers were serving with 115 different missions organizations.[237]

In addition, Ted Limpic provides a helpful breakdown of where Brazilian evangelicals are serving. While a large number are located inside of Brazil (around 750 laborers) or elsewhere in South America (1560 workers), some 456 Brazilians are serving in Africa, while seventy-five

234. Ibid.; also Decker and Keating, "The Radical Project."
235. See Noll, *The New Shape of World Christianity*, 10.
236. See Ekström, "Brazilian Sending," 372.
237. See Ekström, "Missões a Partir do Brasil," 369.

are presently working in Japan. Limpic adds that 20 percent of all Brazilian missionaries serve in the 10/40 window and 281 workers are focused on the Muslim world—both among Arabs and non-Arabs.[238] Based on interviews with Brazilian mission leaders and Brazilian workers in Arab contexts, a conservative estimate is that there are between 120 and 150 Brazilians presently serving in the Arab-Muslim world. The remainder of our study will, of course, discuss the ministry of these Brazilian transcultural workers.

Summary

In this chapter, attention has been given to the rise of evangelical missions in Brazil, a movement that primarily originated in North America in the nineteenth century and that was prompted by evangelical revivals. Though a documented connection between these revivals and evangelical mission work in the South American country is not clear in the literature, a plausible connection has been made by examining the common features between nineteenth-century North American and European revivalist evangelicalism and Brazilian evangelicalism. Though these common features include a high view of Scripture, a call to genuine conversion, a visible faith, a missionary zeal, the priesthood of the believer, and a free church tendency, Brazilian evangelicals have also distinguished themselves by embracing an integrated gospel that includes both verbal proclamation and caring for human needs, and for being more inclusive of other evangelicals (i.e. Pentecostals). Each of these tendencies has propelled the Brazilian church, along with the evangelical church in Latin America, to develop into a missionary-sending church. Brazilians, as noted, presently make up half of the mission force from Latin America. Hence, this chapter, relying largely on the historical narrative, has largely confirmed Luis Bush's statement at COMIBAM in 1987 that "from a mission field, Latin America has become a mission force."[239]

---

238. See Limpic, "O Movimento Missionário Brasilerio (2005)"; also Finley, "Contextualized Training for Missionaries," 5–7. Silas Tostes, in an interview on July 23, 2009, reported that at a recent pre-field training with ten new Antioch Mission candidates, all ten were interested in serving among Muslims.

239. Cited in Prado, "A New Way of Sending Missionaries," 52.

2

Brazilian Workers in Arab Culture, Part 1

Introduction

IN THEIR REPORT ON Brazil at the Lausanne Conference for World Evangelization in 1974, Shedd and Landrey stated, "We understand that the greatest opportunity and responsibility in terms of Brazilian missionary work is in relation to those people with whom we have racial and linguistic affinity (Latin America, Africa, and other Portuguese-speaking peoples)."[1] At this stage in Brazil's history, missions in the Arab-Muslim world was not a stated priority for the Brazilian evangelical church; rather, emphasis was placed on those regions and peoples that shared cultural proximity to Brazil. Indeed, as we have shown, many Brazilians in the twentieth century went to serve in Portugal as well as in the Portuguese-speaking countries of Southern Africa.

In chapters 2 and 3, we raise the question, what does it mean, culturally speaking, to be a Brazilian evangelical missionary in the Arab world? Forty-five past and present Brazilian evangelical workers were invited to comment and reflect upon their own "Brazilianness" and how they have adapted in the Arab world. The perspectives of ten Brazilian mission leaders have also been included. I have treated Brazil as an affinity bloc

---

1. See Douglass, "Brazil National Strategy Group Report," 1344; also Finley, "Contextualized Training for Missionaries," 73.

of cultures in which there is clear diversity as well as some elements of cohesiveness. I have approached the Arab world in the same way. Hence, the framework for discussing Brazilians in the Arab world has been to reflect upon two affinity blocs and to ask members of one group (Brazilians) to share their collective experiences living in a second group (the Arab world) specifically regarding aspects of culture that have clear missiological implications. In chapter 2 we will deal with four areas—race, economics, time, and communication—while in chapter 3 we will consider family, relationships, hospitality, and spiritual worldview. After first consulting the appropriate cultural and missiological literature and then listening to the experiences of Brazilian missionaries and mission leaders, it has become evident, culturally speaking, that Brazilians are not Arabs and that Brazilians must surely work to adapt culturally. However, it also appears that there is generally less cultural distance between the Brazilians surveyed and their Arab contexts than what is normally experienced by Western missionaries in the Arab world, allowing Brazilian evangelical work to be less intrusive.[2]

The importance of studying the relationship of the missionaries' culture and that of their host cultures has been raised by a number of scholars. Finley writes: "Once missiologists start thinking about the factors in the missionary's native culture that should be taken into account in designing their training, the logical next step is to apply those same cultural factors in deciding where in the world missionaries from any given country are likely to be more effective. This could be done by comparing and contrasting characteristics of the missionary's native culture with characteristics of possible host cultures."[3] Keyes and Pate assert that there is a greater general cultural proximity between missionaries from the majority world and their host cultures.[4] Regarding Brazilian missionaries, Mordomo affirms that "Brazilians . . . generally have much more in common culturally with unreached peoples of the world than do the traditional sending nations from North America and Europe."[5] Concerning the relationship between Brazilians and Arab-Muslims, Finley adds that from "both the literature

---

2. For more discussion on reducing the gospel's intrusiveness, see Kraft, *Anthropology for Christian Witness*, 359–60, 400.
3. See Finley, "Contextualized Training for Missionaries," 250.
4. See Keyes and Pate, "Two-Thirds World Missions," 191.
5. See Mordomo, "Unleashing the Brazilian Missionary Force," 219; also Downey, "Ibero-Americans Reaching Arab-Muslims."

and conversations [that] . . . I have had with missionaries and Arab Christians point to similarities between Brazilian and Muslim cultures."[6]

In short, following a brief discussion of culture in general, I will offer some qualifications about the difficult task of describing the cultures of the Arab world and Brazil and then reiterate the theoretical framework that will enable the discussion. As missiological concerns are driving this study, the aspects of culture being discussed in these two chapters are intentionally limited to eight areas. After an initial consideration of the influence of Arab culture on Brazil, which has occurred as a result of significant immigration from the Arab world, these eight areas will be discussed, the Brazilian experiences in the Arab world will be narrated, and the subsequent missiological implications will be explored.

What is Culture?

Though there is a general consensus toward a definition of culture in missiological and anthropological literature within the evangelical tradition—where the present study is focused— it is nevertheless helpful to state what is meant by culture. The drafters of the Willowbank Report propose a helpful and rather thick definition:

> Culture is an integrated system of beliefs (about God or reality or ultimate meaning), of values (about what is true, good, beautiful and normative), of customs (how to behave, relate to others, talk, pray, dress, work, play, trade, farm, eat, etc.) and of institutions which express these beliefs values and customs (government, law courts, temples or churches, family, schools, hospitals, factories, shops, unions, clubs, etc.), which binds a society together and gives it a sense of identity, security and continuity.[7]

Lingenfelter and Mayers assert more succinctly that culture is "the conceptual design, the definitions by which people order their lives, interpret their experience, and evaluate the behavior of others."[8] Finally, Hiebert adds that it is "the set of rules that govern the games of life that

---

6. See Finley, "Contextualized Training for Missionaries," 252. Though her concerns are not missiological, Arabist Margaret Nydell (Nydell, *Understanding Arabs*, 191) concludes a thorough discussion on Arab culture by asserting, "many people find it similar to life in the Mediterranean area and Latin America."

7. See "The Willowbank Report," section 2.

8. See Lingenfelter and Mayers, *Ministering Cross-Culturally*, 18.

we play in our society,"[9] while Nida describes culture as "the rhyme and reason" of life.[10]

In addition to these helpful definitions of culture, it should also be noted that culture is perceived in layers. Kraft correctly asserts that "culture consists of two levels: the surface behavior level and the deep worldview level."[11] That is, a given people group's observed customs and symbols are undergirded by beliefs, feelings, and values which dictate their views on what is appropriate, beautiful, good, evil, right, and wrong.[12] These ultimately refer to the people group's worldview—"the culturally structured set of assumptions underlying how a people perceive and respond to reality."[13] As worldview governs observed behaviors, customs, and symbols, an important strategy toward understanding that worldview is to probe the visible elements of a people's culture. Affirming this methodology, Hiebert writes, "Human behavior and material objects are readily observable. Consequently, they are important entry points in our study of culture."[14] Edward T. Hall well summarizes the relationship between these layers of culture by adding, "The various facets of culture are interrelated—you touch culture in one place and everything else is affected."[15]

The Difficulty of Describing Culture

Before embarking on a discussion of Arab and Brazilian cultures, some qualifications and concessions about the task must be first made. Because of the diversity and complexity present within any given culture, it is admittedly difficult to make definitive conclusions about that culture because, as Kraft asserts, "The inventory of a culture is, of course, very large."[16] Given this, the attempt to have a conversation about two distinct cultures is even more daunting.

Commentators on Arab culture have struggled to reconcile the unity and diversity that exist among Arab peoples. Nydell notes the diversity of Arabic dialects, ethnicity, and customs that exist among the primary

---

9. See Hiebert, "Cultural Differences," 375.
10. See Nida, *Customs and Cultures*, 25, 45.
11. See Kraft, *Anthropology for Christian Witness*, 11.
12. See Hiebert, "Cultural Differences," 376; also Niebuhr, *Christ and Culture*, 33.
13. See Kraft, "Culture, Worldview, and Contextualization," 401.
14. See Hiebert, "Cultural Differences," 375.
15. See Hall, *Beyond Culture*, 16.
16. See Kraft, *Anthropology for Christian Witness*, 360.

regions of the Arab world—the Arabian Peninsula (Saudi Arabia, Yemen, and Gulf State of UAE, Qatar, Oman, Kuwait, Bahrain), the Levant (Lebanon, Syria, Palestine, Jordan, and Iraq), Northeastern Africa (Egypt and Sudan), and the Maghreb (Morocco, Algeria, Tunisia, Libya, and sometimes Mauritania).[17] Arab sociologist and novelist Halim Barakat observes discontinuity within the Arab world because some countries like Algeria have pursued a policy of Arabization in attempting to establish their post-colonial identity, while others have been less aggressive in this regard.[18] Barakat further notes the social, tribal, and religious differences among Arabs—both within the same countries and among neighboring nations—which sometimes has resulted in social unrest and even military conflict.[19] He concludes: "Like other societies, the Arabs have their dominant culture . . . its subcultures . . . and its countercultures . . . As a result of such diversity among constituent cultures, and as a product of new inventions and resources, culture changes constantly."[20]

While acknowledging the complex cultural diversity among Arabs, Barakat still prefers to "view the Arab world as a single, overarching society" rather than "a mere mosaic of sects, ethnic groups, tribes, local communities, and regional entities."[21] At the conclusion of her survey of the various regions of the Arab world, Nydell also affirms that these nations "all have an Arab identity."[22] Indeed, within the Arab world, despite the noted conflicts, there remains a prevailing sense of unity among Arabs in their cultural identity.[23]

In light of the diverse ethnic landscape among Arabs, what are the essential elements of being Arab? The most compelling unifying factor is language. Hourani, reflecting the consensus of scholarship, identifies Arabs as "all those, from Morocco and Spain to the frontier of Iran, who had adopted Arabic as their vernacular language; or . . . those for whom Arabic had become the principal medium of expression of a high literary culture."[24]

---

17. See Nydell, *Understanding Arabs*, 148–49.
18. See Barakat, *The Arab World*, 18; also Patai, *The Arab Mind*, 199–215.
19. See Barakat, *The Arab World*, 32–33; also Nydell, *Understanding Arabs*, 14–16.
20. See Barakat, *The Arab World*, 182.
21. Ibid., xi–xii.
22. See Nydell, *Understanding Arabs*, 13.
23. See Patai, *The Arab Mind*, 14.
24. See Hourani, *A History of the Arab Peoples*, 49; also Patai, *The Arab Mind*, 44; Nydell, *Understanding Arabs*, xxii; and Barakat, *The Arab World*, 33–34.

A second foundational characteristic of Arab culture is the religion of Islam. While Arab Christians have had a presence in the Middle East since before the rise of Islam and continue to exist as significant minority in the present day, Arab culture has come to be dominated by a prevailing Muslim worldview. From a cultural perspective, one of the Qur'an's greatest contributions has been to preserve the Arabic language over the course of time and as the Arab peoples have spread out and dispersed geographically.[25] This inextricable link between the Qur'an, Islam, the Arabic language, and culture is perhaps best expressed by the eleventh-century philologist al-Tha'alib who wrote: "Whomsoever God has guided to Islam . . . believes that Muhammad is the best of the prophets . . . that the Arabs are the best of the peoples . . . and that Arabic is the best of languages."[26] Carmichael comments further on this relationship of religion and culture among Arabs by writing, "As the Arabs gave birth to Islam, so they were, in a way formed by it."[27]

Beginning with this basic foundation of language and religion, Patai suggests that there is an observable national character present among the Arab peoples. Beginning with the work of the medieval historian Ibn Khaldoun (c. 1332–1406) and continuing to assess Arab civilization into the twentieth century, Patai describes this general unity as "the sum total of the motives, traits, beliefs, and values shared by the plurality in a national population."[28] Hence, this overarching unity in Arab culture allows for some general conclusions to be made about Arabs and provides a basis for Arab peoples to be discussed with other cultural groups.

The task of making general conclusions about Brazilian culture may actually be more difficult than describing the Arabs. Though Brazilians reside within a single nation, not including those who have immigrated to other countries, the cultural and ethnic diversity among the country's 291 people groups has led observers to ask, what is Brazil? During my interview with veteran Brazilian missionary Marcos Amado in 2009, he jokingly said, "When you figure out what Brazilian culture is, please let me know." In the following simple but helpful overview, Brazilianist Joseph Page attempts to summarize the various attitudes and values observed in the major regions of Brazil: "*Paulistas* (people from the state of São Paulo) are hardworking and entrepreunerial; *cariocas* (residents of Rio de Janeiro)

---

25. See Patai, *The Arab Mind*, 9–14; and Barakat, *The Arab World*, 35.
26. Cited in Patai, *The Arab Mind*, 46.
27. See Carmichael, *The Shaping of the Arabs*, 2.
28. See Patai, *The Arab Mind*, 19.

carefree and fun loving; *mineiros* (inhabitants of the state of Minas Gerais) cautious and frugal; *nordestinos* (Northeasterners) introverted; and *gauchos* (people from the extreme South) fiercely independent."[29] Schneider appropriately warns students of Brazilian culture that the country "is so diverse that generalizations about it run the risk of being either bland platitudes or the lowest-common-denominator-variety or averages that mask great variations."[30] While such warnings against simplistic conclusions should be heeded, there have still been some attempts to understand "Brazilianness" in general. The most intriguing work has been done by the Brazilian sociologist Roberto DaMatta, who has described Brazil's diversity—"this mixture of Western and non-Western, as well as modern and traditional"— as "the Brazilian puzzle."[31] While DaMatta's paradigm certainly reveals the difficulty of understanding the complex cultural mosaic of Brazil, the puzzle analogy still points to a level of cohesiveness, which will allow the observer to offer descriptions of Brazilianness. Indeed, some clear aspects of shared Brazilian culture will become apparent through the eight areas of culture being discussed in the current chapter.

Theoretical Framework for Discussing Cultures

Given the complexities within Arab and Brazilian culture and being mindful of the danger of drawing simplistic conclusions about these cultures, what will be our theoretical framework for discussing both cultural groups? First, it seems helpful to follow Patrick Johnstone's approach of regarding the Arab world as a cluster or affinity bloc of peoples.[32] That is, as already suggested by Barakat, Patai, and Nydell among others, there is an overarching unity among the Arab peoples even amid significant diversity. My approach has also been to apply this framework to the cultures of Brazil, viewing its melting pot of peoples as an affinity bloc of cultures. Hence, I am inviting one affinity bloc (Brazilians) to reflect on their "Brazilianness" in light of their experiences within another affinity bloc (the Arab world).

Second, in light of culture being understood in terms of layers—observed behaviors and customs which may be traced to values, beliefs, and worldview—I have asked Brazilians to reflect on their experiences in the

29. See Page, *The Brazilians*, 12; also Harrison, *Behaving Brazilian*, 1–3.
30. Cited in Finley, "Contextualized Training for Missionaries," 66.
31. See Hess and DaMatta, *The Brazilian Puzzle*, 2, 23.
32. See Johnstone, "Look at the Fields" 17.

Arab world at the level of observed behaviors, after which potential common areas of worldview may be assessed and analyzed.

Third, as the current study is concerned with Brazilian evangelical mission work among Arabs, the aspects of culture being discussed are deliberately missiological in scope; thus, I have chosen to limit them to the eight noted areas of race, economics, time, communication, family, relationships, hospitality, and spiritual worldview.[33]

With this general framework in mind, my approach has been first to gather data on Arab and Brazilian culture in these eight areas from the relevant cultural and literature. Second, with the literary evidence serving as a theoretical background, I have classified the themes that emerged from the surveys and interviews with Brazilian evangelical workers in the Arab world who have commented on their cultural experience in the Arab world in light of their own cultural background. Finally, after each area of culture has been discussed and analyzed, the missiological implications will be discussed.

The Influence of Arab Culture on Brazil

Before commencing this larger discussion, it would be helpful to consider briefly the historical influence of Arab culture on Brazil. First, it should be noted that Brazilians of pure Portuguese descent are probably quite influenced by Arab culture because of the Arab presence in Portugal for over 500 years—from AD 711 to the middle of the twelfth century.[34] This historical reality probably explains some cultural similarities between Brazilians and Arabs. However, Arabs have also influenced Brazil through the waves of immigration, which have taken place throughout the twentieth century. Today, there are six to ten million Arabs in Brazil—the majority residing in the state of São Paulo—putting Arabs at around 5 percent of the total population.[35] While most are from Christian backgrounds and immigrated from Syria and Lebanon in the earlier part of the twentieth century, in recent years many Lebanese Muslims have also come to Brazil after fleeing civil war in Lebanon.[36] Initially earning a living as ped-

---

33. This approach has been greatly informed by Hiebert's anthropological insights in *Transforming Worldviews*, 81, 103–4.

34. See Page, *The Brazilians*, 42; also Finley, "Contextualized Training for Missionaries," 116.

35. See Karam, "Distinguishing Arabesques," 11–13.

36. Ibid., 180–82, 194.

dlers, Arab immigrants have succeeded in becoming leaders in business, medicine, and politics over the course of the twentieth century.[37]

Brazilian Arabs commonly refer to themselves as "Syrian" (*sírio*), "Lebanese" (*libanês*), "Syrio-Lebanese" (*sírio-libanês*) or simply "Arab" (*árabe*); however, over time these terms have come to be understood generally as "Arab" with little distinction being made over specific Arab origins.[38] However, much of the greater Brazilian population still refers to Arabs as *turcos* (literally "Turks"). Though the early twentieth-century Arab immigrants to Brazil were called *turcos* because the Arab peoples were under Ottoman rule and carried Turkish passports, this quickly became a pejorative term used by Brazilians who did not appreciate the presence of Arab shopkeepers and peddlers.[39] However, as Arabs began to see success in business and politics, they managed to redefine the term and actually use it toward their advantage. Karam notes: "Initially scored as *turcos*, Turks, Syrian-Lebanese merchants rejected the label as degrading Middle Eastern difference in mid-century Brazil. Yet, resignifying the ethnonym of *turco* today, liberal professionals emphasized its nondiscriminatory valence."[40] In light of this, Karam adds that Arabs in Brazil have embraced *turco* for themselves as they "self-identified with what they considered an 'affectionate' or 'caring' ethnonym."[41] Karam quotes a Brazilian Arab physician who remarks, "The Brazilian has a caring way to call you *turco*. It's a form of caring, typically Brazilian . . . that does not have a racist . . . or a discriminatory connotation."[42] While this Brazilian Arab perspective on the term does not seem exaggerated, other Arabs still understand *turco* to be a pejorative term. However, instead of taking it as a racial slur, the latter group interprets *turco* positively—as a sign of Brazilian jealousy on account of the success that Arabs have had in Brazil.[43]

Though Brazilian Arabs have not intermarried with other Brazilians to the extent that the general population has, they have integrated rather well into the fabric of Brazilian society.[44] For instance, Arabs in Brazil have chosen not to become embroiled in the Arab-Israeli conflict because they

---

37. Ibid., 65–85.
38. Ibid., 15, 213.
39. Ibid., 13.
40. Ibid., 9.
41. Ibid., 212.
42. Ibid., 248.
43. Ibid., 163, 224–30.
44. Ibid., 16, 173–75, 208–9.

have had generally good relationships with Brazilian Jews, especially in the area of business.⁴⁵ In addition to finding general acceptance in Brazil, the Arabs also seem to have exercised some influence on Brazilian culture. Arabs, as noted, have been successful in business and have been elected to key national political offices. Through their innovation in the wholesale industry, introducing the sale of goods on credit, and even consulting Brazilian international companies on how to do business in the Arab world, the terms "Arab" and "rich" have nearly become synonymous in Brazil.⁴⁶

Also, Arab food has found a great reception among Brazilians. Each day, 1.2 million *esfihas* (Lebanese meat pies) are consumed in the country and 25 percent of the meals served daily in São Paulo are Arab dishes. The Arab fast-food chain Habib's has grown to be the number two fast-food restaurant in Brazil behind McDonalds with 150 stores located in Rio de Janeiro and São Paulo alone.⁴⁷ Thus, Karam does not overstate his case that "Middle Eastern culinary forms became familiar objects of consumption in contemporary Brazil."⁴⁸

While Arab style architecture has found a place in modern Brazil, Middle Eastern dance has also become wildly popular in the country.⁴⁹ Finally, Brazilians became exposed to aspects of Arab culture through the very popular soap opera (*telenovela*) "The Clone"—a soap opera about a Moroccan family that aired for 221 episodes on the Brazilian Globo Network in 2001-2002.⁵⁰

Indeed, through these noted aspects of culture—let alone the historical relationship between the Arabs and Portuguese of the Iberian Peninsula—Brazilians have been exposed to Arab culture and have arguably been influenced by it as well. This is perhaps best evidenced by the September 23, 2001 edition of *Revista da Folha*, the Sunday magazine of the popular media newspaper, which ran a cover story entitled "Brazil of the Arabias," followed by the caption: "The strong influence of Arab culture in cuisine, music, architecture, fashion, and in the Portuguese language."⁵¹

In light of the Arab presence and influence on Brazilian life and in light of the goals of the present study, it is worth noting a final Brazilian

45. Ibid., 304–5, 330.
46. Ibid., 38, 52, 117–19, 235.
47. Ibid., 2, 17, 33, 256–57, 263, 268–70, 354.
48. Ibid., 269.
49. Ibid., 4, 33, 38, 286, 354.
50. Ibid., 33, 204–7, 352.
51. Ibid., 353.

perspective on Arabs—that of evangelicals. In 1997, João Mordomo and a research team conducted a survey with 100 Brazilian evangelicals. Their results showed that 78 percent would be happy to have an Arab-Muslim neighbor, that 15 percent already had personal relationships with Arab-Muslims, and that 84 percent would be willing to evangelize Arabs or provide financial support to mission work among Arabs.[52] In short, it seems that Brazilian evangelicals are not only aware of the Arab-Muslims that live among them, they also seem to have a missional heart toward them.

Race

Race is typically defined as "a population of a species that differs in the frequency of some gene or genes from other populations of the same species."[53] Though some have argued that racial studies are typically outside of the parameters of cultural anthropology,[54] it does seem worthwhile to raise some pertinent questions about race in the Arab and Brazilian contexts. First, what is the extent of racial diversity within the Arab world and Brazil? Second, is there evidence of racial discrimination in each context, particularly toward minorities? Finally, how have Brazilian evangelical workers encountered and described racial issues in the midst of their mission work and what are the missiological implications?

Arabs and Race

Illustrating the racial diversity present among Arabs today, Peter Mansfield writes: "Because of the admixtures of Turkish, Caucasian, Negro, Kurdish, Spanish, or Berber blood, an Arab today may be coal-black or blond-skinned and blue-eyed."[55] Let us consider further the mosaic of the Arab peoples by surveying the primary regions of the Arab world.

The Maghreb countries are composed of peoples from Arab, Berber, and sub-Saharan African descent. In Morocco, though the vast majority of people are racially Berber, Arab culture has become predominant over time. Today, 25 percent of the population is still culturally Berber.[56] In

---

52. See Mordomo, "The 10/40 Window Moves West," 1–4.
53. Haviland cited in Kraft, *Anthropology for Christian Witness*, 109.
54. See Kraft, *Anthropology for Christian Witness*, 98.
55. See Mansfield, *The Arabs*, 534.
56. See Nydell, *Understanding Arabs*, 149; also Hourani, *A History of the Arab Peoples*, 434.

neighboring Mauritania, around 70 percent of the people are Hassaniya Arabs. The majority of these are the dominant white Moors, while the remainder are the black Moors or Haratine people—an Arabized people who are descended from black slaves. The remaining 28 percent of the Mauritanian population is composed of West African peoples.[57] In Algeria, 70 percent of the population is Arab, many of which are Arabized Berbers. Berber culture continues to flourish among the remaining 30 percent, especially among the proud Kabyle people.[58] In Libya, the vast majority of the population is Arabized; however, there are still significant pockets of Berber culture. Finally, in Tunisia, though there are small vestiges of Jews and Berbers, nearly the entire population is culturally Arab today.[59]

Diversity can also be observed in the Arab countries of Northeastern Africa. In Egypt, though 94 percent of the population is Arab, the remaining 6 percent are racially and culturally Coptic. In Sudan, the country is divided between the dominant Arabs in the North and the non-Arab African peoples in the South. Among the latter, there are nineteen major people groups and 597 sub-groups while some 400 languages are spoken in the country.[60]

In the Levant region, Lebanon makes for an interesting case. The country is over 90 percent Arab, including Arabs from Syria, Egypt and Palestine. However, the Lebanese Arabs are especially proud of their Phoenician origins, which in some ways distinguish them from other Arabs. The rest of the population is made up of Armenians, Persians, and Kurds.[61] In Syria, Arabs make up 92 percent of the country, including pockets of Bedouin peoples and Palestinians. The remaining 8 percent mostly include Kurds, Armenians, Turkmen, and Persians.[62] In Jordan, over 97 percent of the population is Arab, including a massive presence of Palestinians who are, of course, distinct from the Hashemite Arabs. Jordan also has Armenian, Kurdish, Turkmen, and Chechen minorities.[63] In Iraq,

57. See Johnstone and Mandryk, *Operation World*, 434.
58. See Nydell, *Understanding Arabs*, 152.
59. Ibid., 154–56.
60. Ibid., 160; also Hourani, *A History of the Arab Peoples*, 435.
61. See Nydell, *Understanding Arabs*, 163; also Johnstone and Mandryk, *Operation World*, 399.
62. See Nydell, *Understanding Arabs*, 166; Johnstone and Mandryk, *Operation World*, 610.
63. See Nydell, *Understanding Arabs* 169; Johnstone and Mandryk, *Operation World*, 375.

while 75 percent of the people are Arabs, the rest are Kurdish, Turkmen, and Armenian.[64]

Finally, let us consider the racial landscape of the Arabian Peninsula, where Arabs in the truest racial sense are located. However, since the discovery of oil, all of the Gulf States except for Yemen have been flooded by foreign guest workers, including Arabs from neighboring countries. In Saudi Arabia, nearly 84 percent of the population is Arab, including Arabs from Egypt, Yemen, Jordan, and Palestine. The rest include South Asians (Indians, Pakistanis, Bangladeshis, Sri Lankans), Asians (Filipinos), Africans (Nigerians, Sudanese, Somalians), North Americans, Europeans, and Iranians.[65] Similarly, in Kuwait, 64 percent of the people are Arabs from Kuwait and from neighboring Arab countries, while South Asian, Asian, Western, and Iranian guest workers comprise the rest of the population.[66] In Bahrain, one-third of the population is from South Asia, Asia, North America, Europe, and Iran, while 65 percent is made up of Bahraini and other Arabs.[67] Half of the inhabitants of Qatar are Arab—including both Qataris and other Arabs—while the other half are South Asian, Asian, and Iranian.[68] In the United Arab Emirates, only 32 percent of the population is Arab—a little over half being Emirati Arabs—while the rest are South Asian, Asian, Iranian, and European.[69] In Oman, 67 percent of the people are Arabs, including those from surrounding countries, and the rest are South Asian, Asian, African, Iranian, European, and North American.[70] Finally, in Yemen, the Northern peoples are largely Gulf Arabs, while those from the South are a mixture of Arabs who have intermarried with African and Indian peoples.[71]

From this brief survey, it is evident that an abundance of racial diversity exists in the countries of the Arab world. There are certainly observed

---

64. See Nydell, *Understanding Arabs*, 170.

65. Ibid., 173–76; also Johnstone and Mandryk, *Operation World*, 375.

66. See Nydell, *Understanding Arabs*, 182; also Johnstone and Mandryk, *Operation World*, 390.

67. See Nydell, *Understanding Arabs* 184; also Johnstone and Mandryk, *Operation World*, 92.

68. See Nydell, *Understanding Arabs*, 185; also Johnstone and Mandryk, *Operation World*, 532.

69. See Nydell, *Understanding Arabs* , 186–87; also Johnstone and Mandryk, *Operation World*, 647.

70. See Nydell, *Understanding Arabs*, 188; also Johnstone and Mandryk, *Operation World*, 498.

71. See Nydell, *Understanding Arabs*, 179.

differences among the Arab peoples themselves, as has been noted in the example of Yemen. Diversity, of course, also exists between the Arabs and those minorities who have migrated to the Arab countries. Barakat correctly notes that the Arabs have dominated the culture of these minorities.[72] This has clearly been the case in North Africa where expressions of Berber culture have been suppressed by the Arab majority. Ironically, one foundational element to the preservation of culture—language—has often been denied the Berber peoples as books, newspapers, and other means of promoting the written Berber language were largely outlawed in the twentieth century. In Algeria, this issue came to a head in the spring of 1980 as thousands of Kabyle Berber people took to the streets demanding their freedom of cultural expression—a manifestation that was ultimately put down by the government.[73] This Kabyle struggle to overcome Arab dominance has been captured well through the music of Kabyle singers Idir, Lounès Matoub, and others.[74]

Aside from demonstrating cultural dominance, it is no secret that some Arab peoples have also discriminated against the minorities and toward other Arabs. One Lebanese man noted that while growing up in Lebanon, the greatest insult that one could receive was to be called a Kurd. In Tunisia, Arabs commonly refer to Africans or even Arabs from African descent as *abad* ("slaves") or *kahaloush* ("black"). Finally, while living in North Africa, I repeatedly heard discriminatory remarks by Tunisians concerning Algerians and Libyans, while other North Africans have openly criticized the Saudi Arabs for being ignorant Bedouins who happened to discover oil.

Though it may be argued that such discriminatory language is common to any society, in some Arab contexts, these tensions have resulted in violence. While the plight of the Kabyles in Algeria has been noted, the worst case of racially driven violence in the Arab world has surely been that which has occurred in Sudan. Since its independence in 1956, it seems that conflict has abounded among Sudan's diverse peoples. The non-Arab Africans have often cited neglect from the Arab-Muslim government, which has led to continual revolts in the last half century. This, of course, led to the Darfur War in 2003, which essentially turned into a state-sponsored genocide in which it is believed 300,000 people were

---

72. See Barakat, *The Arab World*, 40, 182.
73. See "Le Printemps de Tous Ses Espoirs."
74. See "Idir: Le Site officiel."

killed.⁷⁵ In short, the diversity present among the peoples of the Arab world has been characterized by discrimination and even violence as this brief survey has shown.

Brazilians and Race

The racial diversity present among Brazil's 291 people groups has been previously noted. Azevedo offers the general argument that Brazilians are made up of three streams of race—white, Indian, and African.⁷⁶ However, the white Portuguese were themselves quite diverse before reaching Brazil in the early sixteenth century. Immigrants from Europe in the nineteenth and twentieth centuries, of course, added to the mix of white peoples.⁷⁷ As noted, the "Indians" discovered by the Portuguese were composed of many distinct peoples. Finally, it seems impossible to provide a precise number for the many African people groups that came to inhabit Brazil beginning in the late sixteenth century. These three diverse streams of people freely intermarried, producing *mulattos,* a Portuguese-African mixture, and *cablocos,* those born from Portuguese and Indian parents.⁷⁸ As miscegenation—interracial marriage—has been encouraged by the government throughout the country's history, Brazil's diversity has only been compounded.

The official position of the Brazilian government toward race has been termed "racial democracy"—effectively a denial of racism within the country.⁷⁹ This view was popularized by the Brazilian sociologist Gilberto Freye, who argued that slavery in Brazil was a much more compassionate and humane institution than what was observed in Europe.⁸⁰ In fact, Brazilians have actually embraced aspects of African culture by adopting *feijoada* (black beans, rice, meats, manioc flour) as a national dish and Samba as a national dance, and allowing African influences on the Brazilian Carnival and on popular Roman Catholicism.⁸¹ Azevedo adds that the practice of intermarriage and the acceptance of the resulting diversity

---

75. See BBC News, "Sudan Profile."
76. See Azevedo, *Brazilian Culture,* 31–41.
77. See Vincent, *Culture and Customs of Brazil,* 17–20.
78. See Page, *The Brazilians,* 58.
79. See Levine and Crocitti, *The Brazil Reader,* 352.
80. See Page, *The Brazilians,* 70-74; also Karam, "Distinguishing Arabesques," 6.
81. See Page, *The Brazilians,* 59.

were driven by an underlying racial tolerance on the part of Brazilians.[82] Others assert that Brazil has never pursued any form of racial segregation or apartheid as other nations such as the United States and South Africa have, nor has there ever been a recorded race riot in the country. Finally, the claim of racial democracy is further supported by the fact that Brazilians have at times been given the right to determine their own race, especially during a national census.[83]

Despite the official policy of racial democracy, discrimination does indeed exist in Brazil, though it has been manifested more subtly. Page helpfully summarizes:

> On one level, blacks and whites can display in their dealings with one another a genuine human warmth that blurs color lines and has produced a high degree of social integration, a major achievement—if not *the* major achievement—of Brazilian society. Yet this does not mean that Brazilians live in a "racial democracy," as many have convinced themselves. The manner with which individuals of different racial backgrounds intermingle has served to obscure recognition of the existence of a subtle and not-so-subtle racism that makes it difficult for blacks to enjoy the same political, social, and economic opportunities as whites.[84]

Generally speaking, the Brazilian upper class is much whiter, while the lower classes are much darker.[85] Vincent notes that whites outnumber non-whites three to one in professional jobs and that half of all agricultural and domestic jobs in Brazil are done by non-whites. Finally, Vincent observes that many of the recent Miss Brazil pageant winners as well as some of the famous female television personalities—symbols of Brazilian beauty—are blond-haired, blue-eyed women. He refers in particular to Xusha, the "blond marketing phenomenon of Brazilian television," who spent six years in a relationship with Brazilian soccer icon Pele, who, of course, is black.[86]

Despite the existence of clear racial inequalities in Brazil, Karam writes "what intrigued social scientists was not racism per se, but its

---

82. See Azevedo, *Brazilian Culture*, 129–30.
83. See Vincent, *Culture and Customs of Brazil*, 21.
84. See Page, *The Brazilians*, 11.
85. See Sarti, "Morality and Transgression," 123; also Page, *The Brazilians*, 59–61; and Karam, "Distinguishing Arabesques," 9.
86. See Vincent, *Culture and Customs of Brazil*, 21–23.

seemingly 'smooth preservation' or 'accommodation' in the Brazilian racial order."[87] Indeed, Brazil's racial diversity and the ambiguity between discrimination and racial democracy have contributed to the overall struggle to understand Brazilianness.[88]

Brazilian Perspectives on Race in the Arab World

Having considered the racial diversity in the Arab world and Brazil as well as the unique challenges of racial discrimination in both contexts, how do the racial backgrounds and experiences of Brazilian transcultural workers have a bearing on their ministry in the Arab world? Let us begin to answer this question by consulting some recent literature and then hear the voices of the Brazilian workers in our study.

The first rather obvious implication is that since Brazilians come from a racially diverse background, they tend to be naturally comfortable serving in a diverse Arab context. In his study of Brazilian transcultural workers, Finley observes that Brazilians "have experience dealing with people who look different."[89] He adds that some Brazilian missionaries observed that the common practice of intermarriage in Brazil prepared them to adapt cross-culturally.[90] Another transcultural worker added that coming from a diverse background helps the Brazilian to be less fearful and more compassionate about racial issues in the Muslim context.[91] In 1980, Read and Ineson predicted: "Because of a unique heritage from different peoples and tongues of other nations, Brazil has the potential to become a major Protestant missionary-sending country in the world."[92] This is apparently becoming a reality for Brazilians serving cross-culturally and among Arab-Muslims.

Second, despite the noted inequalities in Brazilian society, even some that have affected the evangelical church and missions movement,[93] it

---

87. See Karam, "Distinguishing Arabesques," 7.

88. See Finley, "Contextualized Training for Missionaries," 72–73; for a further discussion on the race debate in Brazil, see Levine and Crocitti, *The Brazil Reader*, 351–94.

89. See Finley, "Contextualized Training for Missionaries," 215.

90. Ibid., 196; also Mordomo, "The Brazilian Way," 4-8.

91. See L.C., "Mais Missionários Brasileiros," 470.

92. See Read and Ineson, *Brazil 1980*, 6

93. See McLeod, "Transformando Atitudes Raciais," 6; also Murphy, "Etnocentrismo e Racismo," 40.

seems that the racially diverse Brazilian evangelical church has generally been a model for overcoming discrimination. Around 1900, Hugh Tucker, commenting on mission work in Brazil, asserted, "The race or color line is not one that need specially affect the work of a Protestant missionary."[94] Eugene Nida, an imminent anthropologist who certainly had a grasp on the global church in the mid-twentieth century, also found the lack of racial prejudice in Brazil to be remarkable.[95] Willems, a sociologist and outsider to Brazilian evangelicalism, observed that Protestants were indeed successful at planting racially diverse churches.[96] Similarly, Martin, in a more recent study, has noted that Pentecostal churches have been known for actively involving Afro-Brazilians in their congregations.[97]

Some Brazilian workers interviewed indicated that racial discrimination in the Arab world was a real challenge for them. One missionary remarked that "[a difficulty in Arab-Muslim culture is] no acceptance and [respect] as a Latin or non-English speaker," while another added that there was "only one [difficult] aspect [in Arab-Muslim culture]—racial discrimination."[98] Some Brazilians of African heritage especially found this difficult. One woman related, "The mistreatment of black women is difficult for me," and "I don't like the racial discrimination (I am a black Brazilian woman)." Her husband reported that he is often questioned by Arab men about why he married a black woman. Some assume that his desire for the woman's money was the only possible explanation for such a marriage.[99]

Despite these difficulties, it seems that Brazilians, coming from a culture and church experience that is more racially inclusive, might prove to be catalysts of transformation in the Arab world. That is, Brazilians might be helpful in planting churches that are more racially diverse, while encouraging Arab believers to overcome tensions with the minority peoples in their context. One Brazilian worker, modeling these values, related: "We are seeing God work more among the minority peoples despite the fact

---

94. Cited in Beach et. al, *Protestant Missions in South America*, 68.

95. See Nida, *Customs and Cultures*, 64, 284.

96. See Willems, *Followers of the New Faith*, 207.

97. See Martin, *Tongues of Fire*, 67–69.

98. All survey comments that are not otherwise documented are taken from the Brazilian worker and/or mission leaders surveys. The complete list of responses is stored in Appendices B and D of Smither, "Brazilian Evangelical Missions in the Arab World."

99. Related to me in personal conversation, January 6, 2010.

that Arabs can be so racist against them."¹⁰⁰ Another worker, demonstrating his ability to minister to various racial groups and social classes shared, "It's a pleasure to start [relationships] with rich businessmen and poor carpenters." Finally, the same interracial couple mentioned above related that, despite having to endure discriminatory remarks, their marriage has also provided open doors to share the gospel with Arab friends. Specifically, they share with Arab friends that God is pleased with his creation that is ethnically diverse (Gen 1:31) and that this mixed multitude will praise him for all eternity (Rev 7:9).¹⁰¹

A final race related implication for Brazilians serving among Arabs is simply that Brazilians, unlike many North Americans and Europeans, have a "look" that helps them to fit in nicely in many parts of the world, including the Arab world. Ussama Makdisi, in his rather scathing assessment of Protestant missions in the Arab world in the nineteenth and twentieth century, noted that one difficulty for North American missionaries was that their physical appearance alone created barriers for ministry.¹⁰² Having lived for ten years in the Arab world, I (with blond hair and blue eyes) can certainly attest to feeling out of place and uncomfortable at times due to appearance.

One Brazilian worker asserted: "I believe that Brazilians have lots of advantages in serving in the Arab world . . . our physical appearance is also a plus, since a lot of Brazilians have Arab/Turkish physical traits." Another added, "I have been accepted by Arabs rather easily because culturally (including our general appearance) we are similar." Yet, one worker related that having a similar "look" can also have its disadvantages: "It can be difficult because I look very Arab. It is nice to blend in, but I can also get treated badly like locals treat one another." We should not forget that for some Brazilian workers, this resemblance is due to the fact that they are actually of Arab descent.

While this view has often been repeated by the Brazilian mission community as a key aspect for reaching Arabs, Finley asserts with a bit more caution: "If a missionary's physical appearance does not create a barrier in the minds of people, that is a plus."¹⁰³ Yet, he does temper this view

---

100. Ibid.

101. Ibid. Similar values are communicated in a recent article from Ramos in which he argues that no premise for prejudice or racial segregation exists in the Bible. See Ramos, "A Bíblia e as Questões Raciais e Sociais," 174; also Van der Meer, "O Preparo Social," 53–67.

102. See Makdisi, *Artillery of Heaven*, 90.

103. See Finley, "Contextualized Training for Missionaries," 178; also Heikes,

with an appropriate warning: "The danger exists, however, that Brazilian missionaries and mission leaders will make the mistaken supposition that superficial similarities like racial features facilitates identification and contextualization."[104]

Economics

The economic situation within the Arab and Brazilian contexts also makes for an interesting study. Though space does not allow for an exhaustive study of either context, a basic economic overview of the Arab world and Brazil will be presented. Afterward, the perspectives of Brazilian workers and mission leaders regarding economics will be considered, including the implications for mission.

Arab World Economics

Historically, the social structure within the Arab world has been primarily class-based, which has also had economic consequences. The upper or wealthy class was comprised of landowners who later became politicians. In more recent years, the center of wealth has shifted from land ownership to the control of oil production.[105] A second traditional social class was the petite bourgeoisie, made up of small landowners, shopkeepers, self-employed artisans, and farmers. Today, this group includes government workers, teachers, and army officers.[106] The final group was the working class. Historically, these were landless peasants; however, today they include servants, wageworkers, street vendors, and the unemployed.[107] Within this general class structure, the possibilities for social mobility have been rather limited. Barakat illustrates this point by citing the following Arab proverb: "Money begets more money; and poverty begets more poverty."[108] Finally, because Arab identity is based in large part on social

---

"Una Perspectiva Diferente," 76; and Mordomo, "Unleashing the Brazilian Missionary Force," 219.

104. See Finley, "Contextualized Training for Missionaries," 178.

105. See Barakat, *The Arab World*, 81–84, 87–88; also Nydell, *Understanding Arabs*, 67.

106. See Barakat, *The Arab World*, 89–90.

107. Ibid., 91–92.

108. Ibid., 95; see also Nydell, *Understanding Arabs*, 68.

standing, it is common for upper class Arabs to introduce themselves by making reference to their position in society or their family background.[109]

Historically, the Arab economy was based on farming, herding, and, to a lesser extent, mining. Some key crops cultivated and traded by farmers included cereals, beans, lentils, olives, sugar, spices, fruits (including dates and figs), and vegetables. Also, soon after the discovery of coffee in Ethiopia in the sixteenth century, this staple became popular in nearby Mecca where Muslim pilgrims began to buy it and take it home, effectively creating a market for coffee throughout the Arab world.[110]

In arid lands where farming was impossible, Arabs also made a living through herding sheep, goats, camels, and even cattle. While the meat from these animals provided subsistence, the sheep's wool also became the basis for an eventual textile industry.[111] As the pastoralists regarded their work and class as superior, the relationship between farmers and herders was not without tension among the Arab peoples.[112]

With the expansion of the Arab-Muslim empires, commercial activity in each of these domains flourished. Such expanding business also expanded a slave trade that included European, Eurasian, and African servants. In fact, slavery among African peoples can be traced to the Muslim advance on the continent.[113]

Finally, as noted, the economic landscape for much of the Arab world changed forever in the twentieth century with the discovery of oil. Indeed, by the latter half of the century, monies from the sale and export of oil became the primary source of national revenue for Saudi Arabia, the Gulf States, and Iraq.[114]

As a result of the changing economic conditions in the twentieth century, Arab countries, like so many others, experienced rapid urbanization. Barakat notes that the urban population in the Arab world jumped from 10 percent in 1900 to 40 percent in 1970, and it is projected that 70 percent of Arabs will live in cities by 2020.[115] Unfortunately, the economies of the

109. See Nydell, *Understanding Arabs*, 19.

110. See Lewis, *The Middle East*, 158–62, 168–69; also Hourani, *A History of the Arab Peoples*, 100, 111.

111. See Lewis, *The Middle East*, 167–68; also Hourani, *A History of the Arab Peoples* 100, 111–12.

112. See Hourani, *A History of the Arab Peoples*, 100–101.

113. See Lewis, *The Middle East*, 174–76; also Hourani, *A History of the Arab Peoples*, 116–17.

114. See Hourani, *A History of the Arab Peoples*, 378–82.

115. See Barakat, *The Arab World*, 62; also Nydell, *Understanding Arabs*, 5.

Arab cities have not grown as fast as the population and there have been a number of negative side effects.[116] Today, many of the large cities have housing shortages and infrastructure (water, electricity) overload, and the schools and hospitals are simply overwhelmed. Many who have migrated from the villages to the cities in search of work have ended up in the slums in poverty. Nydell reports that 20 percent of Cairo's residents live in illegal housing.[117] While urbanization has had a debilitating effect on the Arab world's impoverished peoples, the educated elite have responded by emigrating to Europe and North America. Nydell reports that this has been the case for 25 percent of university graduates, including 15,000 medical doctors who emigrated between 1998 and 2000 alone.[118] Hence, as economic problems continue, many with the training and expertise to offer solutions are leaving the Arab world.

Reflecting the noted historic class distinctions, another result of the recent economic challenges has been a widening gap between the rich and the poor. Barakat writes, "Extreme concentration of national wealth in a few hands has prevailed in most Arab countries, and disparities are increasing."[119] While this is the case within Arab countries, it is also a reality among the Arab states. Barakat adds, "Growing disparities between rich and poor Arab countries have created further rifts between them, notwithstanding labor migration and other forms of interdependency between oil-producing and non-oil-producing Arab countries."[120] Indeed, in 2003, the Gulf States of Qatar and the United Arab Emirates boasted a per capita income of $30,000 and $19,755 respectively, while families in the non-oil producing countries of Yemen and Sudan earned $520 and $460 respectively.[121]

Finally, it is impossible to separate economic issues from global politics. In particular, Western intervention in the Arab world from the nineteenth century to the present day has impacted the economies of the Arab world.[122] The colonization of Arab countries by European powers in the nineteenth and twentieth centuries implied an economic dominance,

---

116. See Hourani, *A History of the Arab Peoples*, 386, 437–38.

117. See Nydell, *Understanding Arabs*, 5; also Barkat, *The Arab World*, 62; and Hourani, *A History of the Arab Peoples*, 336, 374–75, 390–91.

118. See Nydell, *Understanding Arabs*, 7.

119. See Barakat, *The Arab World*, 10–11.

120. Ibid., 45; also Hourani, *A History of the Arab Peoples*, 384–88, 436–39.

121. See Nydell, *Understanding Arabs*, 148.

122. See Barakat, *The Arab World*, 14, 78.

which included the rights to oil exploration being placed in the hands of Western companies. Even after the Arab nations gained their independence in the latter half of the twentieth century, economic growth in the Arab world actually led to increased economic dependence on the West.[123]

Not surprisingly, this political and economic dominance has led to a great sense of victimization and resentment on the part of Arabs toward the West.[124] Indeed, a hopeless sense of poverty coupled with increasing anti-Western political sentiment has fueled many of the Islamic fundamentalist movements of the last 100 years.[125] Unfortunately, these sentiments have also been directed toward well-meaning North American and European missionaries serving among Arabs over the past century and half as evangelical mission work has been perceived by Arab-Muslims as just another form of imperialism aimed at exploiting the poor and weak.[126] Commenting on the work of American evangelicals in Egypt, Sharkey writes, "Bold, brash, and expansive, the spirit of missionary evangelism resembled the spirit of British imperialism in this period and infused the work of American Presbyterians in Egypt."[127] Hence, the American missionary presence in Egypt in the late nineteenth and early twentieth centuries, which operated under the protection of the British government, probably contributed indirectly to the rise of nationalist and Islamic fundamentalist movements.[128]

Brazilian Economics

The Brazilian economic situation is characterized by significant extremes. On one hand, supported by developed agricultural, mining, manufacturing, and service industries, Brazil's economy dwarfs that of its Latin American neighbors. In fact, the economy of São Paulo alone is larger than that of any other South American country.[129] Brazil has also emerged

---

123. See Hourani, *A History of the Arab Peoples*, 377–78.
124. See Nydell, *Understanding Arabs*, 16.
125. Ibid., 106.
126. See Ryad, "Muslim Response to Missionary Activities in Egypt," 287–98. This reproach to a perceived Western cultural imperialism also forms the basis for Makdisi's work *The Artillery of Heaven*, which seeks to explain why American evangelical missions in the Middle East failed during this period.
127. See Sharkey, *American Evangelicals in Egypt*, 49.
128. Ibid., 4–6.
129. See "Economy: Brazil"; also Vincent, *Culture and Customs of Brazil*, 12–15.

as a world leader in the export of beef, chicken, orange juice, coffee, and other goods.[130] On the other hand, the country is plagued by a massive national debt, has problems with income distribution, and has battled inflation. Beginning in 1981, when Brazil had the eighth largest economy in the world, the country endured thirteen years of crippling inflation until recovery began in 1994.[131]

Similar to the Arab context, Brazilian society has been organized by class more than race—a reality that also has economic implications.[132] The traditional structure included the planter class who dominated the peasants who worked the land.[133] Hess and DaMatta offer this description: "The plantations were controlled by patriarchs who exercised a nearly absolute authority over their dominions in a way similar to that of the king over the realm."[134]

Though Brazil underwent massive industrialization in the twentieth century, which has also led to significant urbanization—from 30 percent in 1940 to 80 percent in 2000—the class hierarchy has largely remained.[135] Hess and DaMatta point out that the new upper class—composed of bankers, industrialists, exporters, and entrepreneurs—often appeal to their status in public contexts with statements like, "Do you know whom you're talking to?"[136] A natural outcome of industrialization was an increase in jobs in engineering and in the technology sector, which has served to develop and strengthen the Brazilian middle class. Members of this sphere of society not only have access to good jobs, but they have the increasing ability to offer their children a better education and future.[137] Industrialization has also given rise to an urban lower class, including those employed in more labor intensive and factory jobs. Finally, such rapid urbanization has also witnessed the emergence of a class of marginalized poor—millions who have immigrated to the cities for work but have taken refuge in the *favelas* (slums) or *invasãos* ("invasions" or squatter communities). Page vividly describes the plight of this group: "About two-thirds of all

130. See Prado, "A New Way of Sending Missionaries," 50.

131. See Vincent, *Culture and Customs of Brazil*, xiv; also Prado, "A New Way of Sending Missionaries," 49–50; Page, *The Brazilians*, 2, 4, 21.

132. See Harrison, *Behaving Brazilian*, 3–5.

133. See Vincent, *Culture and Customs of Brazil*, 23.

134. See Hess and DaMatta, *The Brazilian Puzzle*, 5.

135. See Vincent, *Culture and Customs of Brazil*, 9.

136. See Hess and DaMatta, *The Brazilian Puzzle*, 9; also Vincent, *Culture and Customs of Brazil*, 24.

137. See Vincent, *Culture and Customs of Brazil*, 25–26.

Brazilians have been classified as poor. Of all the families that make up this 'miserable majority,' 71 percent lack running water, 79 percent have no refrigerator, and 85 percent live without sewage disposal."[138] In short, despite great strides in industrial development in Brazil within the last century, including the development of world-class cities, there is a significant gap between the rich and the poor.[139]

Brazilian Perspectives on Economics in the Arab World

From this brief survey of the literature, it seems that there are a number of areas in which Brazilian transcultural workers can relate to the economic context of the Arab world. First, Brazilians understand the class structure which governs Arab society in general and that shapes its economic systems. Thus, Brazilians seem equipped to conduct business and navigate the economic and administrative matrices of the Arab world. Second, Brazilians can intimately relate to the challenges that come with urbanization such as poverty, housing shortages, violence, and the neglect and abuse of children. Missionaries coming from Rio de Janeiro or São Paulo will not be surprised by the social problems of Cairo, Casablanca, or Amman. Third, Brazilians know what it means to live in a society where there is such great disparity between the rich and the poor. Finally, Brazilians and Arabs share a history of being colonized and dominated economically by European and North American political powers.

Given these areas of similarity, it also seems that Brazilian transcultural workers can identify with their Arab contexts because of their own economic challenges. Makdisi argues that historically the high standard of living of North American and European missionaries in the Arab world has proven to be a hindrance to their ministry.[140] Indeed, many affluent missionaries have been unable to identify with the poor around them, and poor Arabs have not felt comfortable in the homes of such upper-class Western Christians. Naja rightly argues that missionaries from the Global South are more closely aligned economically with their target peoples.[141]

---

138. See Page, *The Brazilians*, 6.

139. See Vincent, *Culture and Customs of Brazil*, 26; also Finley, "Contextualized Training for Missionaries," 68–71.

140. See Makdisi, *The Artillery of Heaven*, 189-90. Shaw (Shaw, "Westerners and Middle Easterners Serving Together," 17) also argues that differing standards of living have created misunderstandings between Westerners and Arabs serving in the same Christian organization.

141. See Naja, *Releasing Workers of the Eleventh Hour*, 30–31.

Commenting more specifically on Latin American missionaries, Heikes adds, "Latin Americans live on much less than their Western counterparts . . . the standard of living in Latin American countries is closer to that of any unreached people in the 10/40 window."[142]

The results of the survey with Brazilian workers suggest that many Brazilians serving among Arabs experience some real economic challenges. While affirming the health of his financial situation on the field, Marcos Amado, indicated that his story was the exception because most Brazilian missionaries seemed to struggle financially. Others noted that financial difficulties arose when churches or individuals discontinued financial support or when the Brazilian Real dropped against the currency of their host country. As a result of limited finances, most Brazilian workers have not had health insurance, much less a pension or retirement plan. Others indicated that they were unable to afford language lessons, making it very difficult to gain a proficiency in Arabic. Finally, some were forced to return home while others were somewhat stranded on their field—struggling financially but lacking the means even to return to Brazil.

It should be noted that, in my surveys, I did not ask the participants to indicate their annual income. However, during my three trips in 2009 and 2010, my general observation was that the Brazilian workers lived at a standard of living significantly less than that of North Americans and Europeans in the same contexts. For instance, only eleven of the twenty-nine participants that I met owned a car, and only one could be considered a newer model vehicle. Also, the apartments that I visited had very basic accommodations. Thus, my own observation confirms the repeated themes that have been communicated above.

Despite these difficulties, the Brazilian workers responded repeatedly that their needs were met and that they were not lacking anything. In fact, the vast majority of those surveyed (83.8 percent) indicated that their financial support was very adequate (14 percent) or adequate (69.8 percent). While this report on the economic situation of Brazilian workers may seem ambiguous or even contradictory, Amado's comments and reflections help to interpret the data. He asserts, "'adequate' support for Brazilians is enough to get by every month—but far from the ideal (furlough funds, health insurance, pension)." One single worker affirmed this by sharing that his support is "not what a Brit or American lives on but it is enough," while another couple added, "We have less support than the Americans or Europeans." Thus, it seems reasonable to conclude that most

---

142. See Heikes, "Una Perspectiva Diferente," 72–73.

Brazilian Evangelical Missions in the Arab World

Brazilian missionaries in Arab contexts are struggling financially to some degree; however, their expectations for basic financial support are quite different from those of their North American or European colleagues.

While my aim is not to celebrate poverty or financial difficulties, it does seem that the modest economic background of many Brazilians may actually prove to be an advantage as they serve among Arabs. Finley notes that Brazilians, unlike those missionaries criticized by Makdisi, "can identify with people suffering great economic hardship."[143] Amado adds, "Because of our background of relative poverty and economic crises and inflation, we can identify with [Arab] Muslims." He continues, "People perceive that and it is possible to bond with Arabs in a deep level of friendship." Another missionary affirmed: "They see us as Latinos, partners and similar, not as Westerners, dominant and indifferent. It seems as we share the same struggles, the same pain."[144] While the theological relevance of the economically modest reaching the poor as well as the practical issues of Brazilians cultivating better financial support will be addressed in the next chapters, we can conclude for now that the economic difficulties of Brazilians have actually allowed these workers to identify better with those in their host cultures.

Time

A third area of culture that will be considered is time. Robert Redfield writes, "one cognitive theme found in all societies is a sense of time." Hiebert adds, "Although all people experience repetition and sequence, they organize these differently."[145] In the present section, we will explore the general way in which Arabs and Brazilians view time. After this review of the literature, the perspectives of Brazilian workers will be considered in light of their transcultural mission work.

Arabs and Time

Edward T. Hall's categories of time—namely monochronic (M-time) and polychronic (P-time) time—provide a helpful framework for

---

143. See Finley, "Contextualized Training for Missionaries," 196.

144. See L.C., "Mais Missionários Brasileiros," 470. English translation by Barbara Hubbard.

145. Redford and Hiebert's comments are cited in Hiebert, *Transforming Worldviews*, 51.

understanding how Arabs regard this aspect of culture. Describing the monochronic (M-time) view held by most North Americans and Europeans, Hall writes: "As a rule, Americans think of time as a road or ribbon stretching into the future, along which one progresses. The road has segments or compartments, which are to be kept discrete ('one thing at a time'). People who cannot schedule time are looked down upon as impractical."[146] Hence, "M-time emphasizes schedules, segmentation, and promptness."[147] On the other hand, Hall summarizes the polychronic (P-time) perspective, the predominant view among Arabs, with the following: "P-time systems are characterized by several things happening at once. They stress involvement of people and completion of transactions rather than adherence to preset schedules. P-time is treated as much less tangible than M-time. P-time is apt to be considered a point rather than a ribbon or a road, and that point is sacred."[148] Hall asserts that while North Americans have eight categories of time ranging from an instantaneous event to forever, Arabs have only three—no time at all, now, and forever.[149] This, of course, makes it difficult for Arabs to measure "a very long time" as North Americans would. It also helps to explain why the peoples of traditional Arabia would not be considered late even if they arrived one hour after the agreed upon meeting time.[150] Also, an appointment scheduled for the afternoon could refer to anytime between noon and the late evening. All meetings are made with the caveat *inshallah* ("God willing"), which is also an indication that time is ultimately out of one's control.[151]

Patai observes that the Arabic language also provides some helpful insights for understanding how Arabs view time. For instance, the imperfect tense of the verb can be used for past, present, and even future actions. Also, a verb conjugated in the past can at times have implications for the present. Finally, the perfect tense can also refer to the future. Contrasting this linguistic structure with the typical European language systems, which emphasize a definite past, present, and future, Patai summarizes: "The conclusion from this unavoidably technical presentation of the use of the perfect and imperfect verb forms in Arabic is that for people speaking

---

146. See Hall, *The Silent Language*, 6.
147. See Hall, *Beyond Culture*, 17.
148. See Hall, *Beyond Culture*, 17.
149. See Hall, *The Silent Language*, 149–51
150. See Hiebert, *Transforming Worldviews*, 54; also Matheny, *Reaching the Arabs*, 30.
151. See Patai, *The Arab Mind*, 70.

a language in which the verb has these semantic features, time cannot have the same definite, ordered, and sequential connotation that it has for people speaking a strictly time-structured language."[152]

In short, we can safely conclude that Arabs are largely focused on the present. Patai argues that Islamic determinism actually produces a peace and calm in Arabs that encourages this present orientation. Hence, since much is out of one's control, why not invite a friend spontaneously for a meal or overspend on a wedding or celebration? As one Arab proverb states, "The provision for tomorrow belongs to tomorrow."[153] Barakat adds that the living conditions for traditional Bedouins, including the growing seasons, which essentially ordered their lives, have also contributed to an overall sense of patience and spontaneity. While little could be done to rush the growing of crops, there was also little to inhibit celebration when the harvest had come.[154]

Finally, it should also be noted that Arab time is governed by events and relationships. Patai records the work of one sociologist working in a Lebanese village who discovered that the history of the village was not recorded by dates, but rather by key events—weddings, holidays, and even notorious feuds.[155] While a North American tends to see time in compartments (i.e., time is "up"), Hall observes that an Arab "starts at one point and goes until he is finished or until something intervenes."[156] Hence, a good conversation cannot be abruptly ended for the next appointment nor is an exam necessarily over when time is up.[157] While this event and relationship orientation is true in much of the Arab world, Nydell notes that many Arabs involved in international business in an increasingly globalized world are paying more attention to their watches.[158]

---

152. See Patai, *The Arab Mind*, 72-73.

153. Ibid., 160–61; also Nydell, *Understanding Arabs*, 59.

154. See Barakat, *The Arab World*, 57–60.

155. See Patai, *The Arab Mind*, 76.

156. See Hall, *The Silent Language*, 158.

157. See Matheny, *Reaching the Arabs*, 31. While teaching at a North African university for several years, I observed firsthand the refusal of students to surrender their exam copies when time was "up." This was often encouraged by tolerant Arab professors who allowed students to continue until they were comfortably finished.

158. See Nydell, *Understanding Arabs*, 57.

Brazilians and Time

Brazilians also seem to be rather polychronic in their view of time.[159] While official government events begin at the scheduled time, many events in the rest of society—including parties, concerts, and even classes—may begin thirty minutes to one hour late. Thus, one who arrives at a party thirty minutes late is still considered on time.[160] Social events surrounding the family will not have a specific ending time, and it is not unusual for a weekend party to last until two o'clock in the morning.[161]

Brazilians are also quite focused on the present. Not unlike Patai's arguments for the Arab present orientation, Finley notes that Brazilians are also fatalistic in their worldview. Since the future is out of their hands, they are more content to concentrate on what can be accomplished and enjoyed now. Finley adds that for Brazilians, this focus is driven by a strong sense of *immediatismo* ("instant gratification").[162] Azevedo, contrasting instant pleasure with working toward the future, supports this by adding, "The present is what counts . . . a worthy leisure always appeared more excellent and even capable of conferring nobility than the insensate struggle for daily bread."[163]

Finally, Brazilian time is strongly governed by events and especially by relationships. While parties generally have no official ending time, the Brazilian chapters of Alcoholics Anonymous decided to abandon the internationally prescribed meeting schedule of one hour and continue meeting as long as the leader was willing to remain.[164] Also, in a fascinating study of competitive swimming—a sport necessarily governed by the clock—Conrad Kottak also observed a strong personal element: "In Brazil, racing is more relational: one is racing against the other people in the meet, not against oneself. Swimmers therefore do not walk away from meets with a sense of accomplishment against their own best times; everything is contingent on the relational status of winning or losing."[165]

---

159. See Hall, *Beyond Culture*, 17; also Harrison, *Behaving Brazilian*, 13–14.

160. See Harrison, *Behaving Brazilian*, 44.

161. See Vincent, *Culture and Customs of Brazil*, 83; also Harrison, *Behaving Brazilian*, 45.

162. See Finley, "Contextualized Training for Missionaries," 136–37.

163. See Azevedo, *Brazilian Culture*, 125.

164. See Jarrad, "The Brazilianization of Alcoholics Anonymous," 224.

165. See Kottak, "Swimming in Cross-Cultural Currents," 49-58.

Though appointments are certainly important to Brazilians, the unexpected arrival of a friend will take priority over a scheduled meeting.[166] One Brazilian missionary asserted, "In Brazil, you would sacrifice anything for relationships."[167] Observing that a prompt arrival to an appointment could actually put pressure on relationships, Mordomo helpfully concludes: "In Brazil, punctuality only serves to confound people's schedules! If some were to arrive on time, they would 'lose time' waiting for others to arrive, not to mention that their 'on time arrival' would very possibly be considered impolite! . . . They place a much higher value on the relational activity rather than on achieving certain goals within certain timeframes and thus, time is event or personality related."[168]

Brazilian Perspectives on Time in the Arab World

From this survey of the literature, it is apparent that there is some continuity in the Arab and Brazilian views of time. Both cultural groups are largely polychronic and present-oriented, while events and relationships seem to play a deciding role in how time is organized. The vast majority of the Brazilian transcultural workers surveyed (68.9 percent) affirmed that their view of time was very similar (8.9 percent) or similar (60 percent) to what they perceived in their Arab contexts.

Despite these similarities, some of the Brazilian respondents still shared some monochronic perspectives. One worker related: "Maybe this is just a personal thing, but I value people being on time. If I make an appointment at 5 pm, I do not like to feel trapped at my house waiting for a friend to come whenever he makes it." Another added, "I'm always punctual so for me this would present a difference."

Some Brazilian workers were of the opinion that while both Brazilians and Arabs were flexible about time, Arabs were still more flexible. "Brazilians are late, but not as much as the Arabs," said one worker. The continuity and tension between the two cultures is quite apparent in the following response: "In Brazil you should be late in some cases, not in every situation. If you have a formal appointment you should be on time. Here [in my Arab context], they are late for everything!"

---

166. See Vincent, *Culture and Customs of Brazil*, 83; also Finley, "Contextualized Training for Missionaries," 138.

167. Cited in Finley, "Contextualized Training for Missionaries," 166.

168. See Mordomo, "The Brazilian Way," 13.

A couple of respondents suggested that the view of time shared by Brazilians from the North and Northeast most closely resembled that of the Arabs. One Northeasterner shared, "In my home region of Northeast Brazil, it is okay to be thirty minutes late to an appointment; so I was used to things not starting on time." Nevertheless, he added, "But, it did take some adjustment to people arriving two hours late!"

Though these responses rule out an overly simplistic comparison of Brazilian and Arab views of time, the vast majority of Brazilians nevertheless affirmed an overall cultural proximity in this area. One Brazilian worker shared, "As them [Arabs], we [Brazilians] are almost always late," while another related, "Both Brazilians and Arabs value events more than the actual clock time." Finally, another Brazilian worker summarized: "There is no such thing as being on time for us Brazilians (we are usually late compared to the American view of time), as it is with the Arab culture; also, when we visit someone's house, we forget about time, as we are relational people and could spend the entire day at someone's house talking, having fellowship. I found the Arab culture to be the same in that aspect."

The similar regard for time shared by most Brazilians and Arabs becomes more apparent when compared to the struggles that North Americans and Europeans—those with an M-time perspective—often encounter in similar transcultural work. Hall observes, "Americans overseas are psychologically stressed in many ways when confronted by P-time systems such as those in Latin America and the Middle East."[169] This is particularly evident when transcultural workers attempt to make appointments.[170] Westerners prefer to make them well in advance, record them in a daily planner, schedule only one meeting at a time, do not deviate from the agreed upon time, and try not to break or change the appointment. While Westerners may feel stress when attempting to adapt to a P-time context, Kraft helpfully notes that they might also cause harm to the relationship building process if they impose the M-time values of efficiency and punctuality in more event oriented cultures.[171] Interestingly, one Brazilian respondent shared, "I had conflict with one American colleague because I did not schedule my work day as they did and I was seen as not serious." Hall adds that M-time appointments can often isolate relationships and

---

169. See Hall, *Beyond Culture*, 17.

170. See Hall, *Beyond Culture*, 18. Indeed, I encountered this worldview difference very early on while living in North Africa, which required some uncomfortable adaptation to making appointments according to an Arab, P-time perspective.

171. See Kraft, *Anthropology for Christian Witness*, 384; also Hall, *The Silent Language*, 9.

focus on individuals, while P-time meetings tend to invite more group participation.[172] This aspect of time orientation raises another issue of culture—individualist and collectivist tendencies—which will be discussed later.

Generally speaking, most Brazilian transcultural workers do not seem to encounter the type of cultural stress about time that North American and Europeans will. Rather, given their own polychronic views of time, Brazilians seem quite equipped and poised to adapt well to and thrive within this aspect of Arab culture.[173]

Communication

Intercultural communication is essential to the work of any missionary. Failing to learn the heart language and communication patterns of the host culture will greatly reduce the effectiveness of a transcultural worker and in many cases will result in the worker not continuing long-term in his or her ministry. While the number of studies in intercultural communication theory and practice is vast, the present section will simply deal with three aspects of communication in both the Arab and Brazilian contexts—verbal communication, non-verbal communication, and orality. Following a survey of the literature, the reflections of Brazilian transcultural workers will be analyzed and the missiological implications will be considered.

Arab Verbal Communication

As we have shown, the Arabic language is probably the greatest defining element of Arab culture, and that which unifies the diverse cluster of Arab peoples.[174] It is no secret that Arabs are extremely proud of their language and enjoy the rhetorical nature of their medium of communication.[175] Nydell, a researcher and authority on colloquial Arabic, asserts, "In the Arab world, how you say something is as important as what you have to say." McLoughlin adds, "Arabs take pleasure in using language for

---

172. See Hall, *Beyond Culture*, 20.

173. In his article on incarnational ministry to Muslims, Bashir Abdol Masih observes that an unhurried and free approach to time is key in the Arab-Muslim context. See Abdol Masih, "The Incarnational Witness to the Muslim Heart," 90.

174. See Patai, *The Arab Mind*, 13–14.

175. See Nydell, *Understanding Arabs*, 95.

its own sake."[176] As Arabs are generally gregarious people, their conversations can often be loud, characterized by exaggeration, and filled with emotion—including anger and joy. All of this communication is capably facilitated by the Arabic language.[177] While the average person may exhibit some rhetorical skill, politicians are especially known for citing poetry, proverbs, and passages from ancient books in their speeches as well as being deliberately repetitive.[178] In short, Arabs express themselves with no shortage of words.

Though Arabs are quite verbal, as members of a high context culture, much of their intended meaning is not conveyed in the explicit code of words. Unlike the low context cultures of North America and Europe where communication is more direct and greater value is placed in the actual words, Arabs tend to communicate in an indirect and even non-verbal manner.[179] Hall asserts, "most of the meaning is in the physical context or internalized in the person."[180] So, it is not unusual for a thirsty and famished Arab visitor to repeatedly refuse offers of drink and refreshment before mildly communicating acceptance. Tunisian guests often respond to such an offer with the rather ambiguous word *mesalesh* ("no problem"), which in other contexts would communicate "don't worry about it" or "it's no big deal." However, in the context of hospitality, it communicates indirect acceptance.

Also, Arabs will never respond to a request for help or for a favor with a direct "no." Rather, whether they are willing and able to meet the need or not, they will respond affirmatively, because on one level there is value placed in communicating one's desire to help.[181] Thus, there is not a necessary connection between words and concrete action. Patai summarizes, "The verbal utterance, which expresses such mental functions as feelings, aspirations, ideals, wishes, and thoughts, is quite divorced from the level of action."[182] Therefore, when an Arab says "yes," it may actually mean "perhaps." Again, most communicated intentions are covered with the important caveat *inshallah* ("God willing").

176. Both statements are found in Nydell, *Understanding Arabs*, 97.
177. See Musk, *Touching the Soul of Islam*, 145–49; also Patai, *The Arab Mind*, 170; and Nydell, *Understanding Arabs*, 31–32, 98.
178. See Nydell, *Understanding Arabs*, 97.
179. For a more complete discussion on low and high context cultures, see Hall, *Beyond Culture*, 39.
180. See Hall, *Beyond Culture*, 91.
181. See Nydell, *Understanding Arabs*, 18–19.
182. See Patai, *The Arab Mind*, 173; also Nydell, *Understanding Arabs*, 98.

Arab Non-Verbal Communication

The verbal messages related by Arabs—particularly those of an indirect nature—are supported by a great number of non-verbal signals. How do Arabs communicate in a non-verbal manner? First, Arabs interact with one another within a generally small sphere of personal space. This is especially apparent when the personal space requirements of North Americans are considered. It is not uncommon for Arab men to greet one another with a kiss and, in some contexts, to hold hands for extended periods of time.[183] In Lebanon, Matheny observed "Arabs confronting each other more directly, moving closer together, more apt to touch each other while talking, looking each other more squarely in the eye, and conversing in louder tones."[184] Though focused on one Arab context, Matheny's observations about communication seem to hold true for the Arab world in general.

A second key aspect of Arab non-verbal communication is the use of gestures. Though North Americans and Europeans certainly employ gestures in communication, Arabs use them much more. Nydell writes, "Arabs make liberal use of gestures when they talk, especially if they are enthusiastic about what they are saying. Hand and facial gestures are thus an important part of Arab communication."[185] Robert Barakat, who has catalogued and photographed 247 Arab gestures, adds, "To tie an Arab's hands while he is speaking is tantamount to tying his tongue."[186] Noting that Arab gestures are almost entirely limited to the hands, Barakat further adds that some gestures serve to accompany and enhance verbal communication while others exist to replace speech altogether.[187] Thus, with a single gesture, an Arab might communicate religious devotion, gratitude, respect, an insult, or an obscene remark.[188] For instance, in order to communicate friendship, North Africans will immediately touch their heart after shaking hands. By clicking the back of their upper teeth with the thumbnail, Tunisians communicate that they are completely broke. Finally, other Arabs express general disapproval by clicking their tongue. Though men and women may tend to use different gestures, communica-

---

183. See Nydell, *Understanding Arabs*, 37.
184. See Matheny, *Reaching the Arabs*, 97.
185. See Nydell, *Understanding Arabs*, 37.
186. See Barakat, "Arabic Gestures," 751.
187. Ibid.
188. Ibid., 756–65.

tion in the Arab world would be impossible without this key non-verbal device.[189]

Arabs and Orality

As noted, the Arabic language has served to unify and sustain Arab culture. Though each Arab country has its own dialect of colloquial Arabic, the Arab world is unified by Modern Standard Arabic—also known as *fosha* ("the most eloquent") Arabic.[190] Such high regard for the language of the Qur'an has naturally led to the development of a rich literary tradition. Following innovations in paper production in the ninth century, which facilitated the publication of books, a vast body of works in philosophy, science, medicine, poetry, and prose became available to the educated elite. Hourani notes that Arabs were also early leaders in the science of linguistics. By the twentieth century, Arabic language newspapers began to circulate widely, and books in print became increasingly common.[191] Also, printed materials have become more relevant to Arabs as literacy across the Arab world has increased dramatically since the 1960s. During this period, literacy in the Gulf countries has jumped from 10 percent to 86 percent of the population while at present, 68 percent of all Arabs are able to read.[192]

Despite this rich literary tradition, the peoples of the Arab world have historically been oral communicators and learners. Rick Brown, a linguist and specialist in Arabic, helpfully defines oral learners as "ones who depend mostly on verbal, non-print means to learn, to communicate with others, to express themselves."[193] While some contexts are primary oral cultures, where little or no literacy exists, most of the Arab world would be classified as a secondary oral culture. That is, while many in the society may be able to read and value books and printed materials, the majority still prefer to receive information (e.g., news) and communicate (e.g., making appointments) in an oral manner.[194] According to a recent

---

189. For a list of more common gestures, see Nydell, *Understanding Arabs*, 37–38 and Barakat, "Arabic Gestures," 772–93.

190. See Nydell, *Understanding Arabs*, 94–96, 193–96; also Lewis, *The Middle East*, 245–47.

191. See Hourani, *A History of the Arab Peoples*, 50, 199–200, 338, 393–94.

192. See Nydell, *Understanding Arabs*, 2–3.

193. See Brown, "Communicating God's Message," 122.

194. Ibid., 122–23; also Hourani, *A History of the Arab Peoples*, 425.

study on orality, the majority of the world's cultures operate within this secondary oral paradigm.[195]

How is orality observed in the cultures of the Arab world? First, the affairs of daily life—including business and basic communication—are conducted in colloquial Arabic.[196] This is true for both the educated and illiterate members of Arab society. It is not unusual to observe official speeches or talk show discussions begin in Classical Arabic and then digress into colloquial Arabic over the course of the presentation.

Second, expressions of Arabic art, including "folk stories, folk poetry, proverbs, sayings, riddles, folk songs, [and] folk music" are necessarily oral.[197] Supported by what Patai calls "the mystical allure" of the Arabic language, the canon of poetry possessed by the Arabs is especially rich.[198] Since pre-Islamic times, the Bedouins have transmitted orally their traditional *qasida* poems. Not surprisingly, some of the most capable orators have been illiterate.[199] Hitti adds that poetry has remained a cherished art form for Arabs as "modern audiences in Baghdad, Damascus, and Cairo can be stirred to the highest degree by the recital of poems."[200]

While Arabic poetry is often likened to music, the Arabs also have a rich tradition of song that is also necessarily oral. Hourani notes that in Andalusia, songs were sung to commemorate different seasons, including times of war, harvest, and marriage. While serving to preserve the memories of Andalusian civilization, these songs were passed down orally and a science of preserving music orally was developed.[201]

Second, the religion of Islam itself is quite oral. According to Muslim historians, Muhammad received the Quranic revelations orally over a period of twenty-three years (610–632), and the Muslim holy book was not officially codified until 657 under the reign of Caliph Umar. Resembling an epic poem, which, of course, rhymes in the original Arabic, the Qur'an was received and preserved in a largely oral manner within the first generation of Islamic history. The Hadith tradition, a record of Muhammad's

---

195. See Willis, et. al., *Making Disciples of Oral Learners*, 4–7.
196. See Patai, *The Arab Mind*, 196–98.
197. Ibid., 303.
198. Ibid., 51.
199. See Lewis, *The Middle East*, 250–58; also Patai, *The Arab Mind*, 52, 186; and Hourani, *A History of the Arab Peoples*, 12, 50–51.
200. Cited in Patai, *The Arab Mind*, 51.
201. See Hourani, *A History of the Arab Peoples*, 198.

actions and sayings, was also passed down orally before being committed to writing.²⁰²

Though the Qur'an has been preserved in written form since the seventh century, modern Muslims continue to learn and remember the Qur'an by chanting it. Many Muslims, including children, have attained the status of *hafedh* for having successfully memorized the Qur'an. Orality is also important within the Sufi tradition of Islam as members worship God through *dhikr*—constantly repeating the name of God until a form of spiritual ecstasy is attained.²⁰³

Finally, the oral nature of Arab culture can be observed in how history and legal matters have been recorded. Hourani notes that legal judgments in courts were rendered for hundreds of years solely on the basis of oral witnesses.²⁰⁴ The history of the pre-Islamic Arabian tribes was passed down orally for centuries and, as noted, early Islamic history—especially the record in the Qur'an and Hadith—was initially remembered orally. Patai and Lewis assert that even when written Arab histories began to emerge, they still resembled oral records because of their significant repetition and general lack of sequential organization.²⁰⁵

Though a rich Arab literary tradition cannot be denied, Arabs have historically preferred oral communication. Despite the noted advances in paper technology in the medieval period, which facilitated book publication, Lewis argues that publication did not find broad acceptance among Arabs until the eighteenth century because the language was considered too sacred to be reduced to print on a page. While increased levels of literacy in the twentieth century have certainly benefited the peoples of the Arab world, Patai suggests that it may have endangered some of the noted traditional art forms that are decidedly oral. He concludes, "The spread of literacy militates against the retention in memory of the treasures of oral literature."²⁰⁶

Brazilian Verbal Communication

Like Arabs, Brazilians are generally outgoing people who communicate freely through their words. Phyllis Harrison, in her comparative study of

---

202. See Musk, *Touching the Soul of Islam*, 137–38.
203. See Hourani, *A History of the Arab Peoples*, 199.
204. Ibid., 114.
205. See Patai, *The Arab Mind*, 186–87; also Lewis, *The Middle East*, 262.
206. See Patai, *The Arab Mind*, 303.

Brazilians and North Americans, asserts, "Brazilians feel much freer to express themselves conversationally, through comments and questions."[207] She adds that, "Brazilians do let their emotions show through tone, volume . . . believing that one ought to vent one's feelings for one's own sake and for the sake of others."[208] Gifted at small talk, Brazilians often interrupt one another during informal conversation and make comments about subjects that North Americans would not normally discuss in public (e.g., weight, acne).[209]

While Brazilians are verbal, they also belong to a high-context culture and thus, their intended messages do not rest fully in their words. Harrison adds that, "Because of the value placed on human relations and comfortable interaction, [Brazilians] often approach a subject or a problem indirectly, working toward a solution by degrees."[210] She notes that in an indirect attempt to invite a guest to leave their home, Brazilians will say, "you must be tired."[211] Commenting further on this indirect manner of communicating, one Brazilian missionary added, "If Brazilians want you to leave, they say 'stay.'"

Brazilian Non-Verbal Communication

Similar to Arabs, Brazilians also communicate comfortably with very little personal space.[212] This is very true with greetings. When two Brazilian women meet, they will usually kiss multiple times. Harrison notes that though two women meeting for the first time may greet one another with a handshake, they will commonly say goodbye by embracing.[213] Brazilian men greet one another with a hearty handshake or a "bear" hug. If a man's hand is dirty, then he will offer his forearm to greet a friend. Harrison adds that if two Brazilians know each other well, they will offer extended greetings and embraces.[214] Even after the initial greeting, Brazilians continue to

---

207. See Harrison, *Behaving Brazilian*, 12.
208. Ibid., 24.
209. Ibid., 24–27.
210. Ibid., 17.
211. Ibid., 25–26.
212. Ibid., 20–22; also Vincent, *Culture and Customs of Brazil*, 33.
213. See Harrison, *Behaving Brazilian*, 28–29.
214. Ibid., 27.

communicate through touching, holding hands or arms, and maintaining a good amount of eye contact.[215]

Again, like Arabs, Brazilians communicate non-verbally through gestures. Harrison, who dedicated the longest chapter of her book *Behaving Brazilian* to gestures, states "Brazilians use gestures frequently, far more frequently than the average North American."[216] Harrison's Brazilian friends made statements such as "I am more comfortable when people use their hands," and, "My hands are part of my oral communication."[217] One Brazilian worker that I interviewed affirmed, "We [Brazilians] communicate with our hands a lot," while another went so far as to say, "Brazilians cannot speak without their hands." Hence, Brazilians use gestures to support their verbal messages; however, some gestures succeed in replacing words altogether. For instance, to communicate the idea "more or less," Brazilians shake an open palm or hand sideways. To say "excellent," they give a "thumbs up" or pinch their ear lobe. Finally, to communicate "I doubt it," Brazilians will tilt their head to the side and raise their eyebrows.[218]

Brazilians and Orality

Hess and DaMatta maintain that Brazilian history and culture has been enriched by a strong literary tradition.[219] Azevedo, in his overview of Brazilian culture, offers a helpful summary of Brazil's key writers and their works.[220] On a more popular level, following the emergence of the printing press in the country in 1808, newspapers began to circulate especially as more freedom was granted to the press after 1821. For much of the nineteenth and early twentieth centuries, the print media became a powerful industry and served as a vehicle to communicate political ideas. Though freedom of the press was suppressed by some of the twentieth-century regimes, Brazil's daily newspapers continue to be a key medium of popular communication. They have also become more relevant because, as noted, literacy in the country has increased from 15 percent in 1890 to 88 percent in the present day.[221]

215. Ibid., 12, 20–24.
216. Ibid., 92–118.
217. Ibid., 92.
218. I am indebted to Barbara Hubbard for personally relating these explanations.
219. See Hess and DaMatta, *The Brazilian Puzzle*, 19.
220. See Azevedo, *Brazilian Culture*, 193–228.
221. See Vincent, *Culture and Customs of Brazil*, 95–99.

While affirming Brazil's literary tradition, Hess and DaMatta nevertheless assert, "Brazilians in general tend to prefer oral communication."[222] That is, they prefer to receive information and communicate through oral means rather than print media. Manuel Bandeira's poem the "Evocation of Recife," seems to offer further support:

> Life didn't teach me through newspapers or books
> But came from the mouth of the people,
> Bad speech of the people
> Good speech of the people.[223]

Also, in his study of Brazilian Alcoholics Anonymous, Jarrad reports that members preferred the leader's verbal encouragement and teaching to the organization's literature, which in other contexts occupies a more central role in meetings.[224]

Brazilian orality can be observed in at least a few other ways. First, Brazilian Portuguese is much more of an oral language than a written one. That is, unlike France, Brazil has no official academy of letters that monitors and filters the language for slang and other "barbarisms." Thus, innovation in spoken Portuguese seems to be valued more than upholding the written language.[225] Second, poetry and other forms of drama have maintained a consistent place in Brazilian culture. While these art forms are necessarily oral, Vincent adds that much of Brazilian literature also has a distinctly oral feel to it.[226] Finally, it seems that the media of radio and television have especially connected with and drawn out some oral aspects of Brazilian culture. Following the initial broadcasts in Brazil in 1922, radio has been a key means to transmit news, sports, and radio dramas. By 2001, 90 percent of Brazilians homes had a radio.[227] Television debuted in the country in 1950 and aside from also broadcasting news and sports, the medium has been responsible for delivering probably the most popular cultural text in Brazilian society—the *telenovela* (soap operas).[228] Page asserts that as Brazilian *telenovelas* have gained popularity both within the country and even around the world, there has been a general decline in

---

222. See Hess and DaMatta, *The Brazilian Puzzle*, 19.
223. Cited in Vincent, *Culture and Customs of Brazil*, 27.
224. See Jarrad, "The Brazilianization of Alcoholics Anonymous," 224, 232.
225. See Vincent, *Culture and Customs of Brazil*, 29–30.
226. Ibid., 131–32.
227. Ibid., 102–105.
228. Ibid.,110; also Page, *The Brazilians*, 444–65.

reading among Brazilians.[229] Thus, it seems that Brazilians fall into the category of being secondary oral learners and communicators and that radio and television have stoked these tendencies.

Brazilian Perspectives on Communication in the Arab World

This survey of the literature has shown that there are apparent similarities between Brazilians and Arabs in verbal communication. Both cultures seem to encourage a general extroversion in which ideas and emotions are freely communicated. Despite these apparent similarities, just over half (51.2 percent) of the Brazilians surveyed felt that Brazilian verbal communication was very different (15.6 percent) or different (35.6 percent) from Arab verbal communication, while a slight minority felt that it was very similar (13.3 percent) or similar (35.6 percent).

Some Brazilian transcultural workers reported that communicating with Arabs was not difficult. One worker related, "[I enjoy] their way of expressing their feelings and thoughts. Arabs in general are 'hot blooded,'" while another stated, "They are very loving people; they are transparent and communicate well." In fact, one Brazilian confessed, "I can communicate more easily with Arabs than I can with my colleagues from the U.K."

One clear area of difference is that some Brazilians perceive Arabs to be more aggressive and harsh in how they use their words. This tendency clashes with the cordiality valued by most Brazilians in their verbal interactions. Brazilian workers observed, "It seems though that Arabs are yelling at each other when they are talking," "Arabs shout at each other more than Brazilians," and "Arabs are more aggressive than Brazilians with their words."

Other Brazilians felt that these verbal tendencies were similar. One worker admitted, "They [Arabs] seem to be fighting when verbally communicating. But Brazilians [also] talk very loudly." Another related, "Both cultures are very loud, 'aggressive' in a way, and people talk at the same time (i.e., it's very common to be in a room full of people and multiple conversations happen at the same time)." Finally, one worker who was returning to Brazil after fifteen years in the Arab world made this helpful observation: "I thought it was different but being back in Brazil after fifteen years I find out that Brazilian people are similar. Everybody talks at the same time and they shout!"

---

229. See Page, *The Brazilians*, 448–49.

As noted, both Brazilians and Arabs are members of high-context cultures in which indirect verbal communication is common. However, some Brazilians interviewed expressed some struggles with how Arabs communicate indirectly. One worker stated, "Their indirect communication [was difficult for me]." Others have struggled to interpret the often-used Arab-Muslim caveat *inshallah* (God willing). While this expression reveals a fatalistic worldview, it also seems to be a strategy used by some to avoid a direct response. One Brazilian worker shared, "[it was difficult for me] trusting that North Africans are telling me the truth. The response to everything is *inshallah*." Similarly, another related, "They use the expression . . . *inshallah* a lot, but in a stronger sense . . . it is hard to know if the person makes an effort to do what they say." Finally, some Brazilian workers observed more continuity between Brazilians and Arabs in this area. Describing Arab communication, one worker described it as "Lots of reading between the lines. Not very straightforward; similar to here in Brazil." Another admitted, "Our Brazilian cordiality ("come to see us") is not always a concrete plan. Same in the Arab world. More is communicated by what is not said."

In the area of non-verbal communication, there seemed to be more similarities between Brazilians and Arabs as the survey responses suggest. In all, a healthy majority (73.4 percent) of Brazilians surveyed shared that their non-verbal communication was very similar to (26.7 percent) or similar to (46.7 percent) that of Arabs. While Brazilians disagreed over which cultural bloc uses body language and non-verbal symbols more and pointed out the different meanings communicated by various gestures, there was no question that both Brazilians and Arabs communicate a great deal non-verbally. One worker noted, "We [Brazilians] also use a lot of body language when we talk," while another added, "I believe we are very similar, because they [Arabs] use a lot of gestures when they talk." Another worked related, "Both cultures use hand movements as they talk." Finally, one Brazilian suggested that there was an Arab influence on Brazilian non-verbal communication: "Brazilians have many gestures like Arabs do. In fact, because there is an Arab influence in São Paulo, we Brazilians have probably picked up on some of this."

Though the differences in Arab and Brazilian verbal communication have been noted, Brazilians still seem to be culturally closer to the Arabs in this area than to the low context peoples of North America and Europe. Though needing to adapt to the perceived harshness of Arab communication, Brazilians are generally more expressive, emotional, and outgoing than their North American and European colleagues, and more able to relate to indirect communication. In terms of non-verbal communication, there seems to be some continuity between Brazilians and Arabs. As noted, Brazilians intuitively communicate through body language and gestures and certainly require less personal space in their interactions.

Brazilian Perspectives on Orality in the Arab World

Throughout the history of evangelical missions, most transcultural workers, especially North Americans and Europeans, have been highly literate people who have assumed that their audiences are print learners—those who "depend on reading and writing for the communication of important information."[230] In a recent study by a network of mission practitioners concerned with orality, they concluded that this tendency seems largely unchanged: "Ironically, an estimated 90 percent of the world's Christian workers presenting the gospel use highly literate communication styles. They use the printed page or expositional, analytical and logical presentations of God's word. This makes it difficult, if not impossible, for oral learners to hear and understand the message and communicate it to others."[231] As noted, in the initial North American efforts to evangelize Brazil, missionaries emphasized Bible distribution in a context where the majority of the people were illiterate. Makdisi points out that nineteenth-century Andover Seminary students preparing for ministry in the Arab world received a highly academic and literate education devoid of any contextual study of Arab culture or Islam. Once these North American missionaries arrived in the Arab world, their training translated into a polemical approach with great emphasis on Bible and literature distribution—most of which was largely ineffective in connecting with the host peoples.[232] It seems that the work of Samuel Zwemer—the most famous missionary to the Arab world in the nineteenth and twentieth centuries—had similar outcomes. Sharkey writes, "Zwemer was a driving force behind the American Christian Literature Society for Muslims" which "defined its purpose as 'spreading . . . the gospel through the printed page where Moslems are found.'"[233] Aside from being perceived by some Arab-Muslims as disseminating imperial

---

230. See Brown, "Communicating God's Message," 122.
231. See Willis et. al., *Making Disciples of Oral Learners*, 3.
232. See Makdisi, *The Artillery of Heaven*, 58–59, 88–90, 143–44.
233. See Sharkey, *American Evangelicals in Egypt*, 109.

propaganda,[234] Zwemer's efforts at tract and literature distribution also failed to connect with the oral aspects of Arab culture. Thus, in light of these shortcomings in the history of Western missions to the Arab world, Matheny's suggestion that printed literature remain a key in evangelizing Arabs needs to be reconsidered.[235] Rather, as Musk asserts, "Story-telling should not be feared by Western missionaries to Muslims," but should be regarded as a viable means of communicating Christ and the Scriptures.[236]

To be sure, Western mission movements are rapidly becoming sensitized to the needs of oral learners and are beginning to change their methodologies. A rich literature on orality is developing and groups such as the International Orality Network and the OneStory Partnership are pursuing concrete strategies for communicating the gospel to oral communicators.[237] While the Western church is working to catch up, it seems that Brazilian transcultural workers—themselves secondary oral communicators—already have a natural affinity with Arabs in this area. This seems especially true for those who come from Pentecostal congregations where Bible storytelling is a common approach.[238] Commenting on the work of churches in poor communities in Northeast Brazil, Carlos Mesters writes: "They are using song and story, pictures and little plays. They are thus making up their own version of the 'Bible and the Poor.' Thanks to songs . . . many who have never read the Bible know almost every story in it."[239]

Between their backgrounds and in some cases their experiences, Brazilian transcultural workers seem to identify with many Arabs through developing oral strategies for communicating the gospel. For instance, one Brazilian worker reported: "We created a series of biblical stories with an evangelistic tone, and they were translated to the local dialect and are now available at a website in the internet. Those stories were chosen in order to address the worldview of the people we serve." Another related, "[I am most excited about] storytelling ministry. I like to sit with the women while we work on manual projects and tell them biblical stories that help them grow in their understanding of God and also to prepare the way

---

234. See Ryad, "Muslim Response to Missionary Activities," 285–88; also Sharkey, *American Evangelicals in Egypt*, 1, 21–22, 27–28, 112–16; and Kidd, *American Christians and Islam*, 63, 67.

235. See Matheny, *Reaching the Arabs*, 90.

236. See Musk, *Touching the Soul of Islam*, 154.

237. See "International Orality Network" and "OneStory Partnership."

238. See Martin, *Tongues of Fire*, 177–78, 226–27.

239. Cited in Jenkins, *The New Faces of Christianity*, 29.

for them to come to know Jesus." Finally, a number of Brazilians are using soccer as an approach to ministry—a strategy that will be explored in more detail in an upcoming chapter. It is worth mentioning here that part of the strategy is very much geared toward oral communicators. At the conclusion of each soccer practice, the coach takes time to debrief the team's performance after which he communicates a biblically based life principle relevant to the experience on the field that day.[240]

---

240. I was able to observe this firsthand during a trip to the Middle East in October 2009.

3

Brazilian Workers in Arab Culture, Part 2

Introduction

IN THE PRESENT CHAPTER, we will continue the discussion from chapter 2 and consider how Brazilian evangelical workers reflect on their Brazilianness in the cultures of the Arab world. The aspects of culture explored in this chapter include family, relationships, hospitality, and spiritual worldview. Prior to summarizing the findings from chapters 2 and 3, I will briefly present an aspect of Brazilian culture *(jeintinho)*, which some regard as a key for Brazilians to adapt successfully in other cultures.

Family

Hoebel states, "the family, in one form or another, is the primary unit of human culture and sociality."[1] In nearly every society, the family is the place where children are nurtured, where the division of labor between men and women is established, where relationships with others in the social network are established, and where other social functions are dictated and carried out.[2] While some basic functions of the family can be observed across cultures, there is also much diversity in how the family is

---

1. Cited in Kraft, *Anthropology for Christian Witness*, 291.
2. Ibid., 291–92.

structured, how roles within the family are determined, and, in general, how family values are disseminated.

In terms of transcultural mission work, failing to understand and appreciate the structure, values, and roles present within the Arab family will certainly make evangelism and church planting difficult if not impossible. Thus, in this section, following a survey of the literature on Arab and Brazilian families, the Brazilian perspectives on family in the Arab world will be explored, including the missiological implications.

The Arab Family

Upon hearing the proverb, "You are like a tree, giving your shade to the outside,"[3] Arabs are instantly reminded that family should always remain a priority. When non-Arabs hear the proverb, "I against my brothers; I and my brothers against my cousins; I and my cousins against the world,"[4] they are made aware of the powerful sense of solidarity that exists within the Arab family. Both proverbs underscore the vital role that the family plays within the Arab world. Barakat affirms, "The family unit is the basic unit of social organization and production in traditional and contemporary Arab society, and it remains a relatively cohesive institution at the center of social and economic activities."[5]

In terms of structure, the Arab family is patrilochial; that is, the family continues through the father's line. In one respect, this means that children are identified in official documents as the "son of" *(ibn)* or "daughter of" *(bent)* their father. In another, it signifies that upon marriage, a woman becomes part of her husband's household and often the newlywed couple will live with her husband's parents.[6]

The Arab family also functions largely within an extended family structure, which generally includes a father, his sons, their wives, and their children.[7] Thus, it is not unusual for multiple generations to occupy the same house or property. Compared to the Western nuclear family, which

---

3. Cited in Nydell, *Understanding Arabs*, 101.
4. See Patai, *The Arab Mind*, 44.
5. See Barakat, *The Arab World*, 23; also Nydell, *Understanding Arabs*, 71.
6. See Kraft, *Anthropology for Christian Witness*, 294–95; also Nydell, *Understanding Arabs*, 38; and Barakat, *The Arab World*, 100.
7. See Barakat, *The Arab World*, 23; also Hourani, *A History of the Arab Peoples*, 105; Matheny, *Reaching the Arabs*, 41; and Kraft, *Anthropology for Christian Witness*, 292.

is restricted to a husband, wife, and their children, the notion of family in the Arab world is much broader.[8] Rooted in a Bedouin social structure, the Arab village is merely a network of extended families, and in Palestine, the village is regarded as a "family of families."[9]

Hence, the traditional practice of intermarriage within Arab tribes and clans serves to preserve and promote family solidarity.[10] Patai adds that the networks of extended families provide the basis for solidarity throughout the Arab world in which the "Arab nation" is also referred to as an "Arab family."[11] Even as urbanization challenges the preservation of the traditional Arab extended family, Barakat maintains, "Relatives generally remain closely interlocked in a web of intimate relationships that leaves limited room for independence and privacy. They continue to stay in the same neighborhood, to intermarry, to group together on a kinship basis, and to expect a great deal from one another."[12]

In terms of its authority structure, the Arab family is strongly patriarchal. Traditionally, the father's primary role has been to protect the members of the family, particularly the women.[13] Though the Arab family certainly experiences change, Barakat asserts, "The father continues to wield authority, assume responsibility for the family, and expect respect and unquestioning compliance with his instructions."[14] A second key role for Arab fathers has been providing for the family. Traditionally dubbed "lord of the family" (*rabb al-usra*), the father not only works to provide for the family's needs, but he also controls the family finances—including money earned by other family members.[15] The father's authoritative posture, typically accompanied by a measure of sternness, often leads to his being emotionally distant from the children. Also, it is not unusual for many Arab fathers to spend their evening hours out with other male friends in cafés instead of being at home with their families.[16]

---

8. See Nida, *Customs and Cultures*, 96.
9. See Barakat, *The Arab World*, 55–56.
10. See Musk, *Touching the Soul of Islam*, 46.
11. See Patai, *The Arab Mind*, 44, 300.
12. See Barakat, *The Arab World*, 106.
13. See Musk, *Touching the Soul of Islam*, 25; also Hourani, *A History of the Arab Peoples*, 105.
14. See Barakat, *The Arab World*, 23.
15. Ibid., 98, 101.
16. Ibid., 101; also Nydell, *Understanding Arabs*, 74.

Barakat adds that the father's authoritative role within the family also extends to other spheres within society, including schools and the work place, where a father figure or strong leader emerges to play a dominant role. Hence, leadership structures are quite vertical and subordinates are not only without empowerment, but they seem incapable of functioning without the father figure.[17] For Barakat, this tendency also explains the continued presence of dictators in the Arab world even in the post-colonial twentieth and twenty-first centuries.[18]

What is the woman's role within the Arab family? Traditionally, men and women have been segregated within Arab society—the veil being the clearest indication of this—and women have largely worked and functioned within the home.[19] With the father often absent from the home, the mother is primarily responsible for raising the children. While Arab children respect and fear their fathers, they have a great deal of affection for their mothers, who provide most of the emotional support for the family.[20] Mothers are also responsible for running the general affairs of the home, which certainly includes preparing meals and keeping up the home and often overseeing the household expenditures.[21] Hence, Arab mothers possess a significant behind-the-scenes influence within the home that seems to increase as they grow older.

In many Arab countries, including Morocco, Tunisia, Egypt, Lebanon, Syria, Jordan, and Iraq among others, women have begun to work outside of the home.[22] Despite this development, Barakat argues that women go largely unappreciated as breadwinners and are marginalized both in the work place and in society.[23] Though Arab women have gained more civil rights in the last half-century, including the right to vote, most civil laws in the Arab world still do not favor them.[24] Indeed, some women

---

17. See Barakat, *The Arab World*, 23, 149. Shaw ("Westerners and Middle Easterners Serving Together," 20) also discusses this challenge within Arab Christian organizations.

18. See Barakat, *The Arab World*, 176.

19. See Barakat, *The Arab World*, 30, 102; also Musk, *Touching the Soul of Islam*, 23–24; and Hourani, *A History of the Arab Peoples*, 120.

20. See Patai, 27–28; also Nydell, *Understanding Arabs*, 74; and Musk, *Touching the Soul of Islam*, 33.

21. See Hourani, *A History of the Arab Peoples*, 440.

22. See Nydell, *Understanding Arabs*, 45.

23. See Barakat, *The Arab World*, 30, 102

24. Ibid., 102; also Hourani, *A History of the Arab Peoples*, 441; and Nydell, *Understanding Arabs*, 46–48.

are still victims of honor killings, forced marriages, circumcision, and polygamy in parts of the Arab world, and most women continue to be subservient to their husbands and are certainly not viewed as equal to men.[25]

What are the prevailing values for the Arab family? First, related to the father's primary role as protector, the Arab home and family is a place of protection. This can be taken quite literally in one sense, as Hourani notes that traditional Arab homes were "built to be seen from within, not from outside."[26] Aside from this physical protection, children are also sheltered by the rules imposed by their parents. Barakat adds, "Parents are usually overprotective and restrictive, and children grow up to feel secure only on familiar ground."[27] Consequently, children are not encouraged to assert their independence or to be free in their thinking.

A second, related value is that the Arab family has a group orientation. That is, as Musk has helpfully written, "The proper functioning of a family far outweighs the niceties of individual choice or desire for personal independence."[28] Nydell adds, "Loyalty to one's family takes preference over one's personal preferences."[29] Thus, the individual finds their identity within the family, and it is not unusual for Arabs to introduce themselves by making reference to their family name.[30]

This group value can be observed in how the family maintains itself economically as each member works and sacrifices in order to contribute toward the family's needs. Thus, it is not uncommon for Arab families to operate a family business. Though starting off as dependents, Arab children are expected to grow up, work, and eventually provide support for their own parents—essentially a traditional form of social security. As the family works and dwells together, Barakat notes a prevailing sense of commitment and unity among the members.[31]

A final, essential value for the Arab family is honor *(sharaf)*—maintaining the family's good reputation before the rest of Arab society. Unlike

---

25. See Barakat, *The Arab World*, 102; also Nydell, *Understanding Arabs*, 50–51; Patai, *The Arabs Mind*, 34; and Musk, *Touching the Soul of Islam*, 35–36.

26. See Hourani, *A History of the Arab Peoples*, 126.

27. See Barakat, *The Arab World*, 106.

28. See Musk, *Touching the Soul of Islam*, 57.

29. See Nydell, *Understanding Arabs*, 15; also Musk, *Touching the Soul of Islam*, 127.

30. See Patai, *The Arab Mind*, 107. For a more detailed description of group-oriented societies, see Hiebert, *Transforming Worldviews*, 21 and Moreau et al, *Introducing World Missions*, 274.

31. See Barakat, *The Arab World*, 97–100.

Western societies in which the individual's behavior toward the society is emphasized—resulting in praise or guilt—Arab culture and group solidarity is maintained by this pursuit of honor and avoidance of shame.[32] Musk notes that "hard work, wealth, success [and] generosity" among other efforts and activities are aimed at strengthening and preserving the family's honor.[33] In light of this emphasis on honor, maintaining face *(wajih)* is also a strong value. This helps to explain why some Arabs have a hard time admitting guilt and also why mediators are called upon to resolve a dispute between two parties.[34]

The honor-shame paradigm also helps to explain honor killings—particularly in cases where Arab daughters have been sexually immoral. While the family has failed to maintain its honor by allowing the daughter to make such poor decisions, this violent response is an effort to overcome the family's shame. In a similar way, female circumcision is intended to remove a woman's sexual temptation and thus decrease the potential for the family being shamed.[35] Ultimately, honor serves to maintain solidarity within families, even amid transitions in the broader culture.[36]

The Brazilian Family

Generally speaking, family life is quite important to Brazilians, too. Finley writes that "'Family' is more than a category of Brazilian culture; it is a basic value close to the heart of every Brazilian."[37] Like Arabs, Brazilian families are patrilochial in that families continue through the father's line. Also, even in more urban areas, it is not unusual for a couple to live with the husband's parents for the first few years as they are getting established.[38]

In terms of structure, the traditional Brazilian family functions within the extended family framework. Harrison writes that in Brazil, "Family means parents, children, grandparents, aunts, uncles, cousins, second,

---

32. Ibid., 98; also Nydell, *Understanding Arabs*, 43; Hourani, *A History of the Arab Peoples*, 105; Matheny, *Reaching the Arabs*, 14–16; and Patai, *The Arab Mind*, 95–96.
33. See Musk, *Touching the Soul of Islam*, 68.
34. See Patai, *The Arab Mind*, 111.
35. See Barakat, *The Arab World*, 98; also Musk, *Touching the Soul of Islam*, 28–29, 69–73, 80–81; and Patai, *The Arab Mind*, 101.
36. See Matheny, *Reaching the Arabs*, 15.
37. See Finley, "Contextualized Training for Missionaries," 112.
38. Ibid., 113.

third, and fourth cousins plus spouses and siblings of all of these."[39] Often, this group of people, many of whom already occupy the same dwelling, will traditionally gather on Sunday for a meal.[40] In fact, the Portuguese word for extended family *(parentela)* implies a deep social network within the family. In more conservative areas such as Recife, it is not uncommon for the extended family to be strengthened through the marriage of cousins.[41] While the expressions of family in the regions of Brazil are diverse and the family has certainly become more nuclear in nature in the urbanized areas, the extended family structure is still experienced by many Brazilians and certainly understood by all.

Historically, the Brazilian family has also been patriarchal. The father has been an authoritative figure whose key role is providing protection for the family, especially the women.[42] Sarti adds that this role has been particularly apparent in Brazil's poorer regions.[43] Similar to the Arab world, one element of Brazil's high-context culture is that the leader of an organization (e.g., family, company, organization) takes responsibility for all members of the group.[44] Thus, Jarrad notes that Alcoholics Anonymous group leaders take a very parental posture toward the group members.[45] Finally, authoritarian leadership styles have been observed in Brazil's political leaders as well as its evangelical pastors.[46]

Though today, many Brazilian women pursue careers outside of the home, traditionally they have found their place within the home. Generally subjugated to their husbands, women have been expected to remain morally pure. However, many women have endured marital unfaithfulness as well as physical and emotional abuse from their husbands.[47] While more laws protecting Brazilian women from domestic violence have been enacted, Page remarks, "It is clear that the changes in the law and in law enforcement programs aimed at reducing violence against women can

---

39. See Harrison, *Behaving Brazilian*, 9.

40. See Vincent, *Culture and Customs of Brazil*, 81–82; also Harrison, *Behaving Brazilian*, 9, 84.

41. See Levine and Crocitti, *The Brazil Reader*, 338.

42. See Finley, "Contextualized Training for Missionaries," 116.

43. See Sarti, "Morality and Transgression," 124–28.

44. See Hall, *Beyond Culture*, 113.

45. See Jarrad, "The Brazilianization of Alcoholics Anonymous," 229–31.

46. See Willems, *Followers of the New Faith*, 22–23, 31; also Martin, *Tongues of Fire*, 259; Berg and Pretiz, "Five Waves of Protestant Evangelization," 64; and Comblin, "Brazil: Base Communities," 220.

47. See Page, *The Brazilians*, 254–56.

bring about incremental progress only, but they will not succeed in any way until deeply ingrained societal attitudes evolve."[48] Thus, many women manage to survive through manipulating their husbands and, in turn, their circumstances.[49]

In some poorer regions, the man remains the head of the household while the woman runs its day-to-day affairs.[50] Finally, as the Virgin Mary provides comfort and support to Brazilian Catholic worshippers, the mother is the source of emotional support for children in the home.[51] The role of women in Brazil certainly differs according to the regions, and women definitely experience more rights and freedoms today than they did a century ago. While the tension between the traditional and more modern elements of society should be understood, it seems that most modern Brazilian women can still relate on some level to the plight of more conservative and traditional women in Brazilian society.

What values can be observed in the Brazilian family? First, the most prominent value seems to be that the family is a place of protection. It is where children are nurtured, where family members are provided for materially, and where the elderly can reside when they can no longer care for themselves.[52] Finley adds that "Well-defined families with a high sense of home and group . . . act in defense of their physical possessions, as well as in defense of weaker members of the group, such as children, women, and servants."[53] Even the physical home is built with a protective wall that literally insures the family's protection and privacy.[54] DaMatta argues that this barrier symbolizes the protective nature of the family in a paradigm that he labels the "street and the home."[55] Finley offers the following helpful summary of DaMatta's thought: "The category *street* basically denotes the world, characterized by the unknown, by work, struggle, deception, dirty tricks, and individualization . . . [Home] . . . is a place where harmony should reign, crowding out the confusion, competition and disorder that characterize the street. At home nothing can be bought, sold or exchanged.

---

48. Ibid., 256.
49. See Kraft and Kraft, "Spiritual Warfare in Brazil," 18–19.
50. See Sarti, "Morality and Transgression," 124–28.
51. See Kraft and Kraft, "Spiritual Warfare in Brazil," 19–20.
52. See Vincent, *Culture and Customs of Brazil,* 82; also Harrison, *Behaving Brazilian,* 81.
53. See Finley, "Contextualized Training for Missionaries," 113.
54. See Vincent, *Culture and Customs of Brazil,* 83; also Harrison, *Behaving Brazilian,* 12.
55. See DaMatta, "For an Anthropology of the Brazilian Tradition," 276.

Brazilian Evangelical Missions in the Arab World

Political discussions, which reveal individual differences within the family, are banned from the table and intimate areas of the house."[56]

A second apparent Brazilian family value is its group orientation. That is, as newlyweds initially live with the husband's parents, as multiple generations occupy the same living space, or as every extended family member makes it to every birthday party, Brazilian family members find their identity in the family.[57] Like Arabs, the Brazilian family has traditionally worked together or contributed toward sustaining the family economically.[58] While the Brazilian family's group nature is being challenged through urbanization, all Brazilians can relate to this family value.

Finally, Brazilian families also operate within an honor and shame framework. One Brazilian transcultural worker serving in a Muslim context affirmed, "Brazilian culture is an honor based culture: honor is the base of relationships."[59] Tucker asserts that in the nineteenth century, men had the legal right to murder their wives if they were caught in adultery.[60] While these laws have, of course, been repealed, Page notes that domestic violence is still common, especially in cases when husbands learn of their wives' infidelity.[61] While this is a difficult social problem that cannot adequately be treated here, it should noted that such violence is ultimately undergirded by the family value of honor.

Brazilian Perspectives on Family in the Arab World

As noted, failing to understand the family structure and values within a given culture will certainly hinder transcultural mission work. Sadly, this also seems to have contributed to the failure of Western mission work in the Arab world in the nineteenth and twentieth centuries. Kraft notes that historically, Western missionaries have essentially communicated that the nuclear family structure was the only acceptable model for a Christian family, which has, of course, alienated members of host cultures that value

---

56. See Finley, "Contextualized Training for Missionaries," 119.

57. See Harrison, *Behaving Brazilian*, 9, 49; also Finley, "Contextualized Training for Missionaries," 113.

58. See Page, *The Brazilians*, 184.

59. See L.C., "Mais Missionários Brasileiros," 470. English translation by Barbara Hubbard.

60. See Tucker, *The Bible in Brazil*, 69.

61. See Page, *The Brazilians*, 254–56.

the extended family structure.⁶² Matheny adds that the Protestant emphasis on individual conversion has often been perceived as a threat because it runs counter to the communal values of the Arab extended family.⁶³ Finally, North American evangelical missionaries experienced difficulty in Syria and Egypt in the nineteenth and twentieth centuries by focusing their ministries on children and girls. Though they desired to reach families through these strategies, the Western missionaries ultimately defied the patriarchal structure and protective values of the Arab family.⁶⁴

Kraft correctly asserts, "strategies should work with rather than against culturally appropriate lines of authority, leadership, and decision making."⁶⁵ It seems that Brazilian transcultural workers are able to identify with the Arab family better than their North American or European colleagues. In this brief survey, it has been shown that Brazilians experience or can at least relate to the extended family structure. There is also some resemblance between the traditional roles of men and women in Arab and Brazilian families. Finally, the similar family values of protection, group orientation, and honor and shame have been presented in both contexts.

While only 38.6 percent of the Brazilian transcultural workers surveyed felt that the Brazilian family was very similar (6.8 percent) or similar to (31.8 percent) the Arab family—compared to 61.4 percent who found it to be very different (15.9 percent) or different (45.5 percent)—the narrative responses given by the Brazilian workers revealed that they could still relate to the Arab extended family structure and its communal nature. In fact, a number of Brazilian workers communicated admiration for the Arab family. One worker said, "[I like] their relationship with their family members, [they are] very united, they act as a clan." Others, making specific reference to members of the extended family, commented, "[I like that] they have a love for one another, a strong sense of family, and they care for their elderly," and "[I like the Arabs] respect for the elderly . . . Emphasis in community and family, not in the individual. [I like] the importance of the tradition in community, family, and person."

Some Brazilian workers noted the similarities between Arab and Brazilian families. One worker related,⁶⁶ "We [Brazilians and Arabs] both

---

62. See Kraft, *Anthropology for Christian Witness*, 293.

63. See Matheny, *Reaching the Arabs*, 117–19.

64. See Fleischmann, "Evangelization or Education," 267–68; also Makdisi, *The Artillery of Heaven*, 173; and Sharkey, *American Evangelicals in Egypt*, 123, 127–29.

65. See Kraft, *Anthropology for Christian Witness*, 310.

66. All responses from Brazilian missionaries or mission leaders were gathered from surveys and interviews. See appendices. For a transcript of all surveys and

value the sense of community in the family," while another added, "I am from Northeast Brazil where our family spends lots of time together and [we] have many meals together." Finally, another Brazilian worker confirmed some of the findings in the literature which have been presented: "In both cultures the concept of the immediate family as well as the extended families being very close to each other (emotionally and physically sometimes) is very evident. Also, it's very common in both cultures for family members to work together (share businesses)."

While affirming basic similarities between the Arab and Brazilian family, several Brazilian missionaries suggested that the Arab family was more tightly knit and generally stronger than the Brazilian family. One worker noted, "Brazilians and Arabs both have close families. But the family relationships among Arabs seems much closer," while another added, "Arab families are much more involved with each other."

Though not denying the authoritative role of Brazilian fathers, some workers asserted that Arab men and fathers occupied a more powerful place in family and society. One person stated, "the machismo is much stronger there [in the Arab world]," while another added, "The [Arab] father is more of an authority figure. Men (fathers, uncle) have authority over the women. In the Brazilian family, women are more independent."

Some Brazilians also asserted that the Brazilian family was experiencing more rapid change than the Arab family. "The Arab family feels like the Brazilian family twenty-five years ago. Brazilian families seem to be getting more nuclear, while Arabs still focus on the extended family," stated one worker. Another added, "Family life among Arabs is stronger. I think in Brazil we are losing this."

Finally, one Brazilian added that since the Brazilian family differs from region to region, families from the Northeast of Brazil more closely resemble Arab families, while those from the urban areas do not: "It depends on what part of Brazil you are from. Personally, I see things a bit different because I come from a big city like São Paulo where we are very independent and individualistic. But for example, in the Northeast region of Brazil I see that there are similarities in some aspects."

While some Brazilian workers have pointed out similarities between the Brazilian and Arab family, others have highlighted some clear differences. The first is in the area of raising children. One missionary said, "Raising children [in the Arab world] is very different. The children are

---

interviews, see Smither, "Brazilian Evangelical Missions Among Arabs," 335–408 (appendices B and D).

left to themselves. Discipline is very weak. The entire family and relatives interfere. The children are not so much punished. There are threats but they are not enforced." Another added, "[In the Arab world] everyone can correct a child. In Brazil, no, and never in the parents' presence!"

Another significant difference between Brazilian and Arab families is the difference in the roles of men and women. One worker remarked, "There [in the Arab world] the man is more important! Here [in Brazil] not," while another added, "The Arab family is heavily dominated by the father. He is the one who pressures his children to marry and then to have kids. In Brazil, the father is not the 'king' of the family like this." Commenting specifically on Arab marriages, one Brazilian worker said, "But the marital relationship is different [between Arabs and Brazilians]. The relationship [in the Arab world] is similar to that of master and servant." Finally, another Brazilian missionary observed, "The Arab woman has limitations and a different place in the marriage and society. Their opinion is not valued and their role is different in society. They see women as the personification of sin. Men have extreme freedom and a different role."

For some Brazilian transcultural workers, these differences in the roles of men and women have been some of the most difficult aspects of Arab culture that they have encountered. For example, one worker related, "The husband-wife relationship is very difficult. Also, life is difficult for the girls in the family," while another added, "[It is difficult to] see domestic violence and the extreme dominance of the father in the home." Another worker shared, "[It is difficult to see] oppression towards women and lack of freedom," while yet another said, "The woman's role inside of the family and community [is difficult for me]." While Brazilian women missionaries have found it painful to observe the plight of Arab women, many have also encountered difficulties as Brazilian women living in Arab society—an issue that will be discussed in the next chapter.

While the clear and subtle differences between the Arab family and Brazilian family have been noted, Brazilian transcultural workers still seem quite able to relate to the Arab family structure—certainly much better than their North American or European colleagues can. In light of this, what are the implications for ministry? First, Brazilians are naturally equipped to minister to and evangelize Arabs on a family-to-family basis. Matheny, recalling the Western mistake of focusing too heavily on the individual, urges that ministry in the Arab world should take place at the family level and that group conversions should be celebrated.[67] Indeed,

---

67. See Matheny, *Reaching the Arabs*, 99; also Abol Masih, "The Incarnational

in his study on conversion to Christianity among Palestinian Muslims, Anthony Greenham affirmed that the support and encouragement of family and friends was a leading factor, which helped Palestinians to make this decision to follow Christ.[68] Allen and Duran assert that Brazilians and Latin Americans, because of their own group-oriented backgrounds, actually prefer to communicate the gospel to families instead of individuals, which makes their witness effective in the Arab-Muslim context.[69] In addition, some Brazilian transcultural workers interviewed shared that they had enjoyed ministering to Arabs as a family. One worker related, "Our whole family is involved in ministry," while another added, "As a family we had a great testimony to the Arab families in Southern Brazil. Generally, Arabs have no respect for Brazilian women but they really respected my wife." Thus, in addition to proclaiming the gospel verbally, these Brazilian families have also offered a powerful witness through the quality of their family life.[70] This incarnational witness certainly has the potential to bring transformation to the Arab family as they embrace Christ.

Second, in addition to ministering to Arabs on a family basis, Brazilians also seem poised to facilitate church planting among Arabs. Kraft has suggested that church planting models in communal contexts like the Arab world ought to be developed intentionally around the extended family.[71] Musk adds, "Around the Muslim world today there are many ex-

---

Witness to the Muslim Heart," 91. The relevance and value of group conversion has also been nicely articulated in "The Willowbank Report" (paragraph 7E): "Conversion should not be conceived as being invariably and only an individual experience, although that has been the pattern of Western expectation for many years. On the contrary, the covenant theme of the Old Testament and the household baptisms of the New should lead us to desire, work for, and expect both family and group conversions. Much important research has been undertaken in recent years into "people movements" from both theological and sociological perspectives. Theologically, we recognize the biblical emphasis on the solidarity of each *ethnos*, i.e., nation or people. Sociologically, we recognize that each society is composed of a variety of subgroups, subcultures or homogeneous units. It is evident that people receive the gospel most readily when it is presented to them in a manner which is appropriate—and not alien—to their culture, and when they can respond to it with and among their own people. Different societies have different procedures for making group decisions, e.g., by consensus, by the head of the family, or by a group of elders. We recognize the validity of the corporate dimension of conversion as part of the total process, as well as the necessity for each member of the group ultimately to share in it personally."

68. See Greenham, "Muslim Conversions to Christ," 194–95.
69. See Allen and Duran, "Pre-Field Preparation to Sow," 286.
70. See Finley, "Contextualized Training for Missionaries," 162.
71. See Kraft, *Anthropology for Christian Witness*, 311.

amples of such groups, growing amid pain, founded around families who are able, within their cultural contexts, to help build a new family—the family of the church."[72] Thus, in light of their own cultural background regarding family and the general ability to understand the Arab extended family structure, Brazilians seem prepared to help nurture the church in the Arab context.

Finally, Brazilian men serving among Arabs seem especially able to reach Arab men and the leaders of families. Though it appears that Arab men have more of an authoritative role in the Arab families than Brazilian men do in their families, Brazilian male transcultural workers can still relate to this patriarchal aspect of the family. Thus, they will want to focus on reaching the Arab family with the gospel through the father.[73] As church planting movements are established—ones that remain sensitive to the father's role in the Arab family—Brazilian men, due to their own background, will be able to mentor Arab men toward being strong, yet godly leaders.

Relationships

All Christian ministry—especially transcultural mission—is quite impossible without meaningful relationships. Kraft asserts that if warmth and friendship are present between missionaries and members of the host culture, then cultural change and even conversion to Christianity are much more likely to occur.[74] In the present section, a brief study of relationships in the Arab and Brazilian contexts will be considered. Specifically, how do friendships begin? What are the prominent values observed in friendships? How do Arabs and Brazilians resolve conflicts? After treating these questions in the literature, and considering the input given by Brazilian transcultural workers who serve among Arabs, the missiological implications will be discussed.

Arab Friendships

Because Arabs easily talk to strangers and express themselves freely, spontaneously, and warmly, Nydell asserts, "Friendships start and develop

72. See Musk, *Touching the Soul of Islam*, 65.
73. See Kraft, *Anthropology for Christian Witness*, 311; also Parshall and Parshall, *Lifting the Veil*, 243.
74. See Kraft, *Anthropology for Christian Witness*, 394.

quickly."[75] Even basic greetings and communication are filled with warmth and emotion that may seem rather exaggerated for the average Westerner.[76] For instance, Syrian Arabs will say *nharkoum said* ("may your day be prosperous") for "good morning" to which the response is *nharkoum said wa mubarak* ("may your day be prosperous and blessed"). Also, *kater kheyrak* ("Allah increase your well being") is commonly used to convey thanks.[77]

While friendships may develop quickly among Arabs, it should be noted that Arabs do not regard everyone in the community or society as a friend. Rather, as Nydell notes, "In the Arab way of thinking, people are clearly divided into friends and strangers."[78] Among friends, they can be "polite, honest, generous, and helpful at all times"; however, among strangers in public, it is not uncommon to see pushing in lines, discourteous driving, and even lying and cheating in business.[79]

Once friendships are begun among Arabs, what values help to maintain those relationships? First, Arabs prefer to remain in frequent contact; thus, it is normal for friends to visit and spend time together at least every few days. As conversation is the most popular form of entertainment in the Arab world, frequent meetings do not necessarily mean planned activities that cost money.[80] If friends are unable to see each other, they will call or even send a brief text message to maintain contact until the next face-to-face meeting is possible.

Second, loyalty is also a strong value in Arab friendships.[81] One clear expression of this is the favor system that exists in Arab society. As noted, it is impossible for an Arab friend to refuse verbally a request from a friend—whether or not they are willing or able to meet the need. However, in many cases, Arabs will sacrifice and search for creative solutions to help out a friend—a favor that will certainly be called in sometime in the future. While it seems that Arabs keep fairly good track of favors, this does contribute to loyalty within a friendship.

A final characteristic of Arab relationships is the undergirding value of the group. Stemming from the communal nature of the traditional Arab

75. See Nydell, *Understanding Arabs*, 17; also Barakat, *The Arab World*, 24–25.
76. See Nydell, *Understanding Arabs*, 28.
77. See Patai, *The Arab Mind*, 53; also Nydell, *Understanding Arabs*, 99.
78. See Nydell, *Understanding Arabs*, 26.
79. Ibid.
80. See Nydell, *Understanding Arabs*, 20.
81. Ibid., 17–19.

extended family, friendships should also be understood within this group framework. Barakat asserts, "A highly distinctive feature of Arab society is the continuing dominance of primary group relations" [in which] "individuals engage in an unlimited commitment to one another." He adds that Arabs "derive satisfaction from extensive . . . affiliations and develop a great sense of belonging."[82] As "privacy" is synonymous with "loneliness" in Arabic, Arabs continually default to cultivating relationships within the group context.[83] While the sense of group continues to be stronger in rural settings, family, community, and friendship of a communal nature is still maintained even in larger urban contexts.[84]

How do Arabs approach conflict resolution? Hiebert notes that, as members of a communal society, Arabs prefer to avoid direct confrontation if possible.[85] Despite this, Patai correctly asserts that Arabs, like many other cultures, are quite prone to conflict on family, tribal, as well as national and political, levels.[86] As Arabs freely communicate emotion, it is not unusual for even a small conflict to become explosive rather quickly. The inherited Bedouin values of bravery require them to offer a strong verbal defense in the face of conflict—words that very often do not translate into concrete action.[87]

In light of this tendency to defend one's honor through strong words, how do Arabs concretely resolve a conflict? While one possibility is that the enemy (a rival clan, tribe, or army) might actually be destroyed in the conflict, a more common Arab response is to appeal to a mediator. Traditionally, the mediator *(wasit)* was a man of wealth and prestige whose aim was first to intervene and separate the two fighting parties—an action that actually increased the honor of each group. The mediator's job was not to render a judgment in the conflict; rather, it was to restore and uphold the groups' honor. In fact, a routine strategy was to invite the groups to cease fighting for the sake of their respective families.[88]

On a political level, mediation and conflict resolution often takes the form of conferences attended by delegations from rival Arab nations.

---

82. See Barakat, *The Arab World*, 24.
83. See Nydell, *Understanding Arabs*, 20–21.
84. See Barakat, *The Arab World*, 24.
85. See Hiebert, *Transforming Worldviews*, 21.
86. See Patai, *The Arab Mind*, 232–40.
87. Ibid., 63–69.
88. Ibid., 239–43; also Nydell, *Understanding Arabs*, 25–26. For more discussion on the role of a mediator, see Elmer, *Cross-Cultural Conflict*, 65–79.

From a Western perspective, it seems that these meetings are filled with never ending discourses that result in little concrete action other than scheduling another conference. However, for Arabs, this unhurried time to talk at length restores honor, builds friendship, and offers hope for a peaceful future.[89]

Brazilian Friendships

One of the most distinguishing aspects of Brazilians is their friendly nature and penchant for relationships. Harrison cites a Brazilian friend who relates: "'Friend' likewise means something different in Brazil. 'A friend is like a brother or sister. You share things, be honest with them. They will accept you as you are. They will question you, argue with you. It leads to growth.'"[90] That said, like Arabs, Brazilians are certainly not friends with everyone in society. In light of DaMatta's home and street paradigm, it should be noted that friendship in Brazil is necessarily exclusive and that relationships can be observed on different levels.[91] Many Brazilians remain strangers to one another, while others, such as those who work together, are regarded as colleagues (*colegas*). After some time, a colleague may become a friend (*amigo*), which as indicated in the description above, means that the friend has in a sense become a part of the family.[92]

Given these levels of relationship within Brazil and the process of going from stranger to colleague and possibly to friend, how do Brazilians meet one another? First, Brazilians often become friends through their work. It is not unusual for businessmen working on a deal to strike up a friendship because, as Harrison notes, "Brazilians often approach business as a particular kind of social interaction."[93] Also, it is common for co-workers in a company to go out for drinks after work, even for many years, before consecrating their friendship by inviting one another to their homes.[94] Second, Brazilians also meet in otherwise public places. Friendships have been started on buses, in the market, and of course, at

---

89. See Patai, *The Arab Mind*, 252–60.
90. See Harrison, *Behaving Brazilian*, 10.
91. See Page, *The Brazilians*, 229–58.
92. See Harrison, *Behaving Brazilian*, 10–11; also Finley, "Contextualized Training for Missionaries," 113.
93. See Harrison, *Behaving Brazilian*, 72.
94. See Vincent, *Culture and Customs of Brazil*, 83; also Harrison, *Behaving Brazilian*, 77.

the beach. The latter is a key public place in Brazilian society and it's often where young people, including young men and women with romantic interests, become acquainted and strike up a friendship.[95] Finally, in both work and public places, Brazilians have been known for their warmth, charm, and friendship toward foreigners. Page correctly asserts: "Cordiality is a defining characteristic of their behavior. They radiate an irresistible pleasantness, abundant hospitality, and unfailing politeness, especially to foreigners."[96]

Not unlike Arabs, Brazilian friendships seem to thrive on the favor system. While some colleagues may ask for a favor, such requests happen more often among friends. Sometimes the request, generally communicated in an indirect manner, is actually made to test the friendship. Indeed, if it is within one's power to act, a friend's request for a favor cannot be refused. Even when Brazilians are not able to help, they will rarely communicate this directly.[97]

Also like Arabs, Brazilians build friendships within the context of a largely communal culture. Harrison writes, "The general concern for the group rather than the individual, and an appreciation for the human world around them, all create situations in which Brazilians are rarely alone."[98] A by-product of the traditional Brazilian extended family, the communal nature of Brazilian society can be observed on a number of fronts. Though certainly apparent in the life and business of small towns, the group orientation can also be observed in the cities, for instance, when employees take their coffee breaks.[99] Vincent writes, "[Brazilians] stop their work, come together at the coffee bar or around the coffee server, drink, converse, and then return to previous duties."[100] Outside of work, Brazilians of all races and classes meet and interact on public transportation, at the beach, and, of course, at soccer (*futebol*) matches. Describing the soccer match as a community gathering, Page vividly writes: "Crowds attending major matches are not mere onlookers; they are participants in an ecstatic rite that begins when teams take the field. Waving banners, setting off firecrackers, tossing talcum powder, and chanting cheers, the fans enter into a

---

95. See Harrison, *Behaving Brazilian* 63–67; also Vincent, *Culture and Customs of Brazil*, 89.

96. See Page, *The Brazilians*, 9.

97. See Harrison, *Behaving Brazilian*, 14–15; also Finley, "Contextualized Training for Missionaries," 114–15.

98. See Harrison, *Behaving Brazilian*, 12.

99. See Rosanne Prado's very insightful study in "Small Town, Brazil" 59–82.

100. See Vincent, *Culture and Customs of Brazil*, 85.

symbiotic relationship with the players, who feed off the energy that comes from the stands."[101] Another venue in which Brazilians demonstrate a collective spirit is at Carnival, the pre-Lenten celebration, which officially marks the end of the summer. Page adds, "For five nights and four days, a marathon of merrymaking convulses the city, as delirious celebrants shed all their inhibitions (along with most of their outer garments) and respond to the ubiquitous, nonstop pulsing of drums conveying the infectious beat of the samba."[102] Finally, Brazilians achieve a form of community through popular religion. Though the practices and underlying beliefs of Brazilian Spiritism will be addressed shortly, it is sufficient here to conclude with Wiebe that "Spiritism in Brazil is primarily a group activity."[103]

Some may object to the assertion that Brazil is predominantly a communal culture, arguing for a certain Brazilian individualism. However, Finley helpfully distinguishes Brazilian individualism from that which is observed in North America or Europe. He writes: "Brazilians have a different kind of individualism. Brazil is still a relational culture, and people always sense that they need others. Brazilian individualism consists, therefore, not of isolationism, but of efforts to assert oneself within a group."[104]

Finally, how do Brazilians generally go about resolving conflict? There is a Brazilian proverb that says, "When one doesn't want, two don't quarrel."[105] This saying serves as a reminder that Brazilians are high context people who tend to prefer indirect communication and therefore do not prefer direct, verbal confrontation. Rodriques adds: "The basic Luso-Brazilian personality has a horror of violence and always seeks a way of smoothing things over, a path of moderation that avoids definite breaks. Cleverness, prudence in shunning extremes, an ability to forget, a rich sense of humor, a cool head and a warm heart get the Brazilians through difficult moments."[106] In short, Brazilians continue to value cordiality even in conflicts and will pursue a solution for the problem in a diplomatic and indirect manner. A key value in Brazilian culture, which will be discussed more shortly, is finding a solution (*jeito*) to problems or challenges. Rather than confronting the issue directly, Brazilians will lean on relationships or

---

101. See Page, *The Brazilians*, 392.
102. Ibid., 469.
103. See Wiebe, "Persistence of Spiritism in Brazil," 10.
104. See Finley, "Contextualized Training for Missionaries," 192.
105. Cited in Moreau et al., *Introducing World Missions*, 276.
106. Cited in Harrison, *Behaving Brazilian*, 18.

appeal to favors to resolve it. This approach certainly applies to resolving a conflict with friends.

Brazilian Perspectives on Relationships in the Arab World

While this survey of the literature has revealed some continuity in how Arabs and Brazilians regard friendships, a little over two-thirds of Brazilian workers surveyed[107] felt that the Brazilian approach to relationships was very similar (29.5 percent) or similar to (38.6 percent) that of Arabs. The narrative responses strongly confirmed this data.

A significant number of respondents communicated a general admiration for the value that Arabs placed on relationships. One Brazilian worker said, "[I like] their [Arabs] relational attitude," while another added, "[I like that Arabs] are very loving people, they are transparent and communicate well . . . they are very sociable." Similarly, others shared, "[I like that Arabs] value relationships," and "I enjoy that they [Arabs] are people oriented, open to friendship." One worker showed his appreciation for the Arab emphasis on relationships by contrasting this with how (presumably) Europeans approach relationships: "[I like that Arab] culture is relational. I appreciate the fact that they are warm, and almost always open to deeper relationships. [This is] different from cold climate cultures."

Some transcultural workers noted that Arabs seemed especially open to getting to know Brazilians. One worker said, "[I like that] Arabs are friendly and like to talk. They like Brazilians and we feel welcomed," and another added, "[I like that Arabs] are very friendly. They love Brazilian people . . . They like to talk and eat a lot . . . They are open to relationships."

Other Brazilians affirmed that building relationships with Arabs was generally easy and happened rather quickly. "Arabs make friends quickly," related one worker while another added, "The Muslims are very easy to build friendships with." Another missionary said, "[I like that] there are open doors to relationship and it is easy to make friends and share the gospel."

Once relationships were built, other Brazilian workers affirmed that Arabs were loyal friends. One worker indicated, "Among Arabs, once someone is a friend, they are a very close friend," and another added, "[They are] always in touch." Finally, another missionary shared, "Friendships [with Arabs] tend to last a long time and do not die in spite of the physical distance."

---

107. All responses were gathered from surveys and interviews. See appendices.

A number of Brazilian workers affirmed the communal nature of Arab culture. "[I like the Arab's] people-oriented mentality; they are people who enjoy celebrating," shared one worker. Another added, "[I like that Arabs] are friendly and offer friendship. They are very integrated in the community they live in: [each] one helps one another," while another related, "[I like that Arabs] are laid back and it is easy to spend lots of time together." Finally, one Brazilian worker summarized, "[I like the Arab] emphasis in community and family, not in the individual."

Other Brazilian missionaries interviewed noted some similarities regarding relationship between their own culture and their Arab contexts. One worker said, "Both [Arab and Brazilian] cultures are very relational," and another related, "The way they [Arabs] make friends here is very similar to Brazilians." More specifically, some workers commented on how relationships were begun. "It is easy to make an immediate relationship with Arabs," shared one worker. Another added, "It is very easy for us [Arabs and Brazilians] to make friends, start a conversation, etc.," while another affirmed, "It is very easy to get to know [Arab] people. It is not necessary to have an official reason to meet a new person."

Other Brazilian workers commented on similarities in cultivating and maintaining a relationship that has already started. One worker said, "[I like that Arabs] are very curious to know everything about your life. In Brazil, we do this, too. They [Arabs] are really friendly." Another shared, "A lot of time is spent in building a friendship or a relationship. Simply spending time together without even having much to say has a lot of meaning to both [Arab and Brazilian] cultures." Finally, another Brazilian observed, "Like us [Brazilians], it takes time to gain their [Arabs] trust."

Some Brazilian respondents indicated that there were some slight differences in how Arabs and Brazilians approached relationships, which also reveals some diversity among Brazilians on the issue. Commenting on Brazilian individualism, one worker related, "[I like the Arab's] sense of community. Because I feel that we [Brazilians] are very individualistic. I appreciate it so much even though it is hard for me, like to share a glass, a food, water bottle, etc." Another admitted, "I am more people-oriented than a North American, but not as people oriented as North Africans; North Africans are more status ascribed than myself, so this was challenging." Finally, another worker shared, "In the Arab country where I serve, they take people home so easily! In Brazil, we are more afraid of that (perhaps for me because I am from a big city)."

Other Brazilian missionaries cited some clear differences in how Arabs and Brazilians approach friendship. Indicating that Arabs are more closed than Brazilians, one worker shared, "Arabs are very devoted to the family and family ties. At first, it is not easy to connect with them and create deeper relationships. They appear to be hospitable but it takes time to create trust." Another added, "They [Arabs] are very much among themselves."

Commenting on how relationships begin, one Brazilian noted, "It is different in how we begin the relationship. Brazilians open up more quickly. But, over time Arabs open up, though more slowly." On the other hand, another Brazilian related, "I'm from Minas Gerais. We don't make friends as quickly or easily as they do here in my Arab country." Describing the type of people with whom Arabs and Brazilians make friends, one worker said, "Arabs seem to begin friendships based on appearances and status. In Brazil, we become friends with our work and classmates. In Brazil once you become a friend, you are part of the family." Another added, "Arabs are more likely to build friendships based on social class than Brazilians are. It's slower to start a relationship with Arabs but it gets stronger over time." Finally, another Brazilian commented on the different ways that friendships are maintained: "Arabs call each other all the time; Brazilians give each other a little more space and time."

For some Brazilians, the way that Arabs pursued relationships was challenging for them. Commenting on the lack of privacy in relationships, one worker said, "The concept of privacy [was difficult]. North African's sense of privacy is 'more loose' than mine," while another added, "Lack of privacy [among Arabs is difficult]." Finally, for one Brazilian the communal nature of Arab culture, especially as it affected one's decision to follow Christ, was difficult: "As their identity is in Islam, even those who are open to Christ were very reluctant to believe in Christ. There is a strong pressure from the group."

Regarding conflict resolution, the vast majority (79.6 percent) of Brazilian transcultural workers felt that the Arab manner of resolving conflicts was very different (20.5 percent) or different (59.1 percent) or from the Brazilian approach. Citing similarities between Arabs and Brazilians in resolving conflict, one worker related, "In some cases, Brazilians also have difficulty resolving conflict," and another added, "As Brazilians, the Arabs try to avoid direct conflict." One Brazilian worker admitted, "I was more similar to North Africans . . . in resolving conflict in a roundabout way."

Some of the observations made by Brazilians about Arab communication implied differences in dealing with conflicts. One worker said, "They yell a lot here," while another added, "They [Arabs] talk very loud, scream at each other and get everything resolved in twenty minutes. Only God knows if there was a true repentance, forgiveness and apology." One worker jokingly added, "They love 'fake wrestling' here [and resolve their conflicts like that]." Others commented, "They [Arabs] argue a lot, ask for forgiveness of each other and everything goes back to how it was before," and, "Generally, conflicts are not resolved, and if resolved, it is not done in the best way."

Some Brazilian workers asserted, in contrast to the Arab tendency to shout and argue, that Brazilians tend to maintain their cordiality even during a conflict. One worker related, "Arabs will scream a lot and shout but there is lots of talk and no action. Brazilians do not shout like that," while another said, "Brazilians do not like confrontation; we are generally diplomatic in these things."

Other Brazilian workers indicated that Brazilians are generally more confrontational than Arabs during a conflict. One Brazilian shared, "Brazilians do not like confrontation. But we are more confrontational than Arabs are," while another added, "Brazilians confront each other more than Arabs do. Here [in my Arab country] there is no verbal confrontation." Similarly, one worker related, "In my Arab context there is no direct confrontation. Personally, I prefer to confront someone when there is a problem," and another added, "Brazilians can also be indirect but personally I am more direct in confrontation. Arabs do not want to face a problem and you cannot communicate with them too directly."

Finally, Brazilian transcultural workers affirmed one aspect of Arab conflict resolution that was quite different from the Brazilian way—appealing to a mediator. One Brazilian said, "In Brazil, we can resolve a problem directly with the person. Arabs have to call someone as an intermediary." Another affirmed, "In Brazil, the conflict is between you and the person. In the Arab world, a mediator is needed. In a conflict, Arabs must show themselves to be strong and the mediator serves to boost this strength." Describing this process in a rural context, one Brazilian shared, "Sometimes they make use of a mediator. In the villages where we work they have a meal together. The offending party slaughters a sheep and offers it to the offended party and his family." Finally, one worker highlighted the important role of the mother in conflict resolution: "The mother is

Brazilian Workers in Arab Culture, Part 2

the mediator of disputes in the Arab family and problems are worked out within the family."

In light of the summary from the literature and survey responses given by Brazilian transcultural workers regarding friendship, what are the missiological implications for Brazilians serving among Arabs? First, perhaps the strongest quality that Brazilians bring to transcultural mission is their ability to initiate and cultivate quality friendships. As it has been shown, both Brazilians and Arabs deeply value relationships, and they approach friendships in a similar way. One Brazilian worker illustrated this in sharing some difficulty that he encountered serving under a British mission team leader who exhorted the team to go out and "make friends" with Arabs—in essence, make impersonal contacts in order to share the gospel.[108] However, this worker seemed to find more success in his ministry by approaching relationships in a more Brazilian way. In fact, another Brazilian missionary argued that Brazilians were effective among Arab-Muslims because they were not afraid to develop deep and meaningful relationship with Arabs and because they were able to place people above projects.[109] In short, the Brazilian way of building relationships seems quite meaningful in the Arab context and provides a foundation for authentic evangelism, discipleship, and church planting.

Second, it is quite natural for Brazilians to approach ministry in a group-oriented society. As noted, unlike North Americans and Europeans who can be so focused on personal (individual) evangelism or discipleship, Brazilians are able to build relationships and communicate the gospel to families and groups of friends—a natural basis for a church planting movement.[110] Brazilians also seem naturally equipped to partner with Arabs in ministry teams. In spending time with a mission team composed of Brazilians and Arabs, I observed that the team meeting was planned around a meal and that kids were present. In addition to studying the Scriptures and praying for one another, many personal needs were shared, and very little ministry business was communicated. Indeed, cultivating Christian fellowship was valued more than dealing with ministry projects. For me, this was quite distinct from many mission team meetings in which I had participated where ministry business is the central focus.[111]

---

108. Related to me in personal conversation during a visit, January 5, 2010.

109. See L.C., "Mais Missionários Brasileiros," 470; also Finley, "Contextualized Training for Missionaries," 199.

110. See Allen and Duran, "Pre-Field Preparation to Sow," 286.

111. These observations were made with this team, January 9, 2010.

Brazilian Evangelical Missions in the Arab World

Finally, while Brazilians can relate to Arabs in the general manner of building relationships in a communal culture, there are some clear differences in how conflicts are resolved. Though Brazilians are also from a high-context culture and many may not prefer direct confrontation, most Brazilians will have to adapt significantly in this area when serving among Arabs.

Hospitality

Quite related to the preceding discussions on family and relationships, we now turn our attention to the cultural value of hospitality—the general act of welcoming another into one's home, to one's table, and generally into one's life. A qualification for church leaders in the Pastoral Epistles,[112] offering hospitality is also a vital element for transcultural mission work as it creates an environment for relationships, authentic evangelism and discipleship, and Christian fellowship. In this section, we will examine how Arabs and Brazilians regard and practice hospitality. After analyzing the responses of Brazilian missionaries regarding hospitality in the Arab world, the missiological implications will be explored.

Arabs and Hospitality

Hospitality (*diyafa*) is a defining characteristic of Arab culture.[113] In fact, the basic Arabic greeting for "hello" (*ahhlan wa sahhlan*) literally means that there is a family and a valley of abundance. That is, with the harvest finished and the family present, it is time to sit down and spend some unhurried time together.[114] Hence, a sense of welcoming hospitality is embedded in this daily greeting.

While Islam strongly encourages and informs Arab hospitality, this cultural value can also be traced to the Bedouin roots of Arab culture.[115] Motivated by a desire to increase one's reputation within the community as well as to strengthen group solidarity, Bedouins were obliged to offer

---

112. See 1 Tim 3:2 and Titus 1:8; also 1 Pet 4:9.

113. Patai (see *The Arab Mind*, 93) helpfully points out that *diyafa* is the same word for generosity in Sudanese Arabic.

114. See Nydell, *Understanding Arabs*, 56.

115. See Musk, *Touching the Soul of Islam*, 89–90; also Barakat, *The Arab World*, 52, 60.

Brazilian Workers in Arab Culture, Part 2

protection and shelter to strangers—even fugitives.[116] Thus, it is impossible for Arabs, including the poor, to turn away a visitor and deny him hospitality.[117] Commenting further on the importance of Arab hospitality, one Arab woman helpfully summarized: "For Arabs, hospitality lies at the heart of who we are. How well one treats his guests is a direct measurement of what kind of a person she or he is. Hospitality is among the most highly admired of virtues. Indeed, families judge themselves and each other according to the amount of generosity they bestow upon their guests they entertain. Whether one's guests are relatives, friends, neighbors, or relative strangers, they are welcomed into the home and to the dinner table with much the same kindness and generosity."[118]

In most cases, Arabs show hospitality in the context of their home. Matheny notes that even the shortest visit includes a drink and some food.[119] Often, unexpected visitors are invited to stay for a meal. In Tunisia, such visitors are greeting with the expression *hisanek jiraya* ("your horse makes good time"), meaning that they showed up at just the right moment.

In most Arab contexts, the largest meal of the day is at mid-day or in the early afternoon. As evening meals can be quite late (around ten or eleven o'clock), guests will often arrive a couple of hours before the meal is served to sit, have a drink and snacks, and to talk. When the food does arrive, there is typically much more placed on the table than can possibly be consumed—an opportunity to "feast with the eyes." Guests are generously served food and are constantly urged to eat more.[120] In Moroccan Arabic, the common table expression is *kul ma kliti waylo* ("Eat! You haven't eaten anything!"). As visitors express their intention to depart, the host will protest that it is too early, and the actual leaving process may include another half hour of discussion as the host walks guests to the door.

In the Arab world, there are also occasions that require special and more labor-intensive hospitality. These include weddings, circumcisions, funerals, religious feasts, and the month of Ramadan.[121] While the home

---

116. See Matheny, *Reaching the Arabs*, 17; also Patai, *The Arab Mind*, 90–93.
117. See Patai, *The Arab Mind*, 90; also Nydell, *Understanding Arabs*, 56.
118. Cited in Nydell, *Understanding Arabs*, 57.
119. See Matheny, *Reaching the Arabs*, 18.
120. See Nydell, *Understanding Arabs*, 59–60.
121. See Patai, *The Arab Mind*, 91.

is the common place for offering hospitality, Arabs will also demonstrate this value in public places by paying for a guest at a café or restaurant.[122]

Brazilians and Hospitality

Brazilians are also quite known for their hospitality. In fact, Azevedo argues that Brazilian hospitality, with its implicit kindness and tolerance, is one of the strongest attributes of the culture as a whole.[123] In light of DaMatta's home and street paradigm, Brazilian hospitality is most immediately observed in gatherings of the extended family and friends in the home. The typical Brazilian extended family will gather at least once weekly—often on Sunday—for a traditional meal of *feijoada*.[124] If a family friend should stop by during mealtime, they are expected to stay unless they can offer a compelling reason for why they cannot. In some Brazilian homes, an unexpected visitor is told, "we will put more water in the beans," meaning that there is always plenty of food to go around. Outside of meals, Brazilians also show hospitality by offering coffee, juice, and cookies.[125] Also, outside of the home, Brazilians remain hospitable, as one friend will pay for his invited guest's coffee, drink, or meal.[126]

In terms of food, Brazilians typically eat a smaller breakfast consisting of bread, fruit, and a cup of coffee. Similar to the Arabs, Brazilians eat their biggest meal of the day at mid-day; thus many businesses close for two hours at lunchtime to accommodate this. Finally, Brazilians eat a lighter meal at night between seven and nine o'clock, though this may be even later in the summer. In light of the home being a place of protection and harmony, mealtime discussions are generally light in nature. More serious interactions about business or politics are saved for coffee.[127]

Brazilian hospitality is further observed as guests enter the home. Essentially asking permission to enter, they will say *da licença* ("with your permission"), to which the reply is *fique a vontade* ("be at ease").[128] As guests indicate a desire to depart, the host will also protest that it is too

---

122. Ibid., 93; also Nydell, *Understanding Arabs*, 55–56.
123. See Azevedo, *Brazilian Culture*, 121–23; also Tucker, *The Bible in Brazil*, 70.
124. See Vincent, *Culture and Customs of Brazil*, 83.
125. See Harrison, *Behaving Brazilian*, 87–88.
126. Ibid., 40.
127. Ibid., 84–85; also Vincent, *Culture and Customs of Brazil*, 84–85.
128. See Finley, "Contextualized Training for Missionaries," 120.

early and Brazilians may spend up to thirty minutes at the door saying goodbye.[129]

Though, as noted, Brazilian hospitality is most naturally offered to family and friends, Brazilians certainly have room for new friends—those who go from the street into the home and from being a *colega* to an *amigo/amiga*. Aware of this, a first time visitor to a home will bring a gift while someone invited to a party may send a bouquet of flowers ahead of his arrival.[130]

Brazilian Perspectives on Hospitality in the Arab World

From this brief survey, it seems evident that the cultural value of hospitality is quite similar between Arabs and Brazilians. In fact, this may be the area in which there is the highest degree of cultural proximity between the two affinity blocs. Of the Brazilian transcultural workers surveyed,[131] the vast majority (77.8 percent) felt that that Arab hospitality was very similar (31.1 percent) or similar to (46.7 percent) hospitality in the Brazilian context.

When asked what they liked most about Arab culture, many Brazilians workers indicated that it was the hospitality. One worker noted, "[I like that] they [Arabs] are laid back and it is easy to spend lots of time together. They are very hospitable," while another added, "I appreciate their hospitality. It is an honorable thing here." Another related, "[I like that Arab] families are very welcoming—especially the Bedouin peoples in the villages," while another affirmed, "[I like that] it [my Arab context] is a welcoming and hospitable culture—especially in the poor areas." Finally, another worker shared, "They [Arabs] are very happy to welcome visitors and offer them their best."

A number of Brazilian missionaries affirmed the similarities between Arab and Brazilian hospitality. One worker said, "[For Brazilians and Arabs] food is a reason to gather" and that "we [Brazilians and Arabs] both love to receive people." Another worker asserted, "In general we are similar [in showing hospitality], especially in the rural parts of Brazil/the Arab world."

Workers from the Northeast of Brazil noted a special connection between Arab hospitality and that of their region in Brazil. One worker

129. See Harrison, *Behaving Brazilian*, 88–89.
130. Ibid., 45.
131. All responses were gathered from surveys and interviews. See appendices.

related, "My parents are from Northeast Brazil and the culture is so similar to Arab culture. Sometimes I feel like I am back home. [I like that] they [Arabs] like to talk and eat a lot. They are hospitable. They are open to relationships." Another added, "Arabs in the countryside are like Brazilians in Northeast Brazil. We always have an open door for visitors. If you come to the door in Brazil, you just clap your hands to let someone know you are there. Also, there is a similarity because you do not have to go to the trouble of scheduling visits; you just stop in." Finally, one woman from the Northeast affirmed, "Personally, I grew up in a family where we always had people living with us; so I am used to opening my home."

While no Brazilian workers felt that Arabs were inhospitable, some felt that Brazilians were more adept in this area. One worker related, "Brazilians seem more open to inviting people to their home." Citing differences between the hospitality values in their home region in Brazil to a large Arab urban context, another worker shared, "In the Northeast of Brazil, we invite people a lot. More than in the big Arab city that we live in."

Other Brazilian missionaries felt that, while hospitable, Arabs were more open to welcoming Western visitors. One Brazilian shared, "It seems that Arabs are not as interested in 'Arab looking' foreigners," while another added, "Arabs receive us very well. But they receive white Westerners better."

Some Brazilians related that sociological reasons made hospitality different in the Arab world. Commenting on the different place of women in Brazilian and Arab society, one worker noted, "One difference is that when you go into the Arab home, the women disappear. In a Brazilian home, men and women sit together more freely." Another Brazilian missionary added, "Among Arabs though, if you are single or family without kids, you are limited [which is different from Brazil]." That is, from his point of view, Arabs prefer to extend and receive hospitality from the basis of a complete nuclear family unit (parents and kids) or from the extended family.

Finally, according to the Brazilian workers interviewed, the biggest perceived difference was that Arabs were generally more hospitable than Brazilians. "Both cultures [Brazilians and Arabs] are hospitable but Arabs are more hospitable," shared one Brazilian worker. Another worker added: "Hospitality here [in my Arab context] is extremely important. Here more is given, spent (financially and in terms of time), [and] there are a lot of expressions of one being nice to one another. In fact, many times people spend what they don't have. It is a social burden and the reason of much debt in the family." Finally, a Brazilian pastor ministering to Arabs in Southern Brazil added, "The Arabs are superior to the Brazilians in this area. If they like you, they'll give you anything. Sometimes, it breaks my heart to think that I was often visited more by Muslims than by Christians in the church that I pastored!"

Aside from the value of hospitality, many Brazilians shared that they liked Arab food. Certainly, the noted presence and influence of Arab food in Brazil has contributed to this. One worker shared, "I like the food [in my Arab context]" while another added, "They [Arabs] use lots of butter and oil but I do enjoy the food." Finally, another shared, "I am a Brazilian of Lebanese descent [so I like Arab food]."

Some Brazilian missionaries indicated that the general taste of Arab food was similar to that of Brazilian food. One worker shared, "[Arabs have] Similar foods to what I was used to back in Brazil (i.e., rice, meat)" and another affirmed, "They [Arab and Brazilian food] are similar in the senses that we both use a lot of natural ingredients [and we both] eat lots of grains and nuts, cheese, and olive oil." Similarly, others related, "We have the same basic food: lentils, vegetables, coffee. Also [we have] similar spices," and "Similar foods (rice, beans, meat, and chicken) are consumed by Brazilians and Arabs." Finally, one worker saw particular similarities between Northeastern Brazilian food and that of his Arab context: "North African food is quite similar to that of Bahia."

Other Brazilian workers found the food in their Arab contexts to be quite different. One worker related, "I am from Northeast Brazil. What I like to eat, I do not find here [in my Arab context]." Another shared, "In Brazilian culture, we are a mix of cultures (European, African, Indian). Here [in my Arab context] the food is more limited." Some Brazilian workers noted that Arab food used different spices. One worker shared, "We [Brazilians] use different spices [than Arabs]" and another added, "Some spices they [Arabs] use are different and also the quantity used differs." The fact that some Brazilians had different opinions on the taste and quality of Arab food is surely indicative of the diversity of foods within Brazil itself.

A final difference between Arab and Brazilian food is actually in the preparation process. A number of Brazilian women missionaries shared that personal hygiene and how it related to food preparation was a big difference. One woman shared, "The hardest thing for me [in my Arab context] is that food preparation is not very clean." Another shared, "We [Brazilians] are cleaner in our food preparation."

Brazilian Evangelical Missions in the Arab World

What are the missiological implications for Brazilians serving among Arabs regarding hospitality? Despite some noted areas in which Brazilians need to adapt to the Arab context—different tastes in food and differences in hygiene in food preparation—Brazilian missionaries seem to understand intimately the Arab values of hospitality. Thus, these workers seem naturally equipped to open their homes as well as to receive hospitality from Arabs—a basis for relationships in which authentic evangelism, discipleship, church planting, and Christian fellowship can be pursued. This incarnational value of a hospitality-based ministry was nicely illustrated by a Brazilian pastor ministering to Arabs in Brazil. Realizing that his Arab guests did not care for Brazilian food, he related simply, "Arabs prefer Arab food and we offered them Arab food when they came to our house."

Spiritual Worldview[132]

In this section, we will summarize the general religious worldviews observed among Arab-Muslims, particularly Folk Muslims, and Brazilians. Indeed, in both the Arab and Brazilian contexts, there is an official religion (Islam and Roman Catholicism) to which the majority of people show a nominal adherence. Like most Arab-Muslims, the majority of Brazilians also syncretize the official religion with animistic practices.[133] By surveying the relevant cultural and missiological literature, we will first describe how the official religion is regarded in both contexts, which will be followed by a discussion of the motivations for and practices of popular religion in Brazil and the Arab world. Building on this background, the missiological implications, incorporating the perspectives of Brazilian transcultural workers serving in Arab contexts, will be explored. My aim is to show that Brazilian missionaries in general have a spiritual worldview that allows for the supernatural and demonic; thus, they are not alarmed by the spiritual realities of Folk Islam. Indeed, some members of the Brazilian missionary force have a personal background in Brazilian Spiritism prior to coming to Christ, while the rest, including Pentecostals and non-Pentecostals alike, have grown up around and are quite accustomed to Brazilian popular religion.

132. A version of this section was published as Smither, "Bridging the 'Excluded Middle.'"

133. For a further discussion on syncretism, see Nida, *Customs and Cultures*, 240–41.

Arabs and Islam

Though birthed in a seventh-century Arabian tribal context, Islam spread rapidly and established itself quickly as the official religion of most Arabs. As the majority religion, Islam has also served as a defining and cohesive element for Arab society in general.

As an official religion, Barakat notes, Islam is characterized by "religious texts, the *sharia* (Islamic law), absolute monotheism, the literal interpretation of religious teachings, ritualism, the absence of intermediaries between believers and God, and the religious establishment's close connection with the ruling classes."[134] Based upon sacred books (the Qur'an and Hadith), the religion is characterized by recognized practices (prayer, fasting, almsgiving, pilgrimage), officially sanctioned sacred places (mosques, pilgrimage sites), and recognized religious leaders (imams, muftis). Islamic orthodoxy has been articulated through the centuries through a significant corpus of writings by Muslim theologians; and, as Islam has spread into the world, there have also been theological reform movements such as Wahhabism which have sought to preserve the religion's purity.[135]

Islam has, of course, shaped the spiritual worldview of Arabs. This is best observed in how the name of God is invoked in daily situations. In communicating "please," North Africans will say *b-rabbi* ("by God"), *yaishek* ("God extend your life), and *Allah hamda walidek* ("God bless your parents"). "Thank you" is conveyed with *baraka Allah fik* ("God bless you"), *Allah ybarak fik* ("God bless you"), and again *yaishek* ("God extend your life). "Goodbye" is communicated through *rabbi yawenek* ("God help you"), *Allah yawen* ("God help you"), and *rabbi mak* ("God be with you"). Arabs around the world remember God's provision and blessings throughout the day by uttering *hamdulillah* ("Praise God"). Finally, fatalism—a prominent aspect of the Muslim worldview—is affirmed daily through the oft-repeated phrase *inshallah* ("God willing").[136]

While Islam has served to define Arab society in general, it has also provided an identity for Arab individuals and families who cannot conceive of being anything but Muslim. Indeed, the religion—sustained by the family and community—does not allow for conversion to another

---

134. See Barakat, *The Arab World*, 118–19.
135. See Hourani, *A History of the Arab Peoples*, 348–49, 397–400.
136. See Nydell, *Understanding Arabs*, 28.

belief system. Hence, for the vast majority of Arabs, to be an Arab is to be a Muslim.[137]

Arabs and Folk Islam

Despite the significant work of Muslim theologians, the presence of world-renowned Islamic theological schools such as Al-Azhar (Cairo) and the *Jammat al-Zeitouna* (Tunis), and the efforts of Muslim reformers such as Abd-al Wahhab (1703–1792), most Arab-Muslims are not strict adherents to the official religion. Rather, they practice is what commonly called popular or Folk Islam—"A broad, catch-all phrase that describes the mixing of formal or orthodox Islamic practices with primitive animistic practices."[138] Animism is, of course, understood as "the belief that all of creation is pervaded or inhabited by spirits or souls, that all of creation is in some sense animate or alive."[139] Rick Love asserts that 75 percent of Muslims worldwide practice Folk Islam, and that number increases to 95 percent among women.[140] Though more prevalent in villages, Folk Islam is also commonly practiced in urban centers.[141] Contrasting Folk Islam to the official religion, Barakat writes: "Popular or folk religion . . . refers to a very different religious orientation. This pattern of religious life personifies sacred forces, emphasizes existential and spiritual inner experiences, seeks intermediaries between believers and God, and interprets texts symbolically."[142] Musk adds that while the official religion emphasizes morals, ethics, institutions, and hierarchy, Folk Islam is less institutional and more pragmatic.[143] Indeed, official Islam seeks to answer the religious question "what is true?" while Folk Islam is more concerned with getting at "what works?" Swartley describes official Islam as a "shopping mall" with "neatly organized shops," while folk Islam is "an open market or bazaar, a fluid, free-flowing maze that sprang up without careful pre-planning."[144]

---

137. See Barakat, *The Arab World*, 120; also Patai, *The Arab Mind*, 9–11; and Hiebert, *Cultural Anthropology*, 375–76.
138. See Swartley, *Encountering the World of Islam*, 196.
139. Ibid.
140. See Rick Love, "Power Encounter," 209; also Love, *Muslims, Magic*, 23.
141. See Love, *Muslims, Magic*, 4; also Barakat, *The Arab World*, 118.
142. See Barakat, *The Arab World*, 118.
143. See Musk, *The Unseen Face of Islam*, 180–84.
144. See Swartley, *Encountering the World of Islam*, 196; also Love, *Muslims, Magic*, 21; and Hiebert, "Power Encounter in Folk Islam," 45–46.

Having established that most Arab-Muslims are syncretistic in mixing official Islam with animistic practices, let us now explore the motivations behind such actions. The first motivation seems to be a yearning to connect with the divine. Swartley helpfully writes: "Overall, Muslims are seeking a connection with the spiritual world and with God. In Islamic theology, God is primarily transcendent: He is distant and uninvolved in human affairs . . . This heartfelt need for connection with God (immanence) is a driving force in popular Islam."[145] Barakat affirms, "The role of shrines and saints is to provide mediation between ordinary believers and God, whom official religion has rendered too remote and abstract." Thus, such practices are a "highly personalized and concrete alternative for common people."[146]

Second, Muslims seem driven to animistic practices out of fear. Hiebert asserts that a primary motivation for any religion is the desire for security and comfort, especially during a crisis.[147] Swartley adds: "Many Muslims are fearful of the pressures affecting their daily lives: sickness, death, jealousy, infidelity, and privation, to name a few. They have mounted an unrelenting search for supernatural forces to counteract these forces."[148] Arab-Muslims are particularly afraid of *jinn* (evil spirits or demons), which are generally blamed for many of these difficulties.[149]

Third, in the absence of an immanent deity and with the presence of *jinn*, Folk Muslims are concerned with finding solutions to daily problems. A farmer hopes for rain and an eventual good harvest. Young women long to conceive and give birth to healthy children. A university student hopes to pass his exams and then find a job. A young wife needs assurance that her husband is being faithful and that her jealous neighbor will not put curses on her. Hence, Folk Muslims are concerned with dealing with these heart-felt issues rather than speculating over philosophical or eternal questions.[150] Again, their religion is more motivated by answering "what works?" instead of "what is true?"

---

145. See Swartley, *Encountering the World of Islam*, 194.
146. See Barakat, *The Arab World*, 119.
147. See Hiebert, *Cultural Anthropology*, 375–76.
148. See Swartley, *Encountering the World of Islam*, 194.
149. *Jinn* are mentioned in the Qur'an in Sura 18:50 and 55:14–15. See also Musk, *The Unseen Face of Islam*, 94–96, 174; and Patai, *The Arab Mind*, 154.
150. See Swartley, *Encountering the World of Islam*, 197; also Musk, *The Unseen Face of Islam*, 71, 122; Barakat, *The Arab World*, 59, 119; Love, *Muslims, Magic*, 22; and Hiebert, "Power Encounter in Folk Islam," 47–49.

Fourth, in light of the absence of an immanent deity as well as the fact that Islam is strongly fatalistic, Folk Muslims desire to have some power and control over their lives.[151] In fact, Woodberry argues that "The felt need for power is so great among folk Muslims that their entire worldview is seen through the spectacles of power."[152] In an extended discussion on power, Love asserts that Muslims perceive spiritual power on a number of levels. First, there are powerful spiritual beings—angels and demons—that Muslims desire to appease and manipulate.[153] Second, there are powerful people whose services can be retained in times of need. While they may consult an imam, Folk Muslims are more likely to call upon a shaman (a practitioner of magic).[154] Musk adds that women also figure among the powerful people in Folk Islam, and they include—midwives (*qabila*), who are not only skilled in delivering babies, but also capable of using herbal potions and working magic; sorceresses (*sahhara*) whose powers are believed to diminish or heighten sexual desire; and matchmakers (*shawwafa*) who are helpful in arranging marriages.[155] Love further asserts that Muslims are interested in objects of power (charms, amulets), places of power (saints' tombs, Mecca), times of power (Muhammad's birthday, the period of the hajj), and power rituals (Quranic prayers).[156]

With these motivations in mind, let us now explore further some specific Folk Muslim practices. Love helpfully places such practices into four categories of magic: productive magic, protective magic, destructive magic, and divination. Productive magic is observed, for instance, when a university student consults a shaman for blessing (*baraka*) in order to pass his exams. It is further observed as Muslims—the sick, infertile, and unemployed—visit the tombs of Muslim saints (*marabout*).[157] Commenting on this regard for Muslim saints, Musk writes, "Alive or dead, saints are believed to possess great power. The kind of miracles (*karama*) attributed to them include raising the dead, walking on water, covering great distances in very short times, healing, having knowledge of the future,

---

151. See Nydell, *Understanding Arabs*, 29; also Matheny, *Reaching the Arabs*, 25.
152. Cited in Love, *Muslims, Magic*, 1.
153. See Love, *Muslims, Magic*, 24.
154. See Love, *Muslims, Magic*, 29–30.
155. See Musk, *The Unseen Face of Islam*, 106–111.
156. See Love, *Muslims, Magic*, 30–35.
157. On a hike through the mountains of North Africa, I observed a pregnant woman travel for hours by donkey on a rocky path in order to seek blessing from a famous Muslim saint.

guarding people or tribes, and being in two places at one time."[158] During the shrine visit, Muslims honor the saints and make their petitions known through lighting a candle, making a sacrifice, offering a meal, or leaving a piece of a sick person's clothing at the tomb.[159] In Southern Tunisia, where a significant number of shrines are located, some 20,000 Muslims attend an annual festival in which participants make sacrifices, dance, and even fall into trances as they seek *baraka* from the saints.[160]

Protective magic can be observed when Muslims visit a shaman for *baraka* to ward off a curse.[161] It is also evident when pregnant women visit shrines in hopes that their unborn children will come to full term and will be born healthy. This type of magic is also practiced through the use of certain potions. For instance, in Morocco, a woman will place a drop of her urine in her husband's tea to insure his faithfulness to her. It is said that every man in Morocco, from the king to the poorest peasant, has at some point consumed his wife's urine.[162]

Protective magic is also evident when Muslims attempt to protect themselves from the evil eye—a look of envy that is believed to cause harm.[163] Musk writes, "the fundamental concept of the evil eye is that precious persons or things are constantly vulnerable to hurt or destruction caused by other people's envy."[164] While those most often accused of giving the evil eye are poorer and less fortunate women, those regarded as victims of it include barren women, unmarried women of a higher social standing, the sick, and animals. The latter are cursed because they are the source of a family's livelihood.[165]

To protect themselves against the evil eye, Muslims will hold out their hand (making a "stop" gesture) in the direction of the one suspected of giving the evil eye. Because such a gesture is quite offensive under ordinary circumstances, many Muslims choose to wipe their forehead with the back of their hand in a subtle manner, which gives them protection from the evil eye but also saves them any potential embarrassment if they are mistaken. A second mode of protection against the evil eye is simply

---

158. See Musk, *The Unseen Face of Islam*, 47.
159. Ibid., 47–50.
160. See Love, *Muslims, Magic*, 20.
161. Ibid., 1; also Musk, *The Unseen Face of Islam*, 23.
162. See Love, "Power Encounter," 209–210.
163. See Sura 113:5 of the Qur'an.
164. See Musk, *The Unseen Face of Islam*, 23.
165. Ibid., 18, 94.

repeating the phrase *mashallah* ("God willing"). Finally, Muslims find protection by using amulets—an object worn on the body. Often infused with power by a shaman, amulets include the hand of Fatima, the *nazar* (a replica of the evil eye), a pouch with Quranic verses, a miniature Qur'an, and certain types of jewelry. Also, it is common for families to place an amulet in the home—typically a wall hanging—in order to protect the entire family.[166]

While many Folk Muslims focus on protecting themselves from *jinn* and human enemies, others engage in destructive magic in order to harm others. Such strategies include giving the evil eye and placing curses on others.[167] Love notes that in Yemen, curses are placed on others by stealing some of their hair, while in Tunisia, it happens through taking an enemy's finger nail clippings.[168]

Divination is the final common form of magic practiced by Folk Muslims. Motivated by a desire to know the sex of an unborn child, to have wisdom for important decisions like marriage, and even to know the cause of a certain sickness, Muslims commonly visit fortunetellers in search of answers about the future. While some fortunetellers use tarot cards, others perform a ritual by letting the Qur'an fall open to a random page and then offer an interpretation of that verse.[169]

While Arab-Muslims certainly ascribe to the official expression of Islam with its sacred texts, meeting places, and its recognized leaders, the vast majority still resort to animistic practices for their daily survival. Though it seems apparent that the official religion proves inadequate for daily practice, Patai correctly notes that "the believers are unaware of any incompatibility between their belief in Allah the only God, and these numerous super humans who people their world of the unseen."[170]

Brazilians and Roman Catholicism

Despite significant evangelical growth in the nineteenth and twentieth centuries, Brazil remains one of the largest Roman Catholic countries in the world. Adherence to the church in Brazil has, of course, been weakened by the influence of liberal-minded leaders such as Pedro II, which

---

166. See Love, *Muslims, Magic*, 30–33.
167. See Musk, *The Unseen Face of Islam*, 23.
168. See Love, "Power Encounter," 209.
169. See Musk, *The Unseen Face of Islam*, 61–64.
170. See Patai, *The Arab Mind*, 154; also Musk, *The Unseen Face of Islam*, 202–203.

has encouraged a general free spirit toward religion in Brazilian society.[171] In addition, the shortage of priests—half of whom are foreign born—and the lack of Roman Catholic teaching have resulted in Brazilian Catholicism being largely nominal.[172] Observing Catholic devotion in Recife, one writer commented that "Sunday mass is not an institution, and many regard an annual confession as sufficient."[173] This nominalism is also apparent through the Brazilian expression that a man needs to go to church just three times in his life—to get baptized, to get married, and to die.[174]

Despite the overall lack of devotion to Roman Catholicism, the Catholic Church remains "the institution that defines public religion in Brazil."[175] Hess argues: "Although lay support is soft . . . the Catholic Church is still the hegemonic religion in Brazilian society. Catholicism was the official religion until the end of the nineteenth century, and its hegemony in the religious arena has continued into this century."[176] Ribeiro adds that "it is so difficult, in truth, to separate the Brazilian from the Catholic: Catholicism was the cement of our unity."[177] Indeed, Catholic influence on the Brazilian spiritual worldview can be observed in how God's name is used in daily expressions. When saying goodbye to a friend, Brazilians commonly say, *Deus o acompanhe* ("God be with you") or *fique com Deus* ("stay with God"). In response to a favor or an act of kindness, Brazilians say *Deus te pague* ("God will repay you"). *Graças a Deus* ("thank you God") is used to express gratitude or contentment, while *meu Deus* ("my God") communicates surprise, shock, or disbelief. Finally, Brazilians also reveal a fatalistic worldview when adding the qualification *se Deus quiser* ("God willing"). While Arab-Muslims and Brazilians share a similar practice of using the name of God in daily expressions, some of these expressions actually have similar meanings—especially the example of *inshallah* and *se Deus quiser*.

Another similarity between Islam and Brazilian Catholicism is that, historically, it was unthinkable that a Brazilian would convert to another

---

171. See Vincent, *Culture and Customs of Brazil*, 71–72; also Page, *The Brazilians*, 91; and Finley, "Contextualized Training for Missionaries," 104.

172. See Vincent, *Culture and Customs of Brazil*, 72; also Wiebe, "Persistence of Spiritism in Brazil," 96.

173. See Levine and Crocitti, *The Brazil Reader*, 340.

174. See Vincent, *Culture and Customs of Brazil*, 73.

175. See Finley, "Contextualized Training for Missionaries," 95.

176. See Hess, "Hierarchy, Heterodoxy," 200.

177. See Ribeiro, *The Brazilian People*, 102–103; also Finley, "Contextualized Training for Missionaries," 82.

faith. Writing in the earlier part of the twentieth century, Tucker asserted that "for a native Brazilian, who was brought up a Roman Catholic to apostatize and become a Protestant is intolerable."[178] Though evangelicalism has exploded in Brazil and Latin America, this has not been without resistance from the Catholic Church.

Brazilians and Spiritism

Though Roman Catholicism is Brazil's dominant religion and leaving it is not encouraged, Brazilians certainly mix the official religion with Spiritism.[179] In fact, Neuza Itiokia argues that the Roman Catholicism that came to Brazil in the sixteenth century was already quite syncretistic and included the worship of saints and even witchcraft.[180] This tendency was furthered by the Portuguese authorities who, in an effort to control the African slaves in the colony, encouraged the practice of African religions alongside Roman Catholicism.[181] Finally, Jesuit missionaries, aiming to contextualize the gospel, also accommodated the animistic practices of their target peoples and, as a result, encouraged syncretism.[182] This history has contributed to a prevailing tolerance toward religious syncretism. Illustrating this attitude in reference to the peoples of Bahia, Silverstein writes: "A popular saying describes Bahians as a practical people who go to church in the morning, a Spiritism session in the afternoon . . . and a Candomblé ritual in the evening."[183]

Given the syncretistic nature of Brazilians, let us now define Spiritism, explore the underlying motivations for it, and then describe the various strains of Spiritism in the Brazilian landscape, including their prominent practices. Kloppenburg helpfully describes Spiritism as: "A pretentiously evoked, perceptive communication with spirits from the beyond, whether to receive news from them, to consult them (necromancy), or to place them at the service of men (magic); whether to do good (white magic) or

---

178. Cited in Willems, *Followers of the New Faith*, 60.

179. See Prado, "The Brazil Model."

180. See Itiokia, "O Desafio Da Umbanda," 438–40; also Finley, "Contextualized Training for Missionaries," 79–80.

181. See Silverstein, "The Celebration of Our Lord," 137; also Vincent, *Culture and Customs of Brazil*, 74; and Wiebe, "Persistence of Spiritism in Brazil," 81.

182. See Wiebe, "Persistence of Spiritism in Brazil," 100–103; also Itiokia, "O Desafio Da Umbanda," 443.

183. See Silverstein, "The Celebration of Our Lord," 137.

to perform some evil (black magic). To be Spiritist, therefore, it suffices to accept this minimum doctrine: that spirits exist; that these spirits are ardently interested in communicating with us in order to instruct us or help us; that we can evoke perceptible communication with these spirits."[184] Highlighting its animistic foundations, Park points out that Spiritism involves "the belief [in] innumerable spiritual beings concerned with human affairs and capable of helping or harming men's interests."[185] While Finley asserts that 30 percent of Brazilians are involved in some form of Spiritism, Itiokia argues that this number is as high as 70 percent.[186] Even the more conservative estimates indicate that millions of Brazilians are active participants in Spiritism.

Brazilians seem motivated to practice Spiritism for at least three reasons. First, not unlike the Muslim worldview, the Brazilian Catholic conception of God is distant and uninvolved in daily life. Vincent helpfully writes, "Brazilians are drawn to such religions at least in part because traditional Catholicism seems to offer unsatisfactory answers in a society in flux. With its emphasis on the eternal, on life *after* death, and with a doctrine being advocated by a largely foreign priesthood, Catholicism seems to many Brazilians to offer few answers to more immediate concerns... The perceived failure of Catholicism to respond to such mundane problems is also one of the reasons Brazilians are attracted in ever larger numbers to other religious doctrines."[187]

Second, also like Folk Islam, Spiritism, is "primarily concerned with day-to-day matters, not with metaphysical or other worldly concerns."[188] Itiokia adds that Umbanda adherents are look for something "more tangible."[189] Describing the work of one practitioner, Hess notes that his specialty was dealing with "lover's quarrels, impotent husbands, long strings of financial setbacks, and disease—in short, bad luck."[190] Because problems beset the rich and poor alike, devotion to Spiritism can be observed in every social class. Page asserts: "People from all social classes

184. Cited in Wiebe, "Persistence of Spiritism in Brazil," 13; see also Finley, "Contextualized Training for Missionaries," 84.

185. Cited in Wiebe, "Persistence of Spiritism in Brazil," 14.

186. See Finley, "Contextualized Training for Missionaries," 86; and Itiokia, "O Desafio Da Umbanda," 432; also Anderson, *An Introduction to Pentecostalism*, 70.

187. See Vincent, *Culture and Customs of Brazil*, 77.

188. See Wiebe, "Persistence of Spiritism in Brazil," 15.

189. See Itiokia, "O Desafio Da Umbanda," 478–79.

190. See Hess, "Hierarchy, Heterodoxy," 197; also Wiebe, "Persistence of Spiritism in Brazil," 56, 108–122, 137–42.

belong to Afro-Brazilian cults. Businessmen follow cult rituals before making important deals. The poor find comfort and hope in places of cult worship."[191]

Finally, because Brazilians are open to creative solutions (*jeito*) to such daily problems, they are willing to consider all of the spiritual possibilities available within Brazil's diverse cultural landscape.[192] Commenting further on the appeal of Spiritism, Vincent adds, "It is natural to wonder why such an eclectic religion would enjoy such popularity, but Brazilian society is a fluid and eclectic one, and on reflection it may seem a perfectly logical manifestation of the kind of free-wheeling spirit of the culture."[193] Describing the animistic spiritual worldview of Bahians, Silverstein shows that their involvement in Spiritism is driven by a "who knows what will work?" mentality. He continues, "In a constantly changing and insecure world—a world in which adroit manipulation of one's available social network could mean the difference between having and not having a job, food, or medicine for one's suffering children—all doors must remain open."[194]

Given these motivations, let us now describe the major expressions of Brazilian Spiritism. The first is called Candomblé, though it is also known as Macumba in Rio de Janeiro, Xangô in Pernambuco, and Batuque in Pará.[195] The cult originates from the Bantu and Yoruba peoples of Southern and Western Africa who came to Brazil as slaves.[196] Despite these origins, many white Brazilians have also embraced Candomblé through the influence of African servants and mistresses.

Within Candomblé, there is a belief in ancestral spirits called *orixás*, which are associated with the sea, water, thunder, and ancient kings and queens. Though the Yoruba honored a supreme god named Olorum, the *orixás* developed because Olorum was perceived as being too distant.[197] Candomblé rituals take place at a small shrine within a courtyard *(terreiro)*—a plot of land often donated by a wealthy benefactor. Accompanied by singing in the Yoruba or Bantu languages, animal sacrifices are

191. See Page, *The Brazilians*, 353.

192. See Finley, "Contextualized Training for Missionaries," 79.

193. See Vincent, *Culture and Customs of Brazil*, 77.

194. See Silverstein, "The Celebration of Our Lord," 138; also Finley, "Contextualized Training for Missionaries," 107.

195. See Finley, "Contextualized Training for Missionaries," 86–87; also Vincent, *Culture and Customs of Brazil*, 75–76.

196. See Silverstein, "The Celebration of Our Lord," 135.

197. See Itiokia, "O Desafio Da Umbanda," 445.

offered by a *mãe de santo* ("saint's mother") or by a *pai de santo* ("male priest").[198] Through this, the *exú* (demons) are appeased and leave the shrine and the *orixás* come and take possession of adherents—"sons" and "daughters" of the spirits who attain this status after some months of instruction and practice.[199] Page adds that, once possessed, adherents will go into a trance and "will shake convulsively, scream, gyrate wildly about the room, and flop to the floor like a rag doll."[200]

In general, the rituals are complex and follow a set calendar, surely a practice borrowed from the Catholic Church. Also, many of the *orixás* are named after some of the famous Catholic saints. In addition to these syncretistic practices, Candomblé adherents are encouraged by their leaders to remain in the Catholic Church and deliberately benefit from both spiritual contexts.

A second form of Brazilian Spiritism is called Kardecismo. Developed in the late nineteenth century by a Frenchman named Allen Kardec (1804–1869), Kardecismo is a combination of philosophy, science, Hinduism, and Catholicism.[201] Appealing to educated Brazilians already influenced by French philosophy and culture, Kardec emphasized "rationality without dismissing Catholicism."[202]

Affirming a Deistic doctrine of God in which the creator is no longer involved in the affairs of the world, Kardec emphasized the importance of communicating with spirits in outer space and also with the dead. The latter practice was developed to meet the felt needs of those who had lost loved ones. Communication with spirits and the dead was facilitated through séances performed in the home of a trained Kardecist.[203]

Kardecismo has also been characterized by a strong commitment to morality and charity, which over time has eclipsed communication with the dead in importance. Because of its popularity among the middle class, the educated, and intellectuals—a predominantly white population— the

---

198. Ibid., 451–52.

199. See Wiebe, "Persistence of Spiritism in Brazil," 24; also Page, *The Brazilians*, 362–63; Itiokia, "O Desafio Da Umbanda," 451–52; and Silverstein, "The Celebration of Our Lord," 136.

200. See Page, *The Brazilians*, 362.

201. Kardec was born Denizard Hyppolyte Leon Rivail. See Itiokia, "O Desafio Da Umbanda," 456.

202. See Itiokia, "O Desafio Da Umbanda," 455–56; also Finley, "Contextualized Training for Missionaries," 85; and Hess, "Hierarchy, Heterodoxy," 187–88.

203. See Wiebe, "Persistence of Spiritism in Brazil," 26–27; also Itiokia, "O Desafio Da Umbanda," 457–60.

group has encountered less opposition from the Brazilian Catholic Church.[204]

The final prominent form of Brazilian Spiritism is Umbanda. Having developed in São Paulo and Rio de Janeiro in the mid-twentieth century, it is still regarded as an Afro-Brazilian religion.[205] "The ultimate evolution of Brazilian Spiritism," according to Itiokia, Umbanda is the most definitive expression of Brazilian syncretism as it mixes Roman Catholicism with Candomblé, Kardecismo, and Indian Spiritism.[206] While Umbanda has managed to "whiten" Candomblé and bring it more into the mainstream of Brazilian religious practice, the movement still regards itself as Roman Catholic. Through the influence of Kardecismo's rationality, animal sacrifices and trances have been eliminated in Umbanda. Though Umbanda retains the Candomblé rituals of *orixá* possession, the rituals have come to resemble the Roman Catholic sacraments. Indeed, the *orixás* have been venerated as Catholic saints, while Jesus is depicted as the great *orixá* and the *exu* is reinterpreted as the devil. In addition to these rituals, sorcery is prominently practiced in Umbanda, especially as adherents seek to defend themselves against curses and destructive magic.

While highly syncretistic, Umbanda, which literally means "all of us"[207] or "the limit of limitlessness,"[208] also prides itself on being extremely tolerant. Umbanda leader Jota Alves de Oliveira asserts that "Umbanda does not support any racial prejudice and intends to unite all races and all different social strata and cultures in Brazilian soil."[209] Indeed, Umbanda does appeal to the diversity and creative spirit within the cultures of Brazil. Though Umbanda practitioners must always be mindful of the potential of government repression, the 40,000 Umbanda centers in Rio de Janeiro alone are evidence of its widespread popularity.[210]

---

204. See Itiokia, "O Desafio Da Umbanda," 456–60; also Hess, "Hierarchy, Heterodoxy," 201.

205. See Vincent, *Culture and Customs of Brazil*, 76-77; also Hess, "Hierarchy, Heterodoxy," 195; and Itiokia, "O Desafio Da Umbanda," 462.

206. See Itiokia, "O Desafio Da Umbanda," 464.

207. See Hess, "Hierarchy, Heterodoxy," 198.

208. See Itiokia, "O Desafio Da Umbanda," 462.

209. Ibid., 438.

210. See Hess, "Hierarchy, Heterodoxy," 198; also Finley, "Contextualized Training for Missionaries," 88.

Brazilian Perspectives on Spiritual Worldview in the Arab World

Though the practices of Folk Islam and Brazilian Spiritism differ significantly, some general continuity in the spiritual worldview and motivation for such practices can be observed. First, between their official religions and accompanying popular practices, both Arabs and Brazilians demonstrate a strongly spiritual worldview. Speaking of Brazilians, DaMatta remarks that "we are a people that believes profoundly in another world."[211] One Brazilian transcultural worker, observing this similarity between his home culture and his Arab ministry context, wrote: "Brazilian culture is 'theologically' oriented [and] Brazilians (Christians and non-Christians) refer to God daily in their speech. The use of expressions such as 'God willing,' 'God bless you,' 'God be with you' are very common. Arabs speak much in the same manner."[212] Within this general spiritual worldview, Arabs and Brazilians are both strongly fatalistic—a value expressed in the daily expressions *inshallah* and *se Deus quiser* ("God willing"). Page argues that due to their presence in Portugal until the thirteenth century, the Arabs influenced Portuguese Catholics toward being more fatalistic—a worldview that came to characterize Brazilian Catholicism.[213]

In light of these similar aspects religious worldview, Arabs and Brazilians also share some similar motivations for practicing Folk Islam and Spiritism. First, in Islam and Brazilian Catholicism, God is perceived as distant and uninvolved in the affairs of the world and thus unavailable to help with daily problems. Second and related to the first, adherents to popular practices in both contexts are concerned with felt needs and daily problems rather than eternal, philosophical, or cosmological questions. Finally, though more apparent in the Folk Muslim context, both Arabs and Brazilians engage in animistic practices in order to have some power or control over their lives.[214]

In light of these observed similarities in the spiritual worldview of Folk Muslims and Brazilian Spiritists, what are the implications for Brazilian evangelical missionaries serving among Arab-Muslims? Having been raised in a context of Catholicism syncretized with Spiritism, Brazilian transcultural workers generally possess more of a pre-modern worldview in which they are aware of the supernatural and demonic

---

211. Cited in Finley, "Contextualized Training for Missionaries," 77.
212. See L.C., "Mais Missionários Brasileiros," 470.
213. See Page, *The Brazilians*, 235.
214. See Wiebe, "Persistence of Spiritism in Brazil," 58.

world. Consequently, they are more sensitive to ministering to the needs of Muslims plagued by the spiritual conflicts brought on by Folk Muslim practices.

Before elaborating further, it should be noted that a key shortcoming of Western missions in the Muslim world has been failing to relate to the spiritual world of Folk Muslims.[215] Essentially describing Hiebert's "excluded middle" paradigm in the worldview and ministry of Western missionaries, Love helpfully writes, "Since most Western missionaries come from a materialistic-oriented culture which relegates the supernatural to other-worldly concerns, when faced with the realities of the spirit realm, they often either ignore the issues or offer naturalistic solutions to what are perceived by Folk Muslims as supernaturally-caused problems—so opportunities for ministry are lost."[216] Nevertheless, Hiebert urges that all missionaries serving among Muslims be equipped to minister to the spiritual needs of those practicing Folk Islam— affirming God's presence and care for their daily needs, sharing the availability of God's power for their lives, and encouraging them to call upon the Lord for physical healing and deliverance from evil spirits.[217]

While North American and European workers among Muslims have heeded Hiebert's call and are learning to approach Muslims with a more integrated worldview, it seems that they have much to learn from Christian workers from the Global South in this area. This influence is apparent in the following excerpt from the 1978 Willowbank Consultation:

> A number of us, especially those from Asia, Africa, and Latin America, have spoken both of the reality of evil powers and of the necessity to demonstrate the supremacy of Jesus over them. For conversion involves a power encounter. People give their allegiance to Christ when they see that his power is superior to magic and voodoo, the curses and blessings of witch doctors, and the malevolence of evil spirits, and that his salvation is a real liberation from the power of evil and death. Of course, some are questioning today whether a belief in spirits is compatible with our modern scientific understanding of the universe. We wish to affirm, therefore, against the mechanistic myth on which the typical Western worldview rests, the reality of demonic

---

215. See Hiebert, "Power Encounter and Folk Islam," 45.

216. See Love, *Muslims, Magic*, 6. Itiokia (see "O Desafio Da Umbanda," 482–84) adds that historic Protestant North American missionaries to Brazil in the nineteenth and twentieth centuries also failed to address the spiritual world of Brazilian Spiritists.

217. See Hiebert, "Power Encounter and Folk Islam," 54–60.

intelligences which are concerned by all means, overt and covert, to discredit Jesus Christ and keep people from coming to him. We think it vital in evangelism in all cultures to teach the reality and hostility of demonic powers, and to proclaim that God has exalted Christ as Lord of all and that Christ, who really does possess all power, however we may fail to acknowledge this, can (as we proclaim him) break through any worldview in any mind to make his lordship known and bring about a radical change of heart and outlook.[218]

Brazilian evangelical missionaries certainly number among these Global South peoples and again, their worldview and experiences growing up in a syncretistic Brazilian religious milieu seems to have prepared them to minister in spiritual contexts such of the Folk Muslim world. In his study on pre-field training for Brazilian transcultural workers, Finley offers support by observing that "Brazilians take seriously the subject of spiritual conflict, following the Brazilian tendency to acknowledge the existence of middle-level spiritual beings, but going against the culture in viewing these beings as demonic rather than deities."[219] Commenting further on their preparedness to minister in contexts of spiritual battle, Finley writes, "In terms of worldview, these first- and second-generation Christians usually have little hesitancy in continuing to affirm the reality of spiritual beings beyond the physical senses of the world. This would tend to make them somewhat more prepared for some of the spiritual realities that can be anticipated on pioneer fields, where entrenched non-Christian religious systems sometimes exacerbate the potential for spiritual conflict."[220]

Silas Tostes, present director of Missão Antioquia, affirmed that growing up in an environment of Spiritism has prepared Brazilians for the Folk Muslim context, especially those who had engaged in Spiritist practices themselves prior to professing faith in Christ and pursuing the missionary call. Tostes illustrated this by referring to one such Brazilian church planter serving in a Folk Muslim context in West Africa. While preparing to baptize two believers, he noticed that the men were beginning to vomit and show signs of spiritual conflict. He rather routinely

---

218. See "The Willowbank Report," section 7D; also Jenkins, *The Next Christendom*, 125, 145–47, 257; Noll, *The New Shape of World Christianity*, 34; and Livingstone, "Laborers from the Global South," 54.

219. See Finley, "Contextualized Training for Missionaries," 170.

220. See Finley, "Contextualized Training for Missionaries," 206; see also Kraft, *Anthropology for Christian Witness*, 53–54, 351.

stopped the baptism and began to pray for the men and take authority over the oppressing evil spirits. After the issue was resolved, the Brazilian missionary went ahead with the baptism.[221]

It also seems that Brazilian workers from Pentecostal backgrounds have a particular sensitivity to the spiritual world of Folk Muslims due to their theology and worldview. While observing some similar sociological patterns in Pentecostalism and Spiritism, Freston concludes that, "Pentecostalism is . . . tuned in to an inspirited world."[222] Commenting further on the Pentecostal worldview and how they have engaged Spiritism in Brazil, Itiokia adds, "It was this group [Pentecostals] which acknowledged the supernatural view of reality including the interaction of angels and demons in the everyday lives of people. With [their] emphasis on the Holy Spirit, Pentecostals involved themselves in "power encounters," calling Satan by name and expelling demons . . . Their evangelistic approach toward Spiritism was never polemic."[223]

Though Pentecostals represent less than one-third of the Brazilian evangelical mission force in the Arab world, those that have gone have nevertheless applied a Pentecostal worldview to ministry in Folk Muslim contexts. One worker in the Middle East, who was personally converted in Brazil after his mother was healed from cancer, described his Arab ministry context as spiritually oppressive. He attributed things like his son's constant illnesses and an automobile accident to the spiritual battle around them. Acknowledging that spiritual conflicts are prevalent in both Brazil and the Arab world, he commented that in Brazil the spiritual evils are more outwardly observed while in the Arab context, they go on more in people's hearts. In terms of his ministry strategy, this worker reported that throughout his ministry, he has seen people physically healed after praying for them. While cautioning against sensationalizing these outcomes, he simply emphasized that he has learned to pray with faith and expectation.[224]

A similar worldview and subsequent willingness to engage in spiritual warfare is apparent in the following account from a female Pentecostal missionary in the Arab world. She shared: "Once I was praying for a

221. Tostes related this in personal conversation with me, July 23, 2009.

222. See Freston, "Contours of Latin American Pentecostalism," 255–56; also Finley, "Contextualized Training for Missionaries," 93; Escobar, *The New Global Mission*, 115; and Anderson, *An Introduction to Pentecostalism*, 70.

223. See Itiokia, "O Desafio Da Umbanda," 485; also Anderson, *An Introduction to Pentecostalism*, 201.

224. This was related in personal conversation with me, January 6, 2010.

family. In the family was a boy who was spiritually oppressed. I told my mom in Brazil about this and she had a vision about the family. She prayed and I prayed for the family and the boy's problems were resolved." Finally, another Brazilian Pentecostal worker related that Muslim background believers still experience many spiritual conflicts and it was important that missionaries be prepared to minister to them.[225]

Though it seems logical that Brazilian Pentecostals would be eager to engage in spiritual warfare in the Arab-Muslim world, Brazilian pastors and missionaries from the historic churches and denominations have also demonstrated similar spiritual sensitivities.[226] In 1992, Kraft and Kraft conducted interviews with twelve Brazilian pastors (nearly all were from historic churches) from eight different states around the country. All agreed that spiritual warfare was an important part of church ministry and each pastor reported being personally involved in some form of deliverance ministry. Though none had formulated a specific spiritual warfare strategy, these pastors addressed spiritual conflicts somewhat intuitively and on a case-by-case basis. In short, while certainly sensitive to spiritual warfare, they did not give undue attention to this part of their ministries.[227]

Other Brazilian workers from the historic churches serving in the Arab-Muslim world have affirmed similar values. One woman from a Presbyterian background offered some helpful insights as she correlated her experiences with spiritual warfare in Brazil to her current ministry in the Arab world. She related: "There are lots of evil influences in Spiritism rituals in Brazil. Also, my own brother who was not a believer was possessed. I have had some real experiences praying for him and others and seeing them delivered and this has helped to prepare me for spiritual warfare here [in my Arab context]." Also, a Baptist pastor serving among Arabs in Southern Brazil shared the following moving account of spiritual warfare in a Muslim context: "After eight years, I became deathly ill and felt the spirit of death. I was losing weight everyday and the doctors did not know what to do for me. A group of Christians came and prayed for me. They discerned that a curse had been placed on me by Muslims. They could not stop the work of our church and ministry so they wanted to stop me. The group prayed for me and I was healed and was able to return to ministry." Hence, from these accounts, it seems that Brazilian workers from Pentecostal churches and the historic churches share a similar

---

225. Ibid.
226. See Livingstone, "Laborers from the Global South," 54.
227. See Kraft and Kraft, "Spiritual Warfare in Brazil," 56–61.

perspective on spiritual warfare in the Arab-Muslim context. Indeed, this regard for the spiritual world by non-Pentecostal Brazilians workers affirms a general observation made by Mark Noll about majority world Christianity. He writes: "Westerners who minister in Latin America, China, the Philippines, Africa, or the South Seas consistently report that most Christian experience reflects a much stronger supernatural awareness than is characteristic of even charismatic and Pentecostal circles in the West."[228]

Additional insights were gained after surveying Brazilian missionaries—from both Pentecostal and historic church backgrounds—regarding their views on spiritual warfare in the Arab context. Of those surveyed, about one-third reported that prayer and spiritual warfare ministry were regular aspects of their ministry. Interestingly, not a single respondent indicated that dealing with spiritual conflicts was a difficult or impossible ministry. Also, none reported a lack of spiritual warfare training in their pre-field preparation. This is significant because Western missionaries often feel unprepared and inadequate for the spiritual challenges in a Folk Muslim context.

Brazilian workers indicated a strong awareness of the spiritual battle around them.[229] One worker related, "We know that there is a great battle. We have had some periods of great crises because of this," while another added, "There is a great spiritual battle here. If you have no spiritual life, you will die spiritually." Similarly, others affirmed, "This [attention to spiritual life] is an area of which we need to always pay much attention to in the Muslim world, because we are constantly in spiritual battle in all levels," and "It's fundamental that we are aware of the spiritual battle because we live in it daily. We need to use our spiritual weapons." One worker from a Baptist background asserted, "I try to have a balanced view of the spiritual. Like C.S. Lewis, not give too much attention to the devil, but not ignoring him either." Another affirmed, "We certainly pray against the Evil One; but I am not obsessed with every problem being caused by a demon or the devil."

In addition to the cases already noted, other Brazilian workers attributed health problems to the spiritual battle around them. One missionary shared, "Sometimes I have not felt well but I do understand that there is a spiritual context, especially during the month of Ramadan" while another

---

228. See Noll, *The New Shape of World Christianity*, 34.

229. All responses were gathered from surveys and interviews. See appendices.

related, "I was once very ill during a ministry outreach and after prayer from colleagues, saw myself quickly recover."

Building upon this general awareness for the spiritual world, some Brazilian workers asserted that spiritual warfare differed in various contexts. One missionary who had previously served in North Africa before moving to Southern Brazil asserted, "There is a greater spiritual battle among Muslims in Southern Brazil than there was in North Africa. This is especially true among the Shia Muslims." On the other hand, one worker observed: "It is easier to perceive the evil in Brazil, it is more subtle here [in my Arab context]. The Evil One works in a different way." Similarly, a Brazilian woman shared, "I feel that the spiritual battle is greater here [in my Arab context] than in Brazil (though in Brazil I have been involved in praying for people oppressed by the devil)."

Some of those interviewed observed that Brazilians are generally more sensitive to spiritual warfare than Western missionaries are. The same woman cited in the last quotation related, "I think I feel a greater sense of prayer than my husband (who is from North America)." Describing his organization's training strategy for prayer and spiritual warfare, Mordomo, a North American, admitted: "We do emphasize prayer and spiritual warfare training with our Brazilian workers. Any weakness in this training would be because of shortcomings by our North American leadership." By shortcomings, he was aware that the North American leadership might tend to default to an "excluded middle" paradigm on spiritual warfare issues.

Respondents also offered insights on their strategies and general approaches to spiritual warfare. Most Brazilian workers stated that prayer was their primary strategy. One worker indicated that, "[prayer and spiritual warfare] are necessary for work in a Muslim country. There is an oppression that can only be defeated by prayer," while another added, "Spiritual warfare is very big; so prayer is a necessity." Reflecting on the importance of personal prayer, one missionary shared, "I learned that in order to survive on the field among the Muslims it is necessary to have a strong prayer life, because it is the key of our victory because of the constant spiritual battles that we go through." Another added that prayer and meditating on Scripture was also important: "I have my normal, regular prayer and I also claim the promises of God's Word in prayer." One woman related that intercessory prayer was actually her main ministry in the Arab world: "This is a major part of my ministry; the foundation of all that I am doing here. Prayer is the first thing I do when starting a new project. It is prayer that helps me to love this country and to see change. It is very spiritually oppressive here." Finally, others shared that praying in groups and developing prayer networks were also important strategies. One worker stated, "Prayer is an important concept and we try to pray as a team and with the church regularly. There are moments where the spiritual battle gets stronger, and in those times we pray and fight in the spiritual battles with much effort." Another affirmed, "Prayer is the foundation of the mission agency that I am part of, and that has influenced me a lot in my transcultural ministry. I am part of a prayer network in some countries where there are people praying for our work on the field."

Some Brazilians indicated that fasting with prayer was an important spiritual warfare strategy. The Baptist pastor ministering in Southern Brazil shared, "We had a great dependency on God. Our work was only possible through fasting and prayer. In fact, we prayed and fasted every Friday when the Muslims were at the mosque that there would be a spiritual breakthrough." A Brazilian woman serving in the Middle East added, "My husband and I have experienced separating a period of three days, four times a year, for fasting and prayer. We saw results and need to start doing that again."

Finally, some Brazilian workers reported that deliverance prayer and power encounters were part of their experience with spiritual warfare. For instance, one worker shared, "Arabs have a strong spiritual mindset (demons, spirits, dreams). God works miracles and can speak to Muslims through their dreams and our message speaks to their spiritual mindset." Another added, "It [spiritual warfare] is important in freeing lives from the hands of the enemy, especially when he manifests himself."

In summary, these Brazilian voices seem to affirm that Brazilian transcultural workers possess a spiritual worldview that not only makes them sensitive to the spiritual realities in the Arab-Muslim world but also capable of ministering in this context. Having grown up in a context of Catholicism mixed with Spiritism, Brazilian evangelical missionaries, including ex-Spiritists, Pentecostals, and historic Protestants, seem prone to adapt to the spiritual context of Folk Islam. In this sense, they are not only more prepared than their North American and European colleagues, but they also have much to teach them about spiritual warfare ministry. Their emphases on prayer, fasting, and engaging in appropriate power encounters could also serve as relevant models for ministry.

Jeitinho Brasileiro: A Case Study in Adaptation

Having explored the cultural and missiological literature regarding these eight specific aspects of culture, and having listened to Brazilian missionaries and mission leaders describe how Brazilians adapt in each area, let us consider how Brazilians seem to adapt to culture and new things in general, and how this affects their cultural adaptation in the Arab world.

A vast majority (84.4 percent) of missionaries responded that they felt very comfortable (31.1 percent) or comfortable (53.3 percent) living cross-culturally in the Arab world. Only 15.6 percent said that they were uncomfortable, while no one responded that they were very uncomfortable. The survey comments largely affirmed these numbers. One worker shared, "I am a person who adapts easily to new things." Others related, "I felt no culture shock in Arab culture," and "I didn't have any problems in terms of adaptation." Another shared, "This [my Arab context] has become my second home," while another affirmed, "The things that upset me here are so small compared to how we feel blessed."

Other Brazilian missionaries noted that they adapted with time. One worker shared, "I would say that I am entering the phase of being comfortable here after three years. Cultural and language adaptation bring this comfort, but it takes time." Another added, "In my first impression, it was uncomfortable but soon after it became comfortable."

Finally, the comments of others reflected an ability to adapt even when training is lacking. One worker shared, "I would do my pre-field training again. But you really learn most things on the field." Another related, "I was the first Brazilian missionary to Arabs in Southern Brazil. No one had gone before so there was no set preparation. I wrote the first manual for training. I went with my 'face and courage.'"

Page observes, "Brazilians cope amazingly well. In the face of discomforts and hardships that might drive others to protest or even open revolts, they exhibit forbearance and an extraordinary degree of adaptability."[230] Though his remarks are directed at Brazilians in general, they are also quite relevant to Brazilian missionaries and their efforts to adapt to and thrive within Arab culture. They also point to an aspect of Brazilian culture called *jeitinho Brasileiro*, which will also be explored as it relates to Brazilian transcultural mission work.

---

230. See Page, *The Brazilians*, 10.

While this cultural value has been evaluated at length by anthropologists,[231] let us move toward a definition and consider the underlying motivations for it. While *jeitinho* literally means "a solution," Barbosa further defines it as "a special way of resolving some problem or difficult or prohibited situation; or a creative solution to an emergency, whether in the form of working around an established norm or rule (through trickery or fraud), whether through appeasement, or whether through skill or cleverness . . . the situation must be unforeseen and adverse to the person's objectives."[232] Leonardo Boff adds that Brazilians possess "great creativity . . . to always make a way, [to] find an escape from any problem."[233] On one level, *jeitinho* seems to be a way in which Brazilians cope with a fatalistic view of the world.[234] As noted, Spiritism offers a spiritual *jeito* ("solution") for Brazilians. On another related level, *jeitinho* provides a way for otherwise powerless Brazilians to navigate and survive within the hierarchical and corrupt systems of administration in government and business. Thus, Hess and DaMatta remark that "the *jeitinho* can be an equalizing and humanizing institution."[235] Ultimately, *jeitinho* signifies that relationships—a foundational element of Brazilian culture—trump rules. Barbosa writes, "It [*jeitinho*] also emphasizes the side of Brazilian society that privileges the human and neutral aspects of social reality over the legal, political, and institutional ones. Thus, the *jeitinho brasileiro* expresses the cordial, conciliatory, happy, warm, and human spirit of a country that is young, tropical, sensual, beautiful, and full of possibilities."[236]

In light of this definition and motivations, should *jeitinho Brasileiro* be regarded as a beneficial quality for Brazilian evangelical missionaries? Magaretha Adinawara, a Brazilian mission leader, argues that there are many moral problems implicit in *jeitinho*, including a lack of respect for authority and rules, selfish individualism, a desire for instant gratification, a superficial spiritual life, and an unhealthy desire to always win. Thus, for Adinawara, *jeitinho* is clearly incompatible with the Christian life and

---

231. Some of the most helpful work has been done by Lívia Barbosa. See Barbosa, *O Jeitinho Brasileiro* and Barbosa, "The Brazilian Jeitinho," 35–48.

232. Cited in Mordomo, "The Brazilian Way," 17.

233. Ibid., 11; see also Barbosa, "The Brazilian Jeitinho," 36.

234. See Page, *The Brazilians*, 10.

235. See Hess and DaMatta, *The Brazilian Puzzle*, 23.

236. See Barbosa, "The Brazilian Jeitinho," 46.

missionary call.[237] Similarly, Silas Tostes expressed concern that Brazilian missionaries would compromise their integrity by relying on their *jeitinho*.[238]

On the other hand, given that Brazilian transcultural workers are being transformed by a biblical worldview, it seems that one aspect of *jeitinho*—the ability to adapt and survive in difficult circumstances—ought to be retained. One Brazilian worker asserted, "With *jeito*, the Brazilian missionary is able to make do and find a way around problems."[239] Finley also adds, "The Brazilian missionary, if well-prepared, adapts well because of coming from a culture of improvisation; also, Brazilians are able to adapt to precarious conditions because Brazil is a third world country."[240] Daniel Calze concurs, remarking that "success" in ministry "comes as a result of the [Brazilian's] natural gifts to adapt himself to a context and particularly to Muslim culture. Because of that, they are able to share the gospel in an effective and holistic way."

As Brazilian workers in the Arab world continually face the challenges of limited financial resources, language learning, visa and administration issues, security issues, and (for women) the difficulties of living in a male-dominated culture, this innate ability to adapt is probably a strength. In spite of their difficulties, it is interesting to note that the vast majority of Brazilian workers surveyed plan on spending more than ten years (62.5 percent) or up to ten more years (28.1 percent) in ministry in the Arab world.

Summary

In the last two chapters, the cultural aspects of race, economics, time, communication, family, relationships, hospitality, and spiritual worldview have been discussed in both the Arab and Brazilian contexts. While a study of the relevant literature has been foundational, the theme analysis has been based on the descriptions of Brazilian transcultural workers and mission leaders at work in the Arab-Muslim world. It has become evident that there are some definite differences between the cultures of the Arab world and that of Brazilian missionaries. These have been most notable

237. See Adiwardana, "Treinar Missionários Para Perseverar," 7; also Barbosa, "The Brazilian Jeitinho," 47; and Mordomo, "The Brazilian Way," 19.

238. Related to me in personal conversation, July 23, 2009.

239. Cited in Finley, "Contextualized Training for Missionaries," 181.

240. Ibid.

in the areas of conflict resolution, personal hygiene as it relates to food and hospitality, and the role of women. On the other hand, some aspects of Arab and Brazilian culture are rather similar. The strongest areas seem to be hospitality, relationship building, and a general spiritual worldview that acknowledges the role of demons and spirits. It has also become apparent that transcultural workers from the Northeast of Brazil seem be closest to the Arabs culturally. This was especially evident when considering the cultural aspects of economics, time, family, and relationships. In short, as Brazilians have described their experiences, it seems that there is some favorable continuity between the cultures of Brazilian evangelical workers and the Arab contexts in which they serve. Coupled with the reality that Brazilians seem to adapt well in other cultures, it seems that the contribution of Brazilian transcultural missionaries is important in the Arab world. It also seems that, generally speaking, Brazilians adapt better to ministry in the Arab-Muslim world than their North American and European colleagues.

Marcos Amado agrees that Brazilians have fewer cultural barriers to contend with in the Arab world. However, he reminds Brazilian missionaries that they are still not Arabs and that they must still discipline themselves to learn the language and culture, and not assume that they can adapt without effort.[241] Amado's convictions are further supported in the remarks of a single woman presently serving in the Middle East: "As Brazilians, we think we know more than we do. We need to be humble and learn from others. We cannot rely on our *jeito* but need to work hard on learning the language and culture. We have things in common with the Arab culture so it is easier for us to be here, but we need to be persistent to learn."

---

241. Over the course of his twenty years of service in the Arab world, Amado developed a Transcultural Training Course, which is summarized in Amado, "A Capacitação Contínua do Obreiro," 39–46.

4

Brazilian Approaches to Mission

Introduction

BUILDING ON THE HISTORICAL and intercultural discussions of the previous chapters, let us now pose the question, practically speaking, how are Brazilian evangelicals approaching mission in the Arab-Muslim world? This question will ultimately shed light on how Brazilian evangelicals understand and even define mission. Valuing the collective input of many voices, I have posed this question to individual missionaries and to Brazilian evangelical missions organizations that are working in the Arab world.

Our discussion will be framed by three major questions. First, based on surveys, interviews, and observation, what are the most prominent strategies used by Brazilians missionaries in the Arab world? Second, based largely on missions publications and literature, as well as the data collected from surveys and interviews with mission leaders, what are the philosophies and strategies of six Brazilian missions organizations laboring in the Arab world? Third, after listening to the input of Brazilian missionaries and mission leaders, what are the most apparent strengths and challenges of Brazilian evangelical efforts in the Arab world? This final question will also capture Brazilian thoughts on moving forward in these areas.

Brazilian Evangelical Missions in the Arab World

Ministry Strategies

The results of a survey with forty-five Brazilian missionaries serving in the Arab world showed that their main areas of ministry included evangelism (63.6 percent), discipleship and teaching (63.6 percent), humanitarian aid (45.5 percent), church planting (34.1 percent), prayer and spiritual warfare ministry (29.5 percent), and media ministry (2.3 percent). In addition, some workers added that they were involved in prison ministry, teaching Portuguese, teaching English, distributing the Bible and literature, soccer and sports ministry, children's ministry, orphanage work, Business as Mission, pastoral care, leadership, administration, and training other Latins in ministry. In this section, let us explore these prominent forms of ministry, while taking into consideration the perspectives on these areas of service.

We will begin by discussing three areas of ministry—evangelism, discipleship, and church planting—that may be regarded as classic forms of mission work, especially in contexts of political and spiritual openness to the gospel. After, we will consider how Brazilians are also ministering via humanitarian aid, medical work, business and business as mission, sports ministry, and teaching. On one hand, this second group of ministries has become necessary because most of the Arab-Muslim world is closed to conventional evangelical mission work and so Brazilian workers are required to have a ministry platform in order to access the country. On the other hand, as our upcoming discussion on *missão integral* will show, Brazilians generally regard both categories of ministry (i.e., humanitarian work plus evangelism) as necessarily integrated and of equal value. Hence, in light of this holistic perspective, the following areas of ministry will not be divided into categories such as "front-line" or "hands on" ministry versus "support" or "platform" ministry; rather, it is intentionally integrated.

Evangelism

While most Brazilians surveyed[1] indicated that evangelism was a key part of their ministries, it should be noted that this ministry has occurred largely on a personal or small group level. In part, this is due to the fact that public proclamation is not allowed in most parts of the Arab world. It is also the case because Brazilians seem naturally disposed to personal evangelism because of the relational nature of their culture. After recounting how an Arab friend had come to faith in Christ, one worker shared, "Most of my

---

1. All responses were gathered from surveys and interviews. See appendices.

evangelism has been through building personal relationships." Another added, "I love to build relationships and see people respond to God's love."

In the context of such friendships, some Brazilian workers reflected a strong conviction for incarnational ministry. For instance, one worker related, "When Arabs seek me, they invite me and open their lives to me, telling me personal things and asking for advice. They say that they feel comfortable with me. In that setting, I can communicate some of Jesus' values through my actions." A Brazilian woman who had served in North Africa shared: "I learned after leaving North Africa that our housekeeper had believed in Christ. Even though my language ability was limited, she saw something about our faith and was drawn to Christ." Reflecting on relational ministry, she continued, "I like [these] words, 'preach the gospel always and use words when necessary.' Because Muslims are so serious about their religion, I really need to 'show' the gospel. My ministry must be led by serving and humility." Another worker summarized his journey toward understanding incarnational ministry by relating: "During the past years I've come to learn to look at my friends here as people created according to the image of God, people with human value and dignity, and not as 'contacts' or people to whom I'm trying to win for a specific faith. To love my friends who are part of the major [Muslim] religion is the basis for sharing the gospel."

In light of these values, a number of specific evangelistic strategies can be observed. Though not exhaustive, they certainly offer an idea of how Brazilians are going about proclaiming the gospel message. First, many Brazilians indicated they often shared their faith in the context of offering hospitality—a strong Arab and Brazilian value. One couple shared that they ministered through "opening the doors of our home . . . seeking to always be available to our friends, spending time with them and helping them in what is needed."

Second, in Southern Brazil, in the course of their ministry, some evangelical pastors regularly visit Muslims in the community. One pastor, who planted a bilingual Arabic-Portuguese fellowship shared, "[I] went about ministry through personal relationships. I was known in the community as a pastor and had much freedom to share the gospel." His successor similarly shared, "At the moment I am a local church pastor in Southern Brazil, but at heart, I am a missionary. My position as pastor allows me to be recognized as a religious leader here, even among Muslims. So I have the opportunity to go visit Muslims in their shops and in town and to pray for them and even given them a Bible."

Third, in partnership with some Christian radio and satellite channels that broadcast in the Arab world, some Brazilians have reported being involved in follow-up ministry. That is, they visit Arabs who are corresponding with these media ministries and who have requested to talk with someone personally about the Christian life.[2]

Fourth, in addition to their verbal witness, some Brazilian workers have been involved in distributing the New Testament and Scriptures to those who have expressed interest in the gospel. One worker indicated that he was able to proclaim Christ "through witnessing as a way of life in the context of the personal relationships . . . I was also able to offer these close friends a New Testament in Arabic." Another worker reported inviting friends to her home for an evangelistic Bible study of Luke's Gospel.[3]

Finally, in light of the oral culture of many Arab-Muslim peoples, some Brazilians have approached communicating the gospel and Scriptures in a story format. One worker shared: "We have been seen people coming to the Lord, others having more interest in the gospel. We created a series of biblical stories with an evangelistic tone, and they were translated to the local dialect and are now available at a website on the Internet. Those stories were chosen in order to address the worldview of the people we serve." As noted in the previous chapter, many Brazilians naturally relate to Arabs as secondary oral learners.

How have Brazilians been successful in personal evangelism? Some responded to this question by referring to Arabs who have become followers of Christ. One couple ministering in Southern Brazil rejoiced that "one Muslim girl came to faith and was baptized." While most Brazilians have struggled with the relatively slow response to the gospel in the Arab-Muslim world, especially when their churches back home have expected more significant results, others have measured their success in simply being faithful to build relationships and share the gospel. One worker shared: "I can see how strong my relationships with local people have been and I can see the opportunities God has given me. Even though I can't see the fruits now, I am sure someone will reap them in the . . . future." Another worker shared that successful evangelism was "getting to share the gospel even one time." Finally, another Brazilian celebrated the process of helping Arab-Muslims understand the gospel. That is, success in ministry was "[helping] the people to have a better knowledge of the gospel."

---

2. Related to me in personal correspondence (ministry prayer letter), April 2009.
3. Ibid.

Discipleship

The Brazilian missionaries surveyed also indicated that discipleship and teaching were key aspects of their ministries. In fact, evangelism and discipleship were tied for being the most prominent ministries pursued by Brazilians (63.6 percent). This is probably the case because of the integrative nature of these two ministries in pioneer mission contexts. That is, it would be quite rare for a Brazilian to arrive in an Arab context and find a multitude of believers waiting for discipleship. At the same time, as Brazilian workers are involved in personal evangelism, they certainly would not abandon the relationship once an Arab friend became a follower of Christ; rather, they would begin to focus more on teaching.

Affirming the integrative relationship of evangelism and discipleship, one female Brazilian worker shared, "Well, in a small scale, I can say that in the four years that I've been here, I've seen the fruit in the lives of two young ladies to whom I've invested my life in, as they are walking with the Lord now. . . I have been very much involved in the process of them coming to Christ and in discipling them." Another worker in Southern Brazil shared this account of a young man who had come to Christ: "It is a joy to see him growing in Christ and it blesses me when I hear him speak like me and act like me in the faith. Maybe he will be a Paul, but I am his Ananias (Acts 9:1–19)."

While discipleship is a key value for most Brazilian workers in the Arab world, the forms of discipleship certainly vary according to context. Though certainly not exhaustive, let us consider a few examples. One couple serving in Southern Brazil meets weekly for a Bible study with two new believers from a Muslim background.[4] Another Brazilian couple working in the Middle East are discipling some Brazilian Christians married to Arab non-Christians. By taking a chronological storytelling approach to the Scriptures, they are evangelizing the non-believers while, at the same time, providing useful teaching for the Christians.[5]

Though most discipleship appears to happen on a one-on-one or small group level, one Brazilian worker reported putting on an intensive two-month long discipleship school for around five believers. While the focus was on biblical studies, he is planning a second cycle in the future to address issues such as Christian marriage, parenting, and inner healing. Finally, this worker also organized the first weekend retreat for members

---

4. This was related to me in a personal visit, July 20, 2009.
5. Ibid., October 9, 2009.

of a house church that he is leading. While the weekend getaway included some teaching, it provided an environment for believers to have fun and strengthen their fellowship.[6]

As they contemplated the future of their ministries, some Brazilian workers emphasized the importance of on-going discipleship. One worker indicated that he was looking forward "to seeing our friends grow spiritually, learning with them so that the ministry can be better developed for future relationships." One woman shared her passion and desire to teach children: "[I look forward to] developing my ministry here—discipleship with children. I want to see them discover the love of God. It is neat and interesting to learn that with them."

Church Planting

Just over a third of the Brazilians surveyed related that they were involved in church planting. For many Brazilians, this ministry is quite integrated with evangelism and discipleship. Not unlike discipleship ministry, Brazilian church planting efforts have looked different depending on the context. Let us consider some representative examples of such efforts.

As alluded to briefly, a Brazilian Baptist pastor spent thirteen years serving in the Southern Brazilian city of Foz do Iguaçu, which has the largest concentration of Arabs in Brazil, and planted a small Arabic- and Portuguese-speaking church there. Unlike most other contexts in the Arab world, the church exists openly and the planting pastor and the current pastor have been known in the community as respected religious leaders. From this position in the community, they have evangelized, discipled, and ministered to Arab-Muslims.[7]

On the other hand, due to security and cultural concerns, most Brazilian workers serving in the Arab world have been involved in planting house churches. One Brazilian worker, collaborating with other international workers, reported success in initiating a house church. Comprised entirely of converts from Muslim backgrounds, the group has slowly grown as new believers have been baptized and joined the fellowship. The church has also celebrated the marriage of two of its members. As the family is

---

6. Related to me in correspondence (ministry prayer letter) in April 2009 and January 2010.

7. I visited Foz do Iguaçua July 17–20, 2009. I interviewed the current pastor who invited me to preach at the Arabic Evangelical Church. On July 21–22, I interviewed the planting pastor in Curitiba, where he presently resides and ministers.

a cornerstone of Arab culture, strong Christian families could very well serve to invigorate an Arab house church. While this group has grown and has been strengthened through teaching, discipleship, and retreats, the Brazilian worker has continued to invest time in personal evangelism—a ministry that has also become the conviction of church members. Finally, the Brazilian church planter has not been content to think only about ministry in his current context. Instead, he recently took an exploratory trip to a neighboring country in order to assess the ministry needs there.[8]

Another Brazilian family shared that their ministry has contributed to a church planting movement. That is, an initial group was started which has served as a catalyst for spontaneously multiplying groups of believers. The wife related: "My husband, along with other workers, helped to pastor a small group of national believers . . . From this small group has come a crop of dynamic young leaders who have gone on to lead and multiply the church. They have their own vision for reaching their people and are developing a national structure. Through them the church is taking root in this land."

While most Brazilian church plants among Arabs have resulted from some sort of plan, there is at least one development that seems completely spontaneous. The work of a Brazilian Christian businessman took him to a country in the Middle East. Through the course of getting to know his colleagues and clients and by sharing his faith as a way of life, a number of these friends believed in Christ and a group has begun to meet for worship and Bible study. Though the businessman's schedule makes it difficult to disciple each group member and to prepare adequately for worship meetings (he is praying for someone to come join him in this work), a young church plant still seems to have emerged.[9]

Humanitarian Work

Nearly half of the Brazilian workers surveyed[10] indicated that they were involved in some form of humanitarian work—a definite strength of Brazilian evangelical missions. In a number of Arab countries, Brazilians

---

8. Related to me in personal correspondence (ministry prayer letter), April 2008, January 2009, and October 2009.

9. This account was related to me in personal conversation by a friend of the businessman—another Brazilian transcultural worker in the Middle East—on October 10, 2009.

10. All responses were gathered from surveys and interviews. See appendices.

have established or have affiliated with existing Non-Governmental Organizations (NGOs) to care for the needs of the handicapped, women, and refugees.

In one context, a Brazilian worker directs a team of Brazilian, international, and local volunteers at a cultural center for the handicapped that offers classes in language, arts, and crafts while also offering short excursions. The center, which enjoys a positive reputation with the government and community, cares for around fifty regular members who would otherwise be marginalized in a society that does very little for the handicapped. One Brazilian volunteer in the center related that working among the handicapped was a great way to show God's presence, to build genuine friendships, and to respond to the commonly posed question, why are you so different? That is, through tangibly serving and caring for human needs, this volunteer has also been able to communicate verbally her faith in Christ.

The director also added that Brazilian volunteers—especially those who were handicapped themselves—seemed naturally able to relate to Arab members of the center. One reason is that in both Brazil and this particular Arab context, the handicapped are on the fringes of society and receive little help from the government in the way of programs and assistance. Hence, handicapped Brazilian workers can identify with those to whom they are ministering. Second, according to the director, many Brazilian volunteers—handicapped or not—can relate to the center's poorer members who struggle to scrape together enough money to take public transportation to the center for activities. As many Brazilian workers are struggling with financial challenges, they can certainly identify and empathize with the poor who frequent the center.[11]

In another context, a group of Brazilian women, in partnership with other international workers, have started a center for women. After paying a modest annual fee to the center, participants are offered training in languages, computer skills, and arts and crafts. While some develop skills that will help them to find a job or start a small business, others frequent the center to make friends and have their relational needs met. In an otherwise class-based society, it is an interesting phenomenon to see poor and uneducated women attending the same workshops and activities with university-educated professionals. While addressing the social and economic needs of women in their context, the Brazilian workers are also

---

11. These remarks are based on my observations and conversation with the director and staff during a visit to the center on October 12, 2009.

Brazilian Approaches to Mission

building long-term friendships in which they naturally share the gospel. The women shared that some of these friends have indeed embraced the Christian faith.[12]

Finally, Brazilian missionaries have engaged in humanitarian work by ministering to refugees. One worker, commenting on the general lack of care afforded to displaced peoples in his Arab context, shared, "We are seeing God work more among the minority peoples despite the fact that Arabs can be so racist against them." Another Brazilian described his service in an existing center for refugees: "We have worked in a humanitarian center for refugees in our country that includes a feeding ministry, teaching crafts, [and] home visits." He adds that caring for these real needs has led to opportunities for "evangelism and teaching, and training Christian leaders to run the center." Finally, another Brazilian serving among refugees described the holistic nature of his work: "God has opened doors to work with refugees and we have seen people healed and desiring to follow God."

Medical Work

Quite related to humanitarian aid, some Brazilian workers are caring for the physical needs of Arab peoples through medical work. In one context, two Brazilian women are working as nurses in a historically Protestant hospital in the Middle East. Despite serving in a country that is 94 percent Muslim, in the hospital they have a great deal of freedom to communicate the gospel verbally and to pray for patients as they dispense medicine and care for them. One of the women asserted that serving as a nurse allows her the opportunity to show the gospel in a tangible way—"to be more than to do." She added that it is difficult to be expelled from a country for showing God's love to people. That said, this worker related that even though she is able to communicate her faith quite often, particularly to female patients, she is unsure of the outcomes. The cultural constraints on women make follow-up and ongoing discipleship difficult within her context.[13]

Another medical strategy that some Brazilian workers are beginning to pursue is known as Community Health Evangelism (CHE). Defined

---

12. These remarks are based on a follow-up discussion that I had in Brazil with one of the coordinators (also respondent 1 in the workers survey), July 24, 2009.

13. These remarks were based on my personal conversations with her during a visit, October 9, 2009.

as "a true best practices model for integrating evangelism and discipleship with community based development," CHE volunteers seek to "raise awareness of need and opportunity, and facilitate a process by which the community itself identifies solutions and begins to work together in an organized way." The vision of CHE includes the following outcomes: "Health improves, infant mortality decreases, agriculture becomes more productive, jobs are created, water systems, roads, schools and clinics are built, and churches are established or strengthened. All of this is achieved at the initiative of the people. Peace, justice, compassion, and righteousness are witnessed in the community and God is glorified."[14] Though this is a new and developing strategy among Brazilians, one worker shared that her priority in ministry was "Community health evangelism and thus getting involved more with the humanitarian needs of the community."

Business, Business as Mission, and Business Development

An increasing number of Brazilian transcultural workers are accessing the countries of the Arab world through a business platform and ministering from that basis. As noted, the work of one Brazilian businessman took him to the Arab world. Though not sent through a missions organization or church, this Christian businessman nevertheless has had a fruitful witness that has resulted in a house church being started. His biggest challenge has been having the time to invest in discipleship and teaching with the group.

Similarly, another Brazilian Christian was hired by an international company in the Middle East. Though initially reluctant to speak about his faith, he quickly found that Arabs were very relational and it was easy to share the gospel and even offer a copy of the New Testament to friends. He shared, "There were other Brazilian believers there with me and we began a church fellowship among ourselves. We also reached out and shared the gospel to those with whom we built relationships." That is, the group of international Christians shared their faith on a personal basis but they also enjoyed a collective witness as they invited Arab friends to their small worship gathering.

Though sent by a church and missions agency, Marcos Amado waited until he reached the field and was able to explore the context before he set up a business exporting carpets. Though his livelihood was not completely dependent on the business, he did find that his ability to negotiate for prices in the wholesale market correlated directly to his ability to speak

---

14. See "Global CHE Network."

Arabic. As his command of Arabic improved and as he regularly visited a network of clients, he shared that it was quite natural to communicate the gospel in the context of relationships even during the workday.[15]

More recently, some Brazilian workers have adopted a Business as Mission (BAM) approach. According to Rundle and Johnson, BAM is "the utilization of for-profit businesses as instruments for global mission."[16] Holistic in nature, BAM practitioners endeavor to offer a vibrant gospel witness by running their business according to biblical principles, to create jobs and wealth, and to see communities transformed. One Brazilian worker has successfully started a consulting business in one Arab country and has managed to land some significant clients. He related, "I have had a successful business here. It is a kingdom business." That said, in his reflections on BAM and Kingdom Business—mission models that are certainly continuing to develop—he places more value on proclamation in mission. He asserts: "I am challenged to pursue mission through business rather than Business as Mission. I want to do more direct evangelism. What's wrong with a hybrid business that includes good godly business and sharing the gospel?"

Another Brazilian worker has integrated business with mission by opening a small business development school in one Arab context. As the school operates under the auspices of a registered Christian entity, the worker describes the project as "a Bible school and at the same time, a professional training center."[17] Working from the assumption that evangelism and church planting happen through relationships, and that small business owners are strategically placed people in a community, the worker's goal is to train and set apart business people who will also be able to serve as evangelists and church planters. This worker and his team are especially burdened for the country's rural areas. Trainees come to the school for three months where they take classes in business and Bible, and also serve in various capacities within the church. After this period of training, students spend another three months traveling to different parts of the country where they study the possibilities for opening a business. After working on this project for four years, the worker reported, "We have already trained fifty people and seven small companies have already been established around [the country]." In terms of the leadership of the

---

15. Related to me in personal conversation on Skype, August 4, 2009.

16. See Johnson and Rundle, "Distinctives and Challenges of Business as Mission," 25. For more recent discussions on BAM, see Tunehag et al., "Business as Mission"; Johnson, *Business as Mission*; and Rundle and Steffen, *Great Commission Companies*.

17. Related to me in correspondence (ministry prayer letter) April 8, 2010.

school itself, he added, "At the beginning of this year I was able to pass on the leadership to the locals, and today they lead and I help them."

Sports Ministry

Sport has often been regarded as an international language that breaks down cultural barriers and promotes friendship, and Brazilians—with their excellence in basketball, volleyball, martial arts, and, of course, soccer (*futebol*)—speak this language quite well. Arabs also seem to welcome Brazilian transcultural workers—athletic or not—because Ronaldo, Ronaldinho, and Roberto Carlos (Brazilian soccer stars) are household names in the Arab world.[18] Brazilian workers serving among Arabs are making the most of this strategic connection and have proven to be innovative in using sports in ministry.

At least a couple of Brazilians are employed as physical trainers and also use that as a platform for ministry. One church planter in Southern Brazil recognized this as a viable strategy, and so he returned to the university and earned a degree in physical education. At present, he meets clients daily—many of whom are Arab businessmen. The nature of his work provides an interactive context in which to build relationships and communicate the gospel.[19] Similarly, a female Brazilian worker with significant training and experience is beginning to work in one Arab country as a physical trainer. As physical fitness is becoming more important to many Arab women, this worker's strategy also facilitates personal relationships and opportunities to communicate the gospel.[20]

At least one Brazilian worker, a former professional soccer player and coach in Brazil, has been hired by a school in the Middle East to teach physical education and to coach the school's soccer teams. Though he co-teaches classes with a national teacher while his language abilities develop, this worker still endeavors to communicate in Arabic with students as much as possible. As I visited with him one day at school, I was impressed with a few elements of his work. First, he seemed quite at home and comfortable in the rather chaotic atmosphere of the school. Second, there was

---

18. While traveling with a Brazilian worker in an Arab country, we were stopped at a police checkpoint. Upon seeing my friend's Brazilian passport, the policeman immediately began to name his favorite Brazilian soccer players. Apparently, this is an almost daily experience for Brazilians living in the Arab world.

19. Related to me personal conversation (respondent 9), July 19, 2009.

20. Related to me in personal conversation (respondent 30), October 9, 2009.

an evident mutual affection between him and his students. As a steady stream of children made the effort to greet their teacher (*ustadh*) throughout the day, he greeted them with warmth and affection. Third, he was able to connect quickly with a new afternoon soccer team as the group quickly responded to his instructions on the field. Fourth, he coaches with excellence. In fact, he has a coaching plan laid out for the entire year. Finally, he concluded each class and practice with a moral lesson that emerged from the practice itself. While each lesson is rooted in a biblical teaching or principle, his presentation is less explicit because of the local constraints against open evangelism. Perhaps the greatest affirmation of this Brazilian worker's ministry comes from a local Arab Christian who remarked: "He coaches with passion. Though he has the challenge of learning the language, he is so good with our people."[21]

A number of other Brazilian workers have also used soccer as a basis for ministry. One worker reported using soccer as a means of building relationships with Arab university students studying in the United States.[22] At least a couple of missionaries in Southern Brazil have organized soccer camps as a way of reaching out to Arab children.[23] Another Brazilian in the Middle East has begun a soccer outreach that integrates teaching on purity.[24] One worker serving in North Africa shared, "I . . . started a soccer ministry that one mission organization in the Muslim world has adopted and is using as a strategy." Thus, it is apparent that soccer outreach is such an important strategy that organizations are working to develop reproducible models.[25]

Finally, in one Arab context, a team of Brazilian workers has put on a series of soccer camps in some very conservative and restricted villages, including those inhabited by refugees. One worker reported that with a soccer ball and jersey, they have accessed places where doctors and teachers have never been allowed to enter. After receiving permission to work with the children from tribal leaders, the men have worked with the boys, and their wives have coached the girls. As this group also integrates moral teaching from a biblical foundation in their coaching, each practice ends with some group reflection on what was learned during the experience.

21. These observations were made during a visit with this Brazilian worker, October 10, 2009.
22. Related to me in personal conversation with respondent 18, July 29, 2009.
23. Ibid., respondents 9 and 13, July 19 and 21, 2009.
24. Related to me during personal conversation, October 9, 2009.
25. A similar effort that has developed in the African context and does not seem connected to the Brazilian strategies is called Ubabalo (see "Ubabolo eAfrica").

Apparently, the soccer camps have provided a welcome diversion from the difficulties of daily living for these children and their parents also seem to appreciate the constructive physical activity that their children are receiving. The fact that Arabs like Brazilians and know their soccer players has probably allowed this team of workers access into an otherwise restricted area where Westerners are not welcomed.[26]

In short, Brazilian missionaries are effectively using sports as a means to overcome barriers of mistrust, to build relationships, and to communicate Christian teaching. One worker concluded, "I think that sports ministry in the Arab world is very important and should continue to be used," while another added, "I love using sports—something I really enjoy—for ministry."

Teaching

Some Brazilian missionaries are also getting jobs in Arab contexts as English and Portuguese teachers. Again, while this often provides a platform to access a country not open to Christian missions, teaching also offers an environment in which relationships can be built.

One woman teaches both English and Portuguese to Arab children in Southern Brazil. Regarding her teaching as a tangible way to serve children, she also prays for opportunities to proclaim the gospel. Hence, she asserts, "I love to minister through my work as a teacher." In another Arab context, one Brazilian worker added, "In my English teaching for teens, I have shared the good news." Finally, another Brazilian missionary employed as a teacher shared, "I have been used to touch the lives of my students through words of encouragement."[27]

Training and Mobilization

Some Brazilian missionaries have dedicated part of their ministries to training and mobilizing other Brazilians and Latin Americans for mission in the Arab world. Marcos Amado, a former missionary in North Africa and past director of PMI, developed a transcultural training course for Brazilians entering the Arab world.[28] After serving for over a decade in

26. These efforts were related to me during personal conversation, October 9, 2009.
27. All responses were gathered from surveys and interviews. See appendices.
28. His training strategy is summarized in Amado, "A Capacitação Contínua do Obreiro," 39–46.

Southern Brazil, another Brazilian worker has become the missions pastor of another church in Brazil. He related: "Now I am in a ministry of training others. My desire is to train 150 workers for Arab ministry. Already, we have trained fifty Brazilians who are on the field."[29]

While some Brazilians are reaching out to Arabs in Southern Brazil, others are also convinced that this is a good place to train Brazilian workers before they move to an Arab country. One Brazilian affirmed, "I believe Southern Brazil with all of our Muslims is a good training ground to send others to the Arab-Muslim world." Another added: "I am excited about the potential to minister in Southern Brazil. It is a great place to mobilize and train Brazilians for ministry to Arabs for both here and in Arab countries. I want to teach and train the Brazilian church to have a global focus and to have a heart for Arabs."

In addition to training other Brazilians for Arab-Muslim ministry, some Brazilian workers are also committed to mobilizing others to join them in the work. One Brazilian serving in the Middle East shared: "[I want] to help mobilize Brazilians from my denomination to be well-prepared for work here [in the Arab world]. But I also desire to stay here, too." In considering future ministry, another worker shared his excitement for "mobilizing other Latins to ministry in the Arab world."

Brazilian Missions Agencies

Having considered the primary approaches to mission by Brazilian transcultural workers serving among Arabs, let us now survey the work of six exemplary Brazilian missions organizations involved in ministry in the Arab-Muslim world. While some of the Brazilian workers highlighted in the preceding discussion are affiliated with these agencies, it is also helpful to consider the vision, values, and priorities of each group on an organizational level. The first two organizations—Missão Antioquia and Missão Kairos—are indigenous to Brazil. A third group, PM International, is a distinctly Latin organization that has included Brazilians since its inception. A fourth agency, the Junta de Missões Mundiais da Convenção Batista Brasileira (Brazilian Baptist Convention missions), is a Brazilian national organization that has, of course, historic ties to the North American Southern Baptist Convention. The final two groups, Interserve and CCI-Brasil, are international organizations that have opened offices

---

29. All responses were gathered from surveys and interviews. See appendices.

in Brazil.[30] For each organization, the following questions will be posed: What is the history and vision of the organization? What are the group's core values? What type of pre-field training is provided? Where are the organization's workers serving? What types of ministries are being pursued in the Arab-Muslim world?

Missão Antioquia[31]

In our discussion in chapter 1 on the history of missions from Brazil, Missão Antioquia, founded in 1975, was highlighted for being the first indigenous Brazilian missions agency. According to the organization's web site, the primary vision continues to be "to proclaim His glory among the nations."[32] After some further reflection in 2006, the group added the following value to its vision statement: "bringing about transformation through the Word and good deeds."[33] In addition to these stated values, Missão Antioquia is characterized by a commitment to prayer, especially through an intercessory prayer chapel on the mission's campus that is occupied for most hours of the day.[34] Finally, through his speaking and writing, the group's present director, Silas Tostes, demonstrates a passion for mobilizing the Brazilian evangelical church to becoming more involved in global missions.[35]

Missionary candidates accepted by Missão Antioquia initially spend four months at the mission's campus known as the Valley of Blessing. In addition to receiving training in spiritual disciplines such as Bible study, prayer, and fasting, students take academic courses in the history and theology of missions, world religions, cultural anthropology, contextualization,

---

30. Though international organizations have established offices in Brazil, in 1995, Limpic noted that 69 percent of all Brazilian workers were going with Brazilian denominational or non-denominational mission. This continues to be the case for Brazilian workers serving in the Arab-Muslim world. See Limpic, "Brazilian Missionaries," 145.

31. All information contained in this section that is not otherwise documented is based on Tostes' responses (participant 4) in the mission leaders survey and on my observations and our discussions during my visit with Tostes at the Antioquia headquarters, July 23, 2009.

32. See "Missão Antioquia." I am grateful to Cristina Boersma who translated sections of the website.

33. Ibid.

34. See Itiokia, "Third World Missionary Training," 116–17.

35. Tostes recently published a work called *Brilhe a Sua Luz*, which is a resource intended to motivate pastors toward engagement in global missions.

linguistics, and missionary living.³⁶ Recently, the mission has added the "Perspectives on the World Christian Movement" course to its curriculum along with specialized training in sports ministry and community development.³⁷ As the Valley of Blessing also includes a church, school, orphanage, and day care center, students also have plenty of opportunities for practical ministry involvement. Following the four months of training at the mission headquarters, candidates spend one month in cross-cultural ministry in a neighboring Latin American country after which time they receive an evaluation regarding their suitability for long-term transcultural mission work.

Presently, Missão Antioquia has ninety-two workers serving in nineteen different countries. While only four of its laborers are serving in Arab-Muslim contexts, others are working in Africa and in Asia among non-Arab Muslims. Tostes reports that in its history, the mission has sent around fifteen missionaries to the Arab world. Though Missão Antioquia is not purely focused on the Arab or Muslim world and a majority of its workers are serving elsewhere, the mission does seem to have an increasing Muslim focus. This is certainly due to the fact that Muslim ministry is Tostes's particular burden. After initiating Muslim ministry training at the Valley of Blessing around 1991, Tostes and his wife spent three years (1994–1998) ministering to Muslims in the London area. Since returning to Brazil, he has written three books on Islam to equip Brazilians in reaching out to Muslims.³⁸ While he has no agenda for directing candidates toward Muslim contexts, Tostes reported that an increasing number are interested in Muslim ministry—including all ten graduates from a recent training group.

In keeping with its vision to see transformation occur through preaching the Word and doing good deeds, Missão Antioquia workers in the Arab world are involved in agricultural development projects and efforts to improve the lives of women. While caring for these physical and temporal needs, they are also involved in personal evangelism, discipleship, and the distribution of Scripture.³⁹

---

36. See "Missão Antioquia"; also Itiokia, "Third World Missionary Training," 117.

37. In 2009, the Brazilian Portuguese version of the *Perspectives* text (Bradford et al., *Perspectivas No Movimento Cristao Mundial*) was released.

38. See Tostes, *Jihad e o Reino de Deus*, *O Islamiso e a Cruz de Cristo*, and *O Islamiso e a Trinidade*.

39. See "Missão Antioquia."

Brazilian Evangelical Missions in the Arab World

Missão Kairos

Missão Kairos was founded in 1988 by a group of Brazilian pastors and missionaries with a vision to take the gospel to the world's least-reached peoples.[40] Aside from this general vision, the mission strongly values Christian community. While individuals, married couples, and families are held to a high standard of personal integrity and Christian character, members of the mission work together in teams from the outset of their training and, of course, when they reach the field. As missionaries committed to the Lord and to the task, they are also committed to one another and live in a ministry environment characterized by love, patience, care, respect, and encouragement.

Mission candidates with Kairos initially go through nine months of missiological education. The first six months of study are done by correspondence while the final three are completed in an intensive format at the mission's base in São Paulo. Afterward, candidates make a five-year commitment to an intermediate field where they receive practical training and supervision before being released to serve in a long-term context. Those hoping to go to the Muslim world typically serve in Peru or Mexico.

At present, Kairos has sixty-eight workers—including those in the intermediate and long-term stages—serving in eleven countries. While some are working among Muslims, there are currently no workers with Kairos serving in the Arab world. Why then is Kairos listed among Brazilian agencies serving in the Arab world? Because, through the years, Kairos has consistently partnered with Missão Antioquia and PMI in training and also in seconding workers to these agencies for particular fields. Though Kairos has no workers in the Arab-Muslim world at the moment, the organization has influenced the general Brazilian missions-sending environment toward unreached peoples and toward the Arab world.

PM International[41]

Mentioned briefly in chapter 1, PM International began in 1984 through the initiative of Pablo Carillo, a Mexican missionary who had previously served with Operation Mobilization in several Arab countries. Carillo's

---

40. All of the information in this section comes from "Missão Kairos." I am grateful to Barbara Hubbard for translation.

41. All information in this section that is not otherwise documented is based on the mission leaders responses of Daniel Calze (participant 6) and my observations and our discussions during my visit to the PMI Brazil office in Curitiba, July 21, 2009.

Brazilian Approaches to Mission

initial vision was to place Latin Americans in North Africa and thus, "Project Maghreb" was born. Later, as Ibero-Americans were beginning to serve in the Middle East, Central Asia, and the greater Muslim world, the group changed its name to Povos Muçulmanos International ("Muslim Peoples International") in 1991 to reflect this broader focus. While a number of Brazilians had been involved with PMI since its early years, a Brazilian national office was established in 1998. At present, the international headquarters of PMI is located in Spain, while national offices are located in Argentina, the United States, and Brazil.

The vision of PMI Brazil is to "to cooperate with the Brazilian evangelical church by mobilizing and directing human and financial resources in order to establish the church of Jesus Christ among the Muslims." Daniel Calze, the current director of PMI Brazil adds: "There are approximately 150 thousand evangelical churches of all kinds in Brazil, and some say that there are 25 million evangelicals. As the largest Latin American church, we need to be involved in the biggest missionary challenge of the times—the evangelization of the Muslim world."[42] PMI is unique in that it is the only Brazilian missions organization solely focused on the Muslim world. As an organization, PMI's key values include working together in teams, developing strategic platforms in restricted countries, effective cultural immersion, and ongoing pastoral care—both from the organization as well as from the worker's sending church. Finally, PMI also emphasizes the strategic cultural connection between Brazilians and Muslims, an element discussed in detail in the previous chapter. Calze adds: "Why Latin missionaries or Brazilians? Because the work that has been done so far by Brazilian and Latin missionaries has shown that they adapt very easily to Muslim culture and that they share the gospel very effectively."[43]

In terms of missionary selection, Calze states: "We are not looking for 'perfect' people, but those who have a true missionary calling and are willing to learn and to suffer difficulties because of their love for Jesus Christ, and also to have perseverance meanwhile. We also understand that the local church is the main organization in charge of sending missionaries to the field." Regarding pre-field training for PMI workers, he adds: "We are a receiving mission agency. Our missionaries are trained by our partners in Brazil. Those partners are chosen by us according to their training programs and the level of respect that they have." These partners, which offer

---

42. See "PMI Brasil." English translation by Cristina Boersma.
43. Ibid.

theological and missiological training, include Missão Antioquia, Missão Kairos, and Avante[44] among others.[45]

Though PMI provides pre-field training to its workers through established partnerships, one of the organization's greatest strengths is its five-month Transcultural Training Course that happens once the worker is in the host country. Originally developed by Marcos Amado, the course includes training in observing and analyzing a new culture, developing a plan for evangelism in the worker's specific context, understanding the situation of the national church, as well as understanding the history, geography, economy, and political situation of the worker's host culture.[46] In order to bond adequately with the culture, PMI workers will typically live with a national family during this period of training. In addition to this course, PMI also provides ongoing training for its workers through reading material, retreats, and conferences.

At present, there are approximately 120 workers from fourteen different Latin American countries serving with PMI in the Muslim world. A majority of those are Brazilian and around sixty Brazilians are serving with PMI in the Arab world. With a great commitment to evangelism, discipleship, and church planting, PMI is also quite holistic in its approach; and their workers are involved in sports ministry, medical care, and humanitarian work.[47]

Junta de Missões Mundiais da Convenção Batista Brasileira

As shown in chapter 1, Southern Baptists from North America played a key role in evangelizing Brazil in the nineteenth and twentieth centuries. The founding of the Brazilian Baptist Convention in 1907 was a key step in establishing indigenous leadership of Baptist work in the country. In the same year, the Junta de Missões Mundiais (global missions board) was founded and, as noted, missionaries were immediately sent to Portugal. According to the JMM web site, the organization was founded to faciliate planting Baptist churches outside of Brazil and to strengthen existing

44. See "Avante."
45. Related to me in conversation with former PMI director Marcos Amado, August 27, 2009.
46. See Amado, "A Capacitação Contínua do Obreiro," 39–46. Another earlier description of PMI's in-country immersion strategy is available in Carrasco, "Training Latins for the Muslim World," 1–4.
47. See "PMI Brasil" and "PMI USA." Some thoughts are also based on my discussion with Calze on July 21, 2009.

Baptist efforts.[48] JMM's stated vision is "to serve with excellence and take the gospel to all peoples." With that, its mission is "to serve and to mobilize Brazilian Baptist Churches to make global mission work viable."[49]

Currently, around 600 Brazilians, including long-term and short-term workers, are serving with JMM in fifty-eight countries in the Americas, Africa, Europe, and Asia. The JMM reports that in the last decade, they have made a more concentrated effort in the countries of the 10/40 window. In the last four years, a special initiative has been made to open eighteen new fields of ministry and to send 370 new workers in an effort to plant 200 new churches. The JMM further reports that seventy-eight of its missionaries are serving in North Africa, the Middle East, and Asia with some of these serving in eight countries in the Arab world.

While Brazilian Baptists are committed to the ministries of evangelism, discipleship, and church planting, they are also involved in other strategic and holistic ministries. The organization has made a special effort to recruit educational specialists, health professionals (doctors, dentists, and nurses), and humanitarian aid workers—especially those trained to work with women and children. Finally, the JMM has greatly emphasized sports ministry and has developed a soccer school strategy that integrates soccer skills and the gospel message.[50]

Interserve[51]

Interserve began in 1852 at the initiative of a group of British women concerned with the medical, educational, and spiritual needs of women in India.[52] Presently, workers from around thirty nationalities serve in forty different countries with a particular emphasis on the Arab world and Asia.[53] The Brazilian Interserve office opened in 2003 as an extension of Interserve Canada, which nurtured the new ministry in its initial years. At the same time, Interserve Brasil became official partners with the Centro Evangélico de Missões, a mission training school that was founded in 1983. The partnership is strategic in that mission candidates are able to

---

48. See "JMM." I am grateful to Barbara Hubbard for her translation.
49. Ibid.
50. Ibid.
51. All information in this section that is not otherwise documented is based on the responses of the Interserve leadership (participant 8).
52. See "Interserve."
53. Ibid., also "Centro Evangélico de Missões."

receive quality missiological training through the CEM and then be sent to the field via Interserve.

Interserve's stated vision is "to proclaim by word and action, that Jesus Christ is the Savior of all humanity."[54] Also, in partnership with local churches, Interserve desires to see transformation take place as the poorest of the poor in the Arab world and Asia encounter Christ. Interserve mobilizes Christians with medical, technical, and community development training to care for real human needs while also proclaiming the gospel.[55]

Prior to going to the field, Interserve workers have the opportunity to come to the CEM at Minas Gerais for one- to two-year program that includes studies in Bible, theology, missiology, psychology, world religions, and anthropology. The school also emphasizes training in holistic ministry (*missão integral*) and tentmaking.[56] Once workers are on the field, Interserve has a developing strategy of pastoral care that includes weekly communication, annual visits to workers on the field, and special care for furloughing missionaries, as well as an annual debrief. While this is primarily the work of the home office, Interserve has also set apart a leadership team on the field that oversees pastoral care.

At present Interserve Brasil has seven workers—including married couples and singles—on the field in the Arab world. The Interserve leadership reports that their primary areas of ministry include teaching and discipleship, prayer and spiritual warfare ministry, and developing local leaders. As Interserve workers use their professions to care for real needs, humanitarian work is also central to their efforts in ministry.

CCI-Brasil[57]

In 1987, Crossover Communications International was founded in the United States by Bill Jones and João Mordomo with a vision to "see God glorified among all peoples."[58] Initially focusing on short-term missions from North America, CCI began to emphasize sending long-term workers

---

54. See "JMM."

55. See "Centro Evangélico de Missões."

56. Ibid.

57. All information in this section that is not otherwise documented is based on the mission leaders responses of João Mordomo (participant 5) and my observations and our discussions during my visit at a CCI ministry training in Foz do Iguaçu and at the CCI headquarters in Curitiba, July 17–21.

58. See "CCI Brasil."

Brazilian Approaches to Mission

to Eastern Europe and to the former Soviet Union in 1990. In 1995, CCI began work in Moldova and, after a successful decade of church planting efforts, CCI Moldova was established in 2006 in order to send Moldovans in mission. Currently, CCI has offices in the United States, Australia, Moldova, and Brazil.[59]

Recognizing the great missions-sending potential of the Brazilian church, CCI-Brasil was founded in 1996 by Mordomo and a Brazilian pastor. In 1999, the group sent its first Brazilian workers to Turkey and, presently, CCI-Brasil's sole focus is mobilizing Brazilians for ministry in the Muslim world. Driven by the motto "we love God; we love God's global glory," CCI-Brasil's core values include authentic Christian living, biblical authority, and world evangelization. Also, the group emphasizes reaching Muslim people groups, pioneering church planting, and establishing local ministries out of those churches.[60]

What does CCI-Brasil offer in the way of pre-field training? Mordomo shared, "We do not have a formal training program. Rather, we assess where a candidate is and seek to fill the gaps of their training. Given the needs, we can offer training in Bible, spiritual life, and professional business-type training. Some of these needs can be met through partnering organizations closer to the candidate's home city." He continues, "If needed, we may ask a candidate to come to Curitiba for two years and be a part of a two-year program that includes Biblical training, missiology, church planting experience (inside of Brazil), and business and professional training. We have started a business consultancy to meet this [latter] need." Also, twice a year, CCI sponsors a Muslim ministry training week in the Southern city of Foz do Iguaçu in which participants receive classroom training on Islamic theology and culture as well as practical training in meeting Muslims at the local mosque and in the community.[61]

Presently, CCI-Brasil has sent eight Brazilian workers to serve in five different Arab-Muslim countries. Also, there is a team in Foz do Iguaçu that ministers to Arabs locally, but also facilitates the Muslim ministry training just mentioned. In terms of ministry strategy, CCI's priority is on church planting movements among Muslims—a ministry that implies a great emphasis on evangelism and discipleship. They're also committed to prayer and partnering with other existing mission efforts in a region.

59. Ibid.
60. Ibid.
61. As previously noted, I visited Mordomo in Foz do Iguaçu and observed this training firsthand July 17–20.

Finally, in light of its convictions concerning tentmaking and transformation in mission, CCI-Brasil has been quite innovative in developing Business as Mission strategies.[62]

Summary

While some Brazilian workers are being sent directly by their home churches to minister in the Arab world and other Brazilian organizations are also at work in the Arab-Muslim world,[63] the six organizations surveyed offer a helpful picture of the current status of Brazilian missions sending to this part of the world. In a survey of ten Brazilian mission leaders, including representatives from five of the six organizations just discussed,[64] the most prominent forms of ministry pursued on an organizational level were evangelism (100 percent), discipleship (87.5 percent), church planting (75 percent), humanitarian aid (62.5 percent), and prayer and spiritual warfare ministry (50 percent). Other key ministries include sports ministry and Business as Mission. Hence, these groups have been holistic in their approach in continuing to emphasize proclamation in mission while also ministering to human needs.

Each organization also demonstrates a clear commitment to offering its workers a thorough pre-field training experience. While some agencies have developed their own training and others send their personnel to be trained by partner organizations, the value for training is maintained. Most groups require that their workers spend at least one year in pre-field training, while others require even longer. Reflecting on how training has become more important in the overall Brazilian evangelical missions movement, Calze commented: "Before . . . there was a lot of willpower and not so much maturity, [and] the sending of a missionary was disorganized . . . there was no concern with the formation of the missionary [and] there were no missionary schools. Because of that the missionaries used to remain on the field for a very short time, some would return, which created a negative effect in their lives, and for the sending church. Today the missionaries in general are remaining much longer on the field." The

---

62. Mordomo has become a recognized authority on Business as Mission and his published works on the subject include "Unleashing the Brazilian Missionary Force," 219–39 and "Bossa Nova," 20–21.

63. Some other organizations at work in the Arab-Muslim world on some level include: Jovens Com Uma Missão (Youth with a Mission), Missão Horizontes (World Horizons), and Avante.

64. I was unable to interview the mission leadership of the JMM.

implication, of course, is that increased attention to training has helped Brazilians to remain on the field.

Brazilian missions organizations serving in the Arab world also seem committed to partnership. In a recent article, Bertil Ekström challenged the Brazilian church to pursue partnership in mission. While arguing that partnership leads to a better distribution of resources, guards against duplicating similar efforts, and results in a more efficient and sustainable work, he asserts that it also results in unity that ultimately gives more credibility to the gospel.[65] He writes, "If those who claim to have been transformed by a personal experience with Christ and indwelt by the same Holy Spirit cannot work together and live peacefully, then what type of image of God are they presenting?"[66] The noted Brazilian organizations seem to model what Ekström is advocating. CCI-Brasil and PMI have partnered with Antioquia, Kairos, and Avante for pre-field training, while PMI and Antioquia have also collaborated on the field. Though PMI and Antioquia focus their partnerships on other Ibero-American churches and organizations, they still greatly value collaboration in mission.[67]

Strengths of Brazilian Missions among Arabs

Having discussed the most common approaches to ministry by Brazilian workers as well as philosophies of mission of several Brazilian missions organizations, let us now analyze the apparent strengths of Brazilian evangelical missions among Arab-Muslims. This is largely based on the input of Brazilian missionaries and mission leaders.

First, Brazilians have apparently found success in building meaningful relationships with Arabs. While this shared aspect of Brazilian and Arab culture was laid out in the last chapter, Brazilians seem to have made the most of this cultural similarity in their ministries. Mordomo affirmed that Brazilian workers "take continual initiative in ministry [and] have intentionality . . . our success criteria is less numerical but more based on relationship initiative." Similarly, Amado added, "My definition of success [in ministry] is being able to have Muslims trust you for what you are, for

---

65. See Ekström, "Missões e Cia," 777–81.

66. Ibid., 778. English translation by Barbara Hubbard.

67. In 1994, Carillo reported that partnerships were not always easily formed between Latin American teams and organizations; thus, this observed characteristic of Brazilian missions represents an apparent improvement. See Carillo, "Struggles of Latin Americans," 197.

your life and faith, and through words and deeds, be able to communicate the love of God. Because of that, you see people coming to the Lord, you are discipling them, and eventually they become part of the local church. In light of this goal, most Brazilians have been very successful at building friendship with Muslims and earning their trust." When asked about their success in ministry among Arabs, one worker shared, "We believe that our biggest success in ministry is the true love for what we do and for the people," while another added, "I can look back and see a positive influence in the lives of people; people that I continue to stay in contact with."[68]

Second, many Brazilian workers seem to have done well at adapting to Arab culture. Facilitated in part by the general cultural proximity that exists between the cultures of Brazil and the Arab world, Brazilian workers have also worked to learn and adapt to the culture. Strategies such as PMI's Transcultural Training Course have certainly helped Brazilians to be at home in the host culture. Discussing the success of Brazilian missionaries in Arab contexts, Calze asserted: "I believe that this success comes as a result of the [Brazilian's] natural gifts to adapt himself to a context and particularly to Muslim culture. Because of that, they are able to share the gospel in an effective and holistic way." Timothy Halls, a North American who serves to mobilize Brazilians in global mission added: "They have been pioneers in new fields moving out by faith. They have connected to the local culture a bit faster than North Americans."[69]

Third, Brazilians seem to have also had success in evangelism. While conversion to Christ is often slow in the Arab-Muslim world and the results certainly cannot be compared to that of Brazil or Latin America, Brazilians have nevertheless reported success in seeing Arabs embrace Christ. Amado, who has been involved in Arab-Muslim ministry for three decades, observed: "Most [Brazilians] have been good evangelists. In the first seven to ten years, we did not see many people come to the Lord. Later, however, Brazilians began to see people come to Christ and disciple them." In a recent article, Ekström and Limpic asserted that evangelism was a general strength of the overall Brazilian evangelical missions movement.[70] It seems that the ability of Brazilians to connect relationally in the Arab context has facilitated evangelistic efforts.

---

68. This effective relational connection finds further support in Bertuzzi, *Latinos No Mundo Muçulmano*, 11, 20.

69. Ibid., 10, 14, 22.

70. See Ekström and Limpic, "Signs of Improvement," 32.

Fourth, Brazilians have found increasing success in planting churches among Arabs. In addition to the reports related earlier in this chapter, Brazilian mission leaders have also affirmed that this is an area of ministry where Brazilians have been successful. Halls related that "[Brazilians] have been pretty good at starting churches," while Mordomo affirmed that Brazilian ministry efforts have "often had fed into existing church planting movements."

A final area of strength in Brazilian missions work among Arabs has been excellence in humanitarian work. This is certainly due in part to the general character of Brazilian evangelicalism that has valued integrating gospel proclamation with caring for human needs. Also, it seems that as many Brazilian workers come to the Arab world with limited financial resources, they can more readily identify with the poor and needy that they are serving. One worker, when asked what he most looked forward to in his ministry, summarized the motivation of many Brazilian workers: "To work in social projects that show God's love in practical terms."

As Brazilian workers and mission leaders have reflected on their success in mission in the Arab world, it is remarkable that they have defined success more in terms of faithfulness, obedience, and perseverance as opposed to the concrete outcomes of ministry (i.e., numbers of converts or churches planted). One worker shared: "I believe that in God's eyes, the success is more linked to the faithfulness of the worker than to the numerical result of his ministry. When I am faithful and obedient to God's calling for my life I become successful and obtain success in what I do." Another worker added, "I am faithful everyday and I am being obedient; I do not want to measure success in numbers," while another shared, "[I am successful] knowing that I am just a tool since it is God who is at work in all; so I do not have the pressure of producing numbers." Finally, one Brazilian worker defined success as "when I am obedient and taking steps of faith . . . at these times I feel I have been faithful to my ministry."

From an organizational perspective, Missão Antioquia has also reflected on its criteria for success. Acknowledging that success in ministry can be due to many factors, the Antioquia leadership affirms that "we do not want to bring about success . . . at any cost." Careful not to give undue attention to charismatic personalities or human efforts, Antioquia attributes its success to God's grace and mercy at work in the ministries of a united team. Success in ministry should only result in God being exalted by His people; thus, there is never room for human boasting.[71]

71. See "Missão Antioquia." English translation by Cristina Boersma.

The success criteria of these Brazilian workers and Missão Antioquia certainly challenge some previously held notions of ministry success. Though some Brazilian churches expect their missionaries in the Arab world to have the same success that they would in Brazil—a context where there is a generally healthy response to the gospel—workers and mission leaders have resolved that the outcomes of ministry are outside of their control. Hence, their success criteria have become faithfulness, obedience, and perseverance in the task of mission.

Challenges for Brazilian Missions among Arabs

Having developed rapidly since the early 1970s, the Brazilian evangelical missions movement is still relatively young and not without its challenges. In this section, we will address four major issues facing Brazilian missions efforts in the Arab-Muslim world: Brazilian church support, language acquisition, financial support, and women's issues in the Arab world. Following surveys and interviews conducted with fifty-five Brazilian transcultural workers and mission leaders, these issues emerged as the most critical to Brazilian mission work in the Arab world.

These are certainly not the only issues facing Brazilian missions in the Arab world or in the broader global context. Many leaders are also concerned with pre-field training, ongoing training for current missionaries, combating attrition rates, and ministering to workers on the field (pastoral or member care). Because these issues seem to be receiving adequate treatment elsewhere,[72] the following discussion will be limited to the four noted areas. In each case, the problem will be defined and explored after which I will propose solutions, based on Brazilian perspectives, toward resolving the issue and moving forward.

---

72. The issues of pre-field training have been explored in Itiokia, "Third World Missionary Training," 111–20, many of the editions of the Brazilian missiological journal *Capacitando*, and Finley's dissertation, "Contextualized Training for Missionaries." Also, pre-field training, ongoing training, attrition issues, and member care have been discussed in Lewis, "Designing the ReMap Project," 77–83; Ted Limpic, "Brazilian Missionaries," 143–54; Ekström, "The Selection Process," 183–93; and Adiwardana, "Formal and Non-Formal Pre-Field Training," 207–215. On a practical level, Ted Limpic, after a long career in ministry in Brazil, has relocated to Spain and essentially functions as a member care specialist for Brazilian workers in the region. Finally, a number of Brazilian missions organizations working in the Arab world (Missão Antioquia, PMI, CCI Brasil, and Interserve among others) have developed deliberate member care strategies for their personnel.

Brazilian Church Support

The first major challenge faced by Brazilian workers serving in the Arab world is a general lack of support from their sending churches in Brazil. This can be understood in at least four ways. First, many Brazilian evangelical churches seem to have little vision for global missions. According to one Brazilian missionary from the Pentecostal tradition, the great emphasis on prosperity theology in Brazilian Pentecostal churches has turned church planting into a great competition.[73] As some Brazilian church leaders are pursuing their own agendas, there is little vision for global efforts, especially in the Arab-Muslim world where the response to the gospel is certainly much slower than it is in Brazil. Though some Pentecostal churches are taken by a theology that has little room for missions, other churches (both Pentecostal and historic) define missions as evangelism in their local communities or planting new churches in Brazil within their denomination. Finally, others are simply consumed with the great needs facing their communities and have little energy to think about the global mission task.[74]

Second, many of the Brazilian churches that have sent workers to the Arab world have failed to provide pastoral care and encouragement for their missionaries.[75] Commenting on the general lack of care and support, one worker shared,[76] "Our church gives us very little encouragement and support," while another frankly related, "Church care—what is that?" Other workers have desired that their home churches be more connected to their ministries in the Arab world. One Brazilian shared, "It would have been nice if my home church was more understanding of my ministry," and another added, "[I would like] more involvement from my local church—participating and being part of my work."

Some workers especially long to feel more connected to their home churches as they are serving on the field. One worker related, "In general I should say that the communication could become a lot better . . . with

---

73. This was related to me in a personal conversation during a visit, January 6–9, 2010.

74. These thoughts were related by Calze in conversation, July 21, 2009. See also, Mordomo, "Unleashing the Brazilian Missionary Force," 227. Also, Carillo ("Struggles of Latin Americans," 196) discusses this challenge on a broader Latin American level.

75. Adiwardana (Adiwardana, "Formal and Non-Formal Pre-Field Training," 208) suggests that lack of church support is one of the leading reasons for missionary attrition among Brazilian transcultural workers in general.

76. All responses were gathered from surveys and interviews. See appendices.

the local church." Another worker shared, "My church is not so used to communicating with me by email or letters," but then she added, "When I go back to Brazil I feel their love and encouragement." Feeling a similar sense of "out of sight, out of mind," one missionary stated, "My church has given less care. Once you are gone, you can be forgotten."

Other workers, convinced that their churches have not forgotten them, have recognized that their churches simply do not understand fully how to be missions- sending churches. One worker shared, "Our church prays for us but they do not understand us or missions in general," while another related, "They [the church] only send money; they do not understand these other types of support."

Third, many Brazilian congregations fail to understand the difficulties of ministry in the Arab-Muslim world, including a generally slow response to the gospel. In reality, many Brazilian workers already struggle with feelings of discouragement because of this lack of fruit. Amado said that the biggest issue facing Brazilian missionaries is "discouragement—overcoming the sense of uselessness and struggling with the lack of fruit (e.g., 1–2 people coming to Christ every few years)." Halls added, "Some [workers] have struggled with the lack of fruitfulness in their ministries and they have moved to other fields perhaps prematurely." One Brazilian worker reflected honestly, "Sometimes, we feel discouraged and tired because we do not see immediate results, especially if we compare the results to those of our home country."

Hence, the failure of Brazilian churches to appreciate these challenges only compounds the sense of discouragement for Brazilian missionaries. Mordomo shared that a great challenge for Brazilian workers was "dealing with the expectations of their sending churches in Brazil who expect the results of Brazil in the Arab-Muslim world." Silas Tostes added, "The biggest difficulty is the lack of vision by the churches that want to send missionaries only to areas where there is freedom and churches are able to be planted [freely]." One Brazilian worker shared candidly: "It would be great if our church and supporters understood that work in the Arab-Muslim world is different from Brazil. Our church wants to see immediate results. If they understood our context better, that would be an encouragement to us."

While some Brazilian workers have been discouraged by the lack of understanding from their churches, others have actually felt the pressure to produce results. One missionary shared: "Our sending church was slow to send us out because they want to see quick results. Sometimes, the church pressures us to work more aggressively to see results but we cannot do that here." Another worker admitted, "I worry about sharing a lack of results with the church." Finally, one couple communicated obvious discouragement: "We cannot fail in our mission because we are afraid that our church will not send any more missionaries to the Arab world."

Fourth, many Brazilian churches have not regarded encouraging missionaries as their responsibility; rather, they have abdicated this ministry to the partnering missions organization. One Brazilian missionary shared: "My missions organization gave great support and help. My sending church in Brazil did not understand how to be supportive of a missionary on the field." Another worker shared, "[Pastoral care was] very adequate from the agency; inadequate from the church," while another related, "From the agency [pastoral care] is good; but the local church is non-existent." Though some workers reported that their organizations also failed to provide pastoral care and encouragement, most acknowledged that their missions agencies at least made efforts while their sending churches did very little.

From this survey, it is evident that a great challenge for Brazilian missions in the Arab world is that many Brazilian evangelical churches struggle to have a vision for the Arab-Muslim world, and they often fail to provide pastoral care and encouragement for their missionaries. I would like to suggest three areas for improvement—solutions that are already being pursued in part by Brazilian mission leaders and workers.

First, as many Brazilian evangelical churches (and their pastors) are in need of a greater vision and conviction for engagement in the task of global missions, they must be continually exposed to and educated about the needs of the world. At present, a number of Brazilian mission leaders are hard at work in this task. For instance, Silas Tostes and missions-minded pastor Edison Queiroz regularly speak throughout the country communicating a global vision to churches. Daniel Calze, who refers to Brazilian pastors as an "unreached people group," regularly meets with pastors and speaks at churches about partnering with PMI in the Muslim world. In addition to directing PMI Brasil, Calze also pastors a small Presbyterian congregation that he is endeavoring to mentor in global mission.[77] As noted, beginning in 2009, the "Perspectives" course was offered at the headquarters of Missão Antioquia and in a few other cities around Brazil. This church-based strategy certainly has the great potential to influence pastors and congregations toward being more missions minded.

77. Related to me in personal conversation with Calze, July 21, 2009.

While these strategies for educating churches in missions should certainly continue, two further ideas should be considered. First, it seems important to strengthen the missiological offerings at Brazilian theological seminaries where pastors are being trained. Perhaps "Perspectives," a course rich in theological, historical, cultural, and strategic studies that is also quite reproducible in the local church context, could be offered in the Brazilian seminaries. Second, it would be strategic for Brazilian pastors to visit missionaries sent from their churches on the field in the Arab world.[78] As the pastor's global vision is increased, this will surely translate to the congregation. Also, the visit could serve as a means to encourage and offer pastoral care to Brazilian workers.[79]

Second, as Brazilian workers often feel disconnected from their sending congregations, some of the burden for establishing this connection lies with the missionaries. Prior to going to the field, are Brazilian workers serving faithfully in their local churches and patiently cultivating a global vision? One Brazilian worker shared, "Our church had no vision for missions . . . [so] I worked [for several years] in the missions ministry of the church." Indeed, some aspiring missionaries will need to invest a number of years serving in their local congregation and helping that church to develop a global vision. While PMI encourages churches to develop teams to help missionaries with their finances and to facilitate communication with the church, the missionary can certainly work to establish these teams through his/her network of relationships within the church.[80]

Third, the relationship between the local church and the missions agency needs to be clarified. Recognizing this as a priority for his organization, Mordomo shared, "We need to continue to work on partnerships with Brazilian churches in sending missionaries. Some churches want to control everything that our missionaries do; others simply dump them on us and expect us to do everything. So we want to continue to work on more healthy and strategic partnerships." Similarly, Robson Ramos,

---

78. See Carillo, "Struggles of Latin Americans," 196

79. I observed this strategy modeled well (July 19, 2009) in a small Brazilian congregation in Southern Brazil as the pastor was preparing to visit a missionary couple sent from the church. Prior to the visit, the church organized a fund-raising dinner and collected a generous offering to help the couple in their work. During the Sunday service, their ministry was highlighted and the congregation interceded for them. Church members were also invited to write encouraging notes and send special gifts from home. The pastor, of course, went with the intention of praying for and encouraging the couple.

80. See Carillo, "Struggles of Latin Americans" 196; similar thoughts were realted by Calze in conversation, July 21, 2009.

affirmed the need to "establish a comprehensive understanding of the role of the mission agency and the local church in the missionary's life." While no quick solutions can be proposed, it seems that as mission leaders continue to honor the local churches and initiate ongoing communication with pastors, then trust and partnership will result.

Language Acquisition

A second significant challenge for Brazilians serving in Arab contexts is that many transcultural workers struggle to learn and master the Arabic language. While Arabic is certainly a difficult language for anyone to learn, let us explore the reasons why Brazilians are having difficulty in this area of ministry and, based on the input of Brazilian missionaries and leaders, propose some solutions for moving forward.

In evaluating their own abilities in Arabic, only 7 percent of those surveyed felt that their proficiency in Arabic was excellent, while another 18.6 percent indicated that they were doing well. The vast majority (74.5 percent) reported that their Arabic level was average (46.5 percent), below average (14 percent), or poor (14 percent).

Indeed, some Brazilians have excelled at Arabic, including Amado, who reported that his level of Arabic was "between well and excellent." He continues: "I wanted to learn classical Arabic but I used colloquial Arabic. I later studied Koranic Arabic in England and then studied Modern Standard Arabic in Brazil." He adds, "We did not learn French because it was too easy for us." It should be noted that French is the second language of most of the North African countries and many international Christian workers have been tempted to use French in their ministries because it is easier to learn than Arabic. As Portuguese is similar to French, this could be especially enticing to Brazilian workers serving in the region.

Other Brazilians reported that they are able to use Arabic to communicate the gospel and to interact well in their communities. One worker shared, "I would say that [my Arabic] is good enough for communication in general [and] in order [to do] the ministry we are involved in." Indicating that cultural immersion was a key to his language acquisition, he continued: "There was not a good language school that could teach the Arab dialect in the city I lived in when I first got here (there was no written language), and I moved to the interior right after I got married. I learned by dealing directly with the people." One worker shared, "I can get around (shop, etc.) and I can share my testimony in Arabic," while another added, "I feel free to speak to the children I work with [in my ministry]." Finally, one female worker related, "I can communicate in the market and get by," while another worker jokingly said, "I can even argue with people [in Arabic]."

Some Brazilians related that they had a basic understanding of Arabic but that it was ultimately insufficient for communicating the gospel. One missionary shared: "I can certainly get around but I cannot go that deep in Arabic (e.g., for evangelism or a Bible study). I spent two years studying Arabic . . . and I have not had any Christian vocabulary in my study." Another related, "I can begin to express myself and do my job in Arabic [but] it is difficult to share the gospel in Arabic." Other Brazilians admitted that their limited language ability has forced them to pass up opportunities to minister to Arab friends. One worker shared, "My language ability has been limited which has made me reticent to reach out to people," and another confessed: "Sometimes I pass up opportunities to speak more deeply about the gospel. I want to be better in Arabic."

When asked about their biggest failure in ministry in the Arab world, many Brazilians shared that it was failing to learn the Arabic language well. One worker honestly related, "This has been the most difficult area for me; I truly feel frustrated with my proficiency in Arabic," while another shared, "Learning the language is a huge failure." Another worker commented that "language has been difficult; especially studying classical Arabic and colloquial Arabic at the same time." Finally, one mission leader, reflecting on the work of his personnel on the field, indicated that they "could do a better job if they had . . . if they were more apt to learn different languages."[81]

While many Brazilians have acknowledged their struggles in learning Arabic, let us consider at least six reasons for why this is the case. First, as previously alluded to, some Brazilians have been hindered in their Arabic study due to financial reasons because they have not had the means to pay for Arabic language school tuition or to hire a private tutor. One missionary related: "[I have failed at] language learning due to my low financial support. I can't afford the lessons! What I know now I've learned with my local friends and by myself." Similarly, another worker added: "I have been studying Arabic for one year. The big challenge is that I have not always had financial support for Arabic."

---

81. Both Bertuzzi (*Latinos No Mundo Muçulmano*, 20) and Carillo ("Struggles of Latin Americans," 195–96) affirmed that language learning is a struggle for Latin American missionaries in general in the Arab-Muslim world.

Second, some Brazilians have neglected language study because they have been preoccupied with other activities. This is certainly true for Brazilian women as they endeavor to balance language learning with caring for children and taking care of the home. One woman shared, "Language learning is difficult [for] a mom with kids," while another related, "I have been trying to spend more time in learning the language but my daily activities take too much of my time." Other Brazilian workers indicated that their involvement in ministry activities and humanitarian work prevented them from investing the necessary time in language study. One worker shared: "I studied the local language for only two years, as I was also involved with the activities with the organization I belong to. During my second period here after two years, I got settled in . . . and got busy with the activities with the organization." Even Amado, who eventually attained an excellent level in Arabic, shared, "I was too busy and over committed [in ministry] before I reached a good language level."

Third, some Brazilian workers have admitted that they have simply lacked the focus and dedication to persevere in Arabic studies. One worker attributed his poor level in Arabic to a "lack of dedication in studying the local language," while another confessed, "I can be undisciplined about language learning." Finally, another Brazilian admitted that she was simply "comfortable with communicating the language on an average level" and was therefore not motivated to master the language.

Fourth, some Brazilians have not learned Arabic very well because they have been able to function in another language. One tentmaker employed by an international company in the Middle East shared, "I learned only a little Arabic as Portuguese and English were my work languages." Another Brazilian worker commented: "Unfortunately, this [learning Arabic] is an area where I haven't grown much. I chose to speak English with the local people and because of that I didn't learn the local language as I should have." It became apparent, after surveying several Brazilians working with Arabs in Southern Brazil, that nearly all are using Portuguese as their ministry language. One worker shared, "My ministry in Southern Brazil to Arabs is in Portuguese. I am studying Arabic though." A pastor who planted a bilingual Portuguese- and Arabic-speaking church related: "I carried out my ministry mostly in Portuguese. My sermons in the church (in Southern Brazil) were given in Portuguese and translated into Arabic."

Fourth, many Brazilians have not persevered in mastering Arabic because of a desire for immediate results. This general Brazilian tendency of *immediatismo* has certainly been a hindrance to Brazilians in other areas of ministry and is the reason why some have not continued in ministry in the Arab world. One Brazilian worker offered this critical reflection: "Brazilians come with high expectations and want to see immediate Brazilian results. We need to adjust our expectations. We need to be humble and patient and see how God will use us here. We need to work more with local people. And we need to come and do a better job studying language and culture." While visiting some Brazilian teams in the Arab world, I interviewed one Brazilian couple that was investing time discipling other Brazilians and Portuguese-speaking Arabs. While on one hand, this seems to be a valuable ministry, on the other, it appears that this couple is taken by a desire for immediate results while their progress in Arabic study is certainly suffering. As previously discussed, this tendency is also stoked by Brazilian churches that expect immediate results from their missionaries in the Arab world. One Brazilian couple shared, "They [our sending church] want us to quickly learn Arabic but they don't offer to support us in language classes."

A final reason that Brazilians seem to encounter difficulty in Arabic study is that they struggle with homesickness. Commenting on this sense of yearning (*saudade*)—a particularly strong tendency in Brazilian culture—one mission leader commented that Brazilian missionaries tend to "miss their families a lot (Brazilians are usually very close to their families)." Similarly, one worker shared, "I feel the great distance of being away from my family." As Brazilian workers attempt to cope with missing family and friends, some tend to gravitate toward other Brazilians to meet these relational needs. As a result, cultural immersion, language acquisition, and ministry relationships are hindered.

Having made the case that many Brazilian workers are struggling to acquire Arabic, let us propose some solutions for improvement. First, some Brazilian mission leaders and workers have suggested that a more deliberate program of linguistics and Arabic study should be a part of the pre-field training for Brazilian missionaries. One worker shared, "I regret not having some Arabic studies prior to leaving Brazil for the first time," while a member of the Missão Horizontes Radical Project commented that their pre-field training "could also have included some Arabic language training with it." Mordomo suggested that "pre-field linguistic experience" be added to their organization's pre-field training. He added, "This may take the form of a version of LAMP (Language Application Made

Brazilian Approaches to Mission

Practical)[82] here in Brazil; or, we could send Brazilians to the university here in Brazil to study Arabic."

Second, some Brazilian workers have strongly emphasized that studying Arabic should be the priority of all workers during their initial years in country. While a number of Brazilian organizations take cultural immersion and language study very seriously, one worker still commented that "we need to come and do a better job studying language and culture." Another worker, apparently sensitive to the distractions and challenges of simply living in an Arab country, firmly stated, "I believe that everyone who comes to the Arab world must [completely] dedicate their time to the study of the language during the first two years."

Third, as part of their pre-field cultural training, it would be wise for Brazilian mission candidates to reflect on their "Brazilianness" and to be aware of cultural tendencies such as *saudade* and *immediatismo* that could prove to be a barrier in their cultural adaptation and language acquisition in the Arab world. Don Finley's thesis on contextualized missionary training for Brazilian workers would serve as a great point of reflection in this exercise.

Fourth, Brazilian workers should raise a special budget for language learning for their first two years in country. As they share this need with their sending church and donors, this would also be a great opportunity to educate their senders on the long-term ministry benefits of language learning, which is itself a ministry.

Finally, some international organizations such as World Horizons and Operation Mobilization have sent their Brazilian personnel to Britain in order to learn English—the lingua franca of the mission community in most countries. The problem is that Brazilians are using up precious language learning energy on English before they begin to work on Arabic, which is certainly the more difficult language.[83] My suggestion is that Brazilian teams in the Arab world abandon this practice and focus their energy first on Arabic. While communication with the international mission community is important, one suggestion is that bilingual intermediaries—including Brazilians fluent in other languages—be appointed to facilitate communication.[84]

---

82. LAMP refers to the course and book by Brewster and Brewster, *Language Application Made Practical*.

83. The general difficulty for Latins to learn multiple languages in order to serve on multi-cultural teams has been raised by Bertuzzi ("Internationalization or 'Anglonization' of Missions," 15).

84. In one Arab context, a Spanish-speaking North American serves on a team

Brazilian Evangelical Missions in the Arab World

Financial Support

A third area of struggle for Brazilian missionaries serving in the Arab world continues to be raising adequate financial support. Historically, the Brazilian evangelical church has not seen itself as a financial supporter of missions until relatively recently. Osvaldo Prado recalled the response of a Brazilian church leader in the 1980s when challenged with the idea of involving his church in supporting Brazilian missionaries: "Forget this idea pastor! This business of missions is not for us in the Third World. Mission is for the churches of North America and Europe who have tradition in this area and the financial resources."[85] Yet, Timothy Halls reflected some optimism over how the Brazilian church had advanced in this area. He writes: "Compared to the mid-1970s when no Brazilians were raising support, [today] most are able to raise support from churches on some level. They are becoming support raisers and are finding solutions to this challenge." Both Bertil Ekström and Ted Limpic point to a much stronger Brazilian economy that has put churches in a better financial position to send and support more missionaries.[86]

While there are certainly signs of improvement in the Brazilian church's ability to support its missionaries, it was established in the last chapter that financial struggles continue to plague Brazilian workers in the Arab world. In a study in 1995, Limpic wrote that "Brazilian agencies cite 'lack of financial support' as the great single cause of missionary attrition."[87] In 2009, Halls still admitted that "some [Brazilian workers] have really struggled with their finances—some have had to return because of this; others could not return because of finances and stayed [on the field]." Amado added that the greatest difficulty facing Brazilian workers in the Arab world was "the long-term problem of financial support and future financial planning."

Though Brazil's greatly improved economy is certainly enabling churches to give more generously to missions, most Brazilian workers in the Arab world still struggle financially. Given this reality, what models

---

with Latin Americans. Because he is bilingual, he is able to facilitate communication between his teammates and the broader mission community. The model of this Spanish-speaking team could also be helpful for Brazilians.

85. See Prado, "A New Way of Sending Missionaries," 52.

86. See Ekström, "Brazilian Sending," 371–72; and Limpic, "Brazilian Missionaries," 144.

87. See Limpic, "Brazilian Missionaries," 149; also Downey, "Ibero-Americans Reaching Arab-Muslims."

should the Brazilian missions movement be pursuing for financially supporting its missionaries? Currently, most missions organizations are still employing a Professional Missionary Model (PMM). That is, the missionary, who typically has Bible college or seminary training, raises his or her support from churches and individuals.[88] The perspectives of mission leaders currently mobilizing Brazilians for work in the Arab world are particularly insightful. Amado, emphasizing a conviction that funds should not be raised from North America, stated: "Each worker raise[s] his/her own support. Brazilians are to raise 100 percent of their support from Brazil." Another leader, highlighting the sending church's role in raising support for the missionary, related, "The local church should be the main supporter of any missionary, with help from other people and organizations." Calze concurred, "We believe that the local church is the main organization in charge of raising support for the missionary. Their priority and privilege is to send out missionaries to the field, and also to support them materially and spiritually in all they need while serving abroad. As an organization we help the missionary to raise support, but we do not take full responsibility for it."

While it is impressive that mission leaders long for Brazilian churches to be the primary senders and supporters for Brazilian missionaries, there seem to be some problems with the PMM in the Brazilian context. First, Robson Ramos argues that this model is based on a nineteenth- and twentieth-century North American model of missions—a socio-economic reality that Brazil has never experienced.[89] Mordomo adds that in the history of Christian missions, the North American paradigm has certainly not been normative. Second, Mordomo argues that though the Brazilian economy has significantly recovered from its crises of the 1980s and 1990s and has even become a leading exporter of goods, the country is still greatly affected by poverty, unemployment, and inflation.[90] Thus, he is skeptical that the Brazilian evangelical church could be the sole source of financial support for missions, especially as the number of Brazilian workers continues to increase. He concludes rather frankly: "Any Brazilian missionary who seeks to serve in the PMM mold faces an uphill battle and runs a significant risk of never achieving critical financial mass and finally being able to serve among the people to whom he or she is called. And any

---

88. See Mordomo, "Unleashing the Brazilian Missionary Force," 224–25; also Ekström and Limpic, "Signs of Improvement," 31–32.

89. See Ramos, "Tentmaking and Missions," 49.

90. See Mordomo, "Unleashing the Brazilian Missionary Force," 226.

Brazilian mission agency that chooses to perpetuate this model will very possibly continue to struggle year after year to place even a single worker or family in a cross-cultural ministry."[91]

Concluding that the PMM is not a viable paradigm for Brazilian workers, Ramos and Mordomo have proposed other models. While not objecting to the church providing some level of support for missionaries, Ramos suggests "a bi-vocational model" in which "only a few should be fully financially supported." He insists that all mission candidates receive a university degree and develop marketable skills—the basis for a career in Brazil as well as in the countries of the Arab world. Also, he is quite burdened that Brazilian professionals who have already proven themselves in the marketplace in Brazil would go as tentmakers to the Arab world.[92]

Reflecting on the current strategy of his organization (CCI-Brasil), Mordomo relates, "More and more because of the economic situation of Brazil, we are taking more of a Business as Mission approach to help with support." Though a thorough discussion of this philosophy is beyond the scope of the present work, let us highlight some of Mordomo's key thoughts on BAM as it relates to Brazilians serving in the Arab world. Emphasizing that BAM is a holistic strategy that integrates work and mission, Mordomo supports BAM's philosophy of pursuing profit and sustainability.[93] The business platform enables the worker to leave Brazil more quickly, to gain access into an otherwise restricted country, to live there with credibility, and ultimately, to use the business platform as a means of transformation.[94] While international business is undoubtedly a daunting task, even for those with business experience in their own country, Mordomo is confident that with their entrepreneurial spirit (*jeitinho brasileiro*), Brazilian workers will be successful in BAM initiatives.[95]

Though tentmaking and Business as Mission strategies are still rather new concepts for the Brazilian missions movement, some workers have reported success. One worker shared "[I enjoy] using my tentmaking job as a place to show God's love and speak about it . . . just letting God work in my life." One fully self-supported tentmaker in Southern Brazil shared,

91. See Mordomo, "Unleashing the Brazilian Missionary Force," 225. Ramos expresses similar concerns in Ramos, "Tentmaking and Missions," 49. See also Mordomo, "Bossa Nova," 20; and Heikes, "Una Perspectiva Diferente," 80.

92. Related to me in personal conversation, July 29, 2009; see also Ramos, "Tentmaking and Missions," 50–51.

93. See Mordomo, "Unleashing the Brazilian Missionary Force," 231–32.

94. Ibid., 227–29.

95. See Mordomo, "Bossa Nova," 21.

"I have a good place in the community with my tentmaking job; it is a credible platform." Finally, reflecting on the value of developing a sustainable platform, one worker related that he looked forward to "building strong platforms to give more [opportunities] for others who will come."

The majority of Brazilian missionaries in the Arab world continue to pursue the traditional North American model of raising support and, as noted, the majority still struggle financially. While Brazilian churches ought to continue giving financially to support missionaries, alternative strategies such as tentmaking and Business as Mission should also be embraced. In light of this, let us consider six suggestions for moving forward in this area. First, in addition to theological and missiological training, Brazilian missionary candidates ought to receive a university diploma and professional training in order to have marketable skills to work in the Arab world. Ramos has made a strong case for this in his writing and teaching since the early 1990s.[96] Though this paradigm shift does seem to be slow in the making, some organizations such as Missão Antioquia are encouraging their personnel to receive more professional skills.

Second, more Brazilian churches and organizations will want to follow the model of Interserve, which seeks to help Brazilian professionals find jobs in the Arab world.[97] Able to support themselves financially, these workers are more naturally integrated into the community and are able to minister in word and deed.

Third, the BAM ideas of CCI-Brasil and others seem to have much promise. Mordomo asserts that Brazilian workers should strategically plan to market Brazilian products such as coffee, soccer, and Brazilian martial arts, and even consider opening Brazilian churrascarias (barbecues) around the Arab and Muslim world.[98] As CCI-Brasil develops their business consultancy strategy, they might consider networking with Brazilian Christian businessmen, including Arab-Brazilians, who are already doing business in the countries of the Arab world.[99]

---

96. See Ramos, "Tentmaking and Missions," 48, 51; also Ekström and Limpic, "Signs of Improvement," 32; and Ekström, "The Selection Process," 189–90.

97. See Ramos, "Tentmaking and Missions," 50–51.

98. See Mordomo, "Bossa Nova," 21. The idea of opening a Brazilian churrascaria is not at all strange. While visiting one city in the Middle East in 2010, I learned that there were two churrascarias there.

99. Karam ("Distinguishing Arabesques," 335–36) shows that some Arab-Brazilians have been involved in consulting non-Arab Brazilians in doing business in the Arab world.

Fourth, it would be strategic for Brazilian missions organizations and teams to network and partner with Brazilian professionals already contracted to work in the Arab world. Teams could provide fellowship, encouragement, and even training in skills such as evangelism, discipleship, and church planting. On the other hand, established professionals could mentor new teams and organizations on how to work successfully in an Arab country. One Brazilian Christian whose job took him to the Arab world, reflected this need: "I worked in an international company in the Middle East . . . It would be good for Brazilian tentmakers to have more training and preparation to minister in similar contexts to ours."

Fifth, BAM projects could be pursued through Brazilians partnering with North American and other international Christian workers. Halls shared that the greatest struggle of his teams was being able "to establish a viable, long-term platform." Though Silas Tostes has argued that Brazilian missionaries should only raise financial support within Brazil, he is in favor of Brazilians accepting jobs and collaborating in businesses with North Americans or other internationals who may have a network of investors to help launch a new business venture.[100] Hence, some BAM and tentmaking projects may serve to facilitate appropriate partnerships between the Northern and Southern countries in global mission.

Finally, while the first five suggestions have related to alternative forms of raising financial support (BAM, tentmaking, etc.), I would like to propose one idea that is actually closer to the traditional model. In light of Timothy Halls's assertion that "there are probably 1000 Brazilian evangelical churches in the U.S., many of these with missions minded pastors and congregations," what if North American Brazilian congregations began to support their fellow Brazilians in global mission? These churches are certainly economically stronger and in a much better position to support missionaries than the churches in Brazil. Though money would be coming from Brazilians in North America, it would not be coming from North Americans and thus, dependency from the North would be avoided.

Brazilian Women in the Arab World

A final significant challenge for Brazilian missions in the Arab world relates specifically to the difficulties faced by Brazilian women in Arab contexts. In the previous chapter, it was shown that Brazilian women struggle with how Arab women are treated in male-dominated societies; however,

---

100. Related to me in conversation, July 23, 2009.

Brazilian women missionaries also face similar obstacles. Mordomo indicated that the greatest challenge faced by CCI-Brasil missionaries was "our women missionaries suffering harassment [by men] in Arab contexts."

What are the specific issues faced by Brazilian women? First, they have reported feeling a great sense of disrespect from Arab men. This has most often been communicated through harassing words, gestures, and even inappropriate touching. Though Harrison reports that such behavior is not uncommon in Brazilian culture, Brazilian women missionaries—particularly single women—maintain that this treatment can be quite unbearable at times.[101] One single worker shared, "It was really hard to live in [my Arab context] as a single woman; [there is] no respect from the men," and another added: "It has not been easy being a single woman working in the Arab culture. We suffer discrimination, lack of respect, etc., that forces us many times to do things that are not allowed for a woman to do so that we can be respected."

While some of this discrimination is certainly due to a traditional Arab disregard for women in general, it also seems that Brazilian women are portrayed through the media as being morally loose. Van der Meer writes, "Brazilian women are viewed in other countries and cultures as sensual and easy, thanks to Globo (TV) soap operas and Carnival."[102] Karam adds that Brazilian Arabs inside of Brazil also tend to look down on Brazilian women. In the country's famous Arab clubs, Brazilian women are hired to entertain through traditional Arab dance because the men want to preserve the modesty of Arab women.[103] A Brazilian pastor of Lebanese descent also affirmed this Arab lack of regard for Brazilian women in Southern Brazil.[104]

For many Brazilian women serving in the Arab world, this lack of respect has led to feelings of insecurity and fear and has rendered some women less effective in their ministries. One worker shared honestly, "Sometimes we feel so insecure and scared and because of that you don't do as much as you can."

A second area of struggle for Brazilian women is that they feel restricted by the lack of social freedom in the Arab world. Finley writes, "The issue of gender roles and restrictions presents challenges for female

---

101. See Harrison, *Behaving Brazilian*, 60–61.

102. See Van der Meer, "A Vida dos Missionários," 35. English translation by Barbara Hubbard.

103. See Karam, "Distinguishing Arabesques," 286.

104. Related to me in personal conversation, July 21, 2009.

missionaries going to serve in Muslim countries, especially among Arabs."[105] For example, many Brazilian women find it difficult because they cannot express themselves freely in public or in mixed company. Others encounter difficulty with more traditional Arab cultures that frown upon women leaving the house without a male guardian. Finally, some women have felt restricted by having to adopt a more modest dress code in the Arab world, while others have continued dress in a more Brazilian manner, which has resulted in more harassment.[106] These issues of social freedom seem especially difficult for single Brazilian women.

In light of these difficulties faced by Brazilian women, which has often resulted in many workers not continuing in their ministries,[107] let us explore six suggestions for moving forward—some of which have originated from Brazilian women themselves. First, in terms of perspective, some Brazilian women have reported that reflecting on their own difficulties in the Arab world has actually helped them to empathize with the plight of the Arab women whom they desire to reach with the gospel. While not diminishing their own difficulties, these Brazilian women have allowed their suffering to become a source of compassion. When asked what she most looked forward to in her ministry, one worker replied, "seeing Arab women recovering their self esteem, recovering their happiness, and the feeling that they are important."

Second, also in terms of perspective, some Brazilian women are regarding this cultural difficulty as an opportunity to persevere by faith. Reflecting on her ministry, one woman shared her hope of "overcoming the fear of being here as a single woman especially because of the men [being] able to trust God with the security challenges and to be discerning; knowing that God has me here not just to survive but to live well regardless of the results; and seeing doors open and seeing women respond to Christ."

Third, it seems imperative that Brazilian missions organizations working in the Arab world would include a special track for women's issues in their pre-field training. Perhaps using Nida's three-culture model as a point of reference,[108] Brazilian women mission candidates should first reflect on their Brazilianness and what it means to be a woman in Brazil.[109]

105. See Finley, "Contextualized Training for Missionaries," 162.

106. See Bertuzzi, *Latinos No Mundo Muçulmano*, 17, 50–51.

107. In 1995, Ted Limpic ("Brazilian Missionaries," 148) reported that the attrition rate was particularly high among single women.

108. Cited in Hesselgrave and Rommen, *Contextualization*, 200.

109. Finley's thesis ("Contextualized Training for Missionaries") would certainly serve as a helpful starting point in this exercise.

Second, they would benefit from studying the Arab family and gaining a profound understanding of the roles of women in their host culture. Also, it would be helpful to reflect on how Brazilian women are perceived in the Arab world. Finally, they ought to study the Scriptures for perspectives on the Christian family and what it means to be a Christian woman. As this process continues, Scripture should serve as the basis for evaluating and transforming both Brazilian and Arab culture.

Fourth, Brazilian women missionaries—aware of their own Brazilianness and the roles of women in Arab culture—should enter the host culture with a learner's posture and a willingness to adapt. While organizations like PMI have been innovative with its in-country Transcultural Training Course, at least one Brazilian woman feels that the women need to be more deliberate in this area. She asserts: "We need to come and do a better job studying language and culture. Most Brazilian women come and hate the Arab culture at first." Specifically, Brazilian women must be willing to identify with Arab women in their general social freedoms (e.g., not traveling out alone after dark). Also, they should endeavor to dress according to the standards of modesty in the host culture. Though it is not necessary that Brazilian women take the veil or adhere to a strict Muslim dress code, it is imperative that they relinquish the right to dress as they would in Brazil.[110] As they reflect on biblical principles of modesty, Brazilian women ought to seek guidance from mature Arab Christian women in the host culture on matters of dress as well as other women's issues.

Fifth, Brazilian women should plan to overcome the negative and immoral perception of Brazilian women through a winsome moral testimony. One pastor in Southern Brazil remarked that over time, his wife began to be greatly respected by Arab men in the community because of her good testimony as a woman, wife, and mother. Bertuzzi reports that some Latin American single women have been a vibrant witness to single Arab women on account of their evident hope, peace, and joy in Christ as well as their contentment with being single.[111]

Finally, in light of the high rate of attrition among single Brazilian women missionaries, Brazilian missions organizations, mission teams, and churches should especially consider the needs of single women in their member care strategies. One single worker shared, "It would be good for the Brazilian church to appreciate the role and work of single Brazilian

---

110. Bertuzzi (*Latinos No Mundo Muçulmano*, 57) reports that some Latin American women missionaries in the Arab and Muslim world have successfully worked though such challenges by embracing the local culture as much as possible.

111. See Bertuzzi, *Latinos No Mundo Muçulmano*, 7.

women in the Arab world," while another added, "We single female workers in the Arab world need more support and help." As single Brazilian women seem to struggle the most in the Arab world, caring for these needs does not seem unreasonable.

Summary

In this chapter, a practical summary of Brazilian evangelical approaches to mission in the Arab-Muslim world has been offered. This included some prominent historic mission strategies employed by Brazilian workers (evangelism, discipleship, and church planting) as well as a summary of integrated support ministries, which include humanitarian work, medical work, sports ministry, and Business as Mission among others. In addition, the work and core values of six Brazilian missions organizations that work in the Arab world were considered. These included two groups that are indigenous to Brazil (Missão Antioquia, Missão Kairos), one that is indigenous to Latin America (PMI), one historic denomination (Junta de Missões Mundiais da Convenção Batista Brasileira), and two international organizations that have opened offices in Brazil (CCI-Brasil, Interserve).

Based on this survey of Brazilian mission strategies in the Arab world, the apparent strengths (as described by Brazilians) were discussed. It was argued that Brazilian missionaries are doing particularly well at building relationships, adapting to culture, communicating the gospel, planting churches, and offering humanitarian aid. It was further observed that Brazilian workers and missions organizations tend to measure their success in terms of their ability to persevere and to build relationships. Finally, the chapter concluded by exploring the four most apparent challenges facing Brazilian evangelical missionaries in the Arab world—church support, language acquisition, financial support, and women's issues. In each case, an effort was made to understand and define the problem clearly after which some suggestions—based largely on Brazilian reflections—were offered toward resolving the problem. In short, this chapter has demonstrated that after a few decades, Brazilian evangelical missions efforts the Arab world are focused, innovative, courageous, and still developing.

5

Toward a Brazilian Theology of Mission

Introduction

BUILDING ON THE PREVIOUS chapters, which have considered Brazil's missions-sending history, the cultural experiences of Brazilian transcultural workers in Arab contexts, and Brazilian approaches to mission in the Arab world, let us now explore how Brazilians are thinking theologically about mission, especially in the Arab world.

For Mordomo, this endeavor will be difficult because he argues that "there is no comprehensive Brazilian theology of mission to be found."[1] While acknowledging the strides made by Latin American theologians and missiologists in the last forty years, Mordomo maintains that a distinctive Brazilian theology of mission has yet to be articulated. On the other hand, Valdir Steuernagel—a Lutheran missiologist who presently serves as minister at large with World Vision and has played an influential role in the Lausanne Movement—is persuaded that Brazilian missiologists continue to "drink from the streams of Padilla and Escobar."[2] That is, they remain indebted to these innovative thinkers within the Latin American Theological Fellowship (FTL).[3] Hence, Steuernagel, a leading Brazilian missiologist who has been an active member of the FTL and regards

---

1. See Mordomo, "Unleashing the Brazilian Missionary Force," 224.

2. Related in conversation with Steuernagel and Mordomo, July 22, 2009.

3. Ironically, Padilla asserted in the 1980s that Latin America was without its own articulated theology. See Padilla, *Mission Between the Times*, 95–96.

himself as a disciple of Escobar,[4] sees more continuity between Brazilian and Latin American missiology than Mordomo does. Indeed, it is difficult to read an article by a Brazilian missiologist in which Padilla, Escobar, or Orlando Costas are not cited.

To be sure, Brazilian missiology, not unlike Latin American missiology in general, is continually emerging and is supported by the more well known works of Steuernagel and Ronaldo Lidório as well as through the reflections of missiologists who contribute to journals such as *Capacitando*. While a Brazilian theology of mission can certainly be appreciated through articulated thought in published articles and books, it can be understood more strategically through the observed practice of Brazilian transcultural workers, which, in the present study, focuses on those serving in the Arab-Muslim world. Indeed, as Timothy Tennent has recently asserted, "missions and missiology each stimulate, support, and lead to the other."[5] Similarly, Costas reflected, "[missiology] is a critical reflection that takes place in the praxis of mission" and that "it emerges out of mission and leads to mission."[6] Perhaps Steuernagel best summarizes this approach by suggesting that theology of mission develops "at the kitchen table" and in the context of relationships—not in libraries.[7] In short, our approach to understanding Brazilian missiology, especially in the Arab-Muslim world context, will be informed through published articulated thought as well as through the observed practices of Brazilian evangelical missionaries—including that which has been summarized in the last chapter.

Any discussion of Brazilian missiology must first be understood in light of the general characteristics of Brazilian evangelicalism that were presented in chapter 1: a high view of Scripture, a call to genuine conversion, a visible faith, a missionary zeal, the priesthood of the believer, and a free church tendency. As Brazilian evangelical transcultural workers have gone from this matrix to serve in the Arab-Muslim world, four particular aspects of theology of mission have been apparent and will be discussed in this chapter: *missão integral* (the whole gospel), a church-centered missiology, missions from below, and spiritual awareness.

4. See Steuernagel, "Learning from Escobar," 123–25.
5. See Tennent, *Invitation to World Missions*, 496.
6. Cited in Smith, "The Essentials of Missiology," 236, 241. Smith helpfully relates that the leading FTL thinkers all theologized from a place of practical ministry. Escobar was a Peruvian missionary to Argentina, Brazil, and Spain, while Padilla and Costas have both been pastors (see Smith, "The Essentials of Missiology," 304–5, 307–12, 320–35).
7. See Steuernagel, "Learning from Escobar," 124–25.

Missão Integral (The Whole Gospel)

The most prominent aspect of Brazilian theology of mission is *missão integral*, which can best be translated as the "whole gospel" or "holistic mission." As this aspect has been central to Latin American missiology in general, let us first recount how *missão integral* has developed historically through the work of the Latin American Theological Fellowship (FTL). Next, a theological overview of *missão integral* will be given based largely on the articulated thought of FTL theologians, including Brazilians and other Latin Americans. Finally, we will explore how *missão integral* is being reflected on and applied by Brazilian missions organizations and missionaries.

Historical Development of Missão Integral

For much of the twentieth century, Western evangelicals struggled to reconcile the relationship between kerygmatic proclamation and social action. Historically, evangelicals—including those who went to Latin America in the nineteenth century—were quite concerned with ministering to human needs.[8] However, beginning in the late nineteenth century, North American evangelicals in particular became preoccupied with the challenges of liberal theology, science, and modernity.[9] In addition, as North American evangelicals were becoming increasingly individualistic culturally and premillenial theologically, this led to the so-called "great reversal" in which a dichotomy between proclamation and social action emerged, especially after World War I.[10] Hence, for many evangelicals, caring for social needs meant compromising the gospel and giving in to the aims of liberal theology. As a result, this North American contextual theology, which emphasized evangelism as mission, prevailed at global evangelization congresses in Berlin in 1966 and in Bogota (CLADE I) in 1969.[11]

---

8. See Steuernagel, "The Theology of Mission in Its Relation to Social Responsibility," 51.

9. Ibid., 46.

10. Ibid., 51–52, 60–65; also Campos, "Premillenial Tensions and Holistic Missiology," 150; Tizon, *Transformation After Lausanne*, 23–26; and Padilla, *Mission Between the Times*, 88.

11. See Steuernagel, "The Theology of Mission in Its Relation to Social Responsibility," 100–101, 104, 110, 126–27, 157, 160.

Following the Bogota congress, the Latin American Theological Fellowship (FTL) was founded in 1970 and was nurtured by a diverse group of evangelical theologians, including Escobar, Costas, Padilla, Emilio Núñez, Pedro Arana, Peter Savage, Andrew Kirk, and later Steuernagel.[12] In reality, the FTL was initiated as a response to what was regarded as two unsatisfactory streams of thought—Liberation Theology, which developed in the Roman Catholic Latin American context, and evangelical fundamentalism, which, of course, originated in North America. In rejecting the hermeneutics and presuppositions of Liberation Theology, including an ecumenical theology that regarded Latin America as thoroughly Christian, the FTL thinkers maintained the noted evangelical distinctives of the need for genuine conversion, visible faith, and a high view of Scripture.[13] Observing the authoritative place of Scripture in the theological method of the FTL leaders, Bonino correctly notes, "Assent to the authority of the Bible could be considered as one of the most general features of the evangelical movement in Latin America."[14] Summarizing Escobar's critique of the ideological basis of Liberation Theology in light of his Biblicist convictions, Sharon Heaney writes: "Escobar is forced to ask whether liberation thinkers actually believe the Bible is the revealed and inspired fruit of divine initiative. If they do not believe in the true significance of the Bible and its subsequent authority, then Escobar makes the suggestion that the theology of liberation should concentrate on Marxist texts instead."[15] This value is maintained by Steuernagel who, in a recent article, admonishes evangelical missiologists to recapture the primacy of Scripture in their missiological reflection.[16]

---

12. See Escobar, *Changing Tides,* 119–20; and Bonino, *Faces of Latin American Protestantism,* 48. With the exception of Kirk—an Anglican missionary who spent many years in Latin America—each key FTL leader has been of Latin origin. Also, Smith's dissertation, "The Essentials of Missiology," offers a thorough history of the movement until 1983.

13. See Escobar, "Latin American Theology," 204; also Bonino, *Faces of Latin American Protestantism,* 49. See Tizon, *Transformation After Lausanne,* 53–55 for a brief and useful summary of Liberation Theology.

14. See Bonino, *Faces of Latin American Protestantism,* 49; also Escobar, *Changing Tides,* 114; Smith, "The Essentials of Missiology," 20–21; and Costas, *Christ Outside the Gate,* 33.

15. See Heaney, *Contextual Theology for Latin America,* 103. For further discussion of the FTL members' regard for Scripture and their hermeneutics, see Heaney, *Contextual Theology for Latin America,* 94–125; Smith, "The Essentials of Missiology," 95–104; and Padilla, *Mission Between the Times,* 106–7.

16. See Steuernagel, "Learning from Escobar," 130.

While the FTL rejected Liberation Theology for promoting ideology over authentic Christian faith, they also faulted North American evangelicals serving in Latin America for failing to develop a theology of mission that took the Latin American context seriously. Steuernagel wrote that mission could no longer be "an exercise in linear, one-way hermeneutics—from here to there, from the North to the South, from the individual missionary to an individual person, and from a verbal language to a single soul."[17] Rather, Padilla affirmed that the "aim [of the FTL] was to offer a new open-ended reading of Scripture with a hermeneutic in which the biblical text and the historical situation become mutually engaged in a dialogue whose purpose is to place the church under the Lordship of Jesus Christ in its particular context."[18] Escobar added that what was needed was "a fresh exploration . . . into the depths of the biblical text, with the questions raised by the Latin American context."[19] That is, Scripture should be read in light of Latin America's very real social problems, including poverty, injustice, and oppression—issues that have been addressed in Scripture and in the earthly ministry of Jesus.[20] Acknowledging the contextual concerns of liberation theologians—concerns largely ignored by North American evangelicals in the twentieth century—Padilla asserts, "The question for me is not how do I respond to Liberation Theology . . . but rather, how do I articulate my faith in the same context of poverty, regression, and hopelessness out of which Liberation Theology has emerged?"[21] The FTL's commitment to proclaiming the kerygmatic gospel and applying the authoritative Scriptures within the concrete Latin American context naturally led to an organic integration of proclamation and social action—a *missão integral*.[22]

17. See Steuernagel, "The Theology of Mission in Its Relation to Social Responsibility," 17.

18. Cited in Escobar, "Latin American Theology," 204–205; see also Smith, "The Essentials of Missiology," 14–15; and Heaney, *Contextual Theology for Latin America*, 84.

19. See Escobar, *Changing Tides*, 114.

20. See Escobar, "Latin American Theology," 205; and Steuernagel, "The Theology of Mission in Its Relation to Social Responsibility," 7.

21. Cited in Smith, "The Essentials of Missiology," 117; see also Heaney, *Contextual Theology for Latin America*, 46–47.

22. This excerpt from the "Evangelical Declaration of Bogota" of 1969 (cited in Steuernagel, "The Theology of Mission in Its Relation to Social Responsibility," 129) shows the development of this theology of mission: "The process of evangelization must occur in concrete human situations . . . The time has come for us evangelicals to take seriously our social responsibility. In order to do this, we must build on a biblical

As the FTL thinkers forged a holistic theology of mission for Latin America, they also began to influence some global conversations on evangelization—most notably the 1974 Lausanne Congress. As theology of mission—including the relationship between social action and proclamation—was among the planned topics at the meeting, Padilla and Escobar gave papers that raised difficult questions and challenged the delegates' missiological paradigms.[23] In his paper, Padilla argued, "Concern for man's reconciliation with God cannot be separated from concern for social justice ... I refuse, therefore, to drive a wedge between a primary task, namely the proclamation of the gospel, and a secondary (at best) or even optional (at worst) task of the church."[24] Warning against creating a false dichotomy between evangelism and social action, Escobar added, "To give only ... spiritual content to God's action in man or to give only a social and physical dimension to God's salvation are both unbiblical heresies."[25] Years after the 1974 Lausanne gathering, Steuernagel helpfully summarized the Latin American position by asserting, "Word and deed cannot be separated from each other at the cost of sacrificing the rich wholeness of the gospel."[26] The missiology presented by Padilla and Escobar encountered strong opposition from other evangelicals at Lausanne who championed the priority of proclamation. However, it seems that without the FTL influence at Lausanne, article five of the Lausanne Covenant ("Christian Social Responsibility") would not have been drafted:

> We affirm that God is both the Creator and the Judge of all people. We therefore should share his concern for justice and

---

foundation, which implies evangelical doctrine and the example of Jesus Christ carried to its logical implications. Christ's example must become incarnated in the critical Latin American situation of underdevelopment, injustice, hunger, violence, and despair. Men cannot build the Kingdom of God on earth, but evangelical action will contribute toward the creation of a better world as a foreshadowing of that Kingdom who coming we pray for daily." See also Smith, "The Essentials of Missiology," 194–202; and Bonino, *Faces of Latin American Protestantism*, 50.

23. See Steuernagel, "The Theology of Mission in Its Relation to Social Responsibility," 136, 141.

24. Ibid., 144.

25. Cited in Smith, "The Essentials of Missiology," 212. The "Radical Discipleship" group which convened during Lausanne 1974 added this declaration (cited in Padilla, "Holistic Mission," 157): "There is not a biblical dichotomy between the Word spoken and the Word made flesh in the lives of God's people. Men will look as they listen and what they see must be at one with what they hear."

26. See Steuernagel, "The Theology of Mission in Its Relation to Social Responsibility," 257; see also Escobar, *The New Global Mission*, 149–54.

reconciliation throughout human society and for the liberation of men and women from every kind of oppression. Because men and women are made in the image of God, every person, regardless of race, religion, color, culture, class, sex or age, has an intrinsic dignity because of which he or she should be respected and served, not exploited. Here too we express penitence both for our neglect and for having sometimes regarded evangelism and social concern as mutually exclusive. Although reconciliation with other people is not reconciliation with God, nor is social action evangelism, nor is political liberation salvation, nevertheless we affirm that evangelism and socio-political involvement are both part of our Christian duty. For both are necessary expressions of our doctrines of God and man, our love for our neighbor and our obedience to Jesus Christ. The message of salvation implies also a message of judgment upon every form of alienation, oppression and discrimination, and we should not be afraid to denounce evil and injustice wherever they exist. When people receive Christ they are born again into his kingdom and must seek not only to exhibit but also to spread its righteousness in the midst of an unrighteous world. The salvation we claim should be transforming us in the totality of our personal and social responsibilities. Faith without works is dead.[27]

In the aftermath of the 1974 conference, the Lausanne Movement continued to struggle to strike a balance between proclamation and social action. In some cases, such as at the 1989 Lausanne Congress in Manila, social action was virtually ignored.[28] On the other hand, at the 1982 Grand Rapids gathering—a meeting chaired by John Stott, who had come to appreciate the FTL theology—the delegates had a healthy discussion regarding the integral relationship between word and deed. At the conference, three possibilities were affirmed: first, social action could be regarded as a consequence of evangelism; second, that it could serve as a bridge to evangelism; third, that social action was an equal partner with evangelism.[29]

Over the last three decades, The FTL thinkers have continually argued for the theological legitimacy of the third possibility leading Padilla

27. See "The Lausanne Covenant"; see also Steuernagel, "The Theology of Mission in Its Relation to Social Responsibility," 143–44, 151, 169–70; Escobar, *Changing Tides*, 113; and Heaney, *Contextual Theology for Latin America*, 212–14.

28. See Steuernagel, "The Theology of Mission in Its Relation to Social Responsibility," 170–236.

29. See Stott, "Evangelism and Social Responsibility"; also Bosch, *Transforming Mission*, 403–408; Tizon, *Transformation After Lausanne*, 43–49.

to affirm that "social involvement has finally been granted full citizenship in evangelical missiology, mainly under the influence of people from the Two-Thirds World."[30] While holistic mission has been debated within the global church, it has been embraced much more by the Latin American and Brazil evangelical church. Steuernagel notes that following Lausanne 1974, Latin Americans delegates who gathered at Curitiba (Brazil) in 1976 engaged in rigorous and stimulating missiological reflection in light of their context.[31] Referring to the declaration adopted at Curitiba, Brazilian missiologist Antônia Van der Meer stated that in mission, "We are called to take the presence of Jesus Christ, proclaiming his redeeming gospel, serving the world and changing it by his love, patient in the hope of a new creation that he will bring."[32] Commenting on the work of the Brazilian Congress on Evangelization that met in Belo Horizonte (Brazil) in 1983, Steuernagel observed that "the commitment of the congress was to identify the needs of the Brazilians and present to them a word of 'faith and hope through the redemptive cross of Christ.'"[33] Finally, following the 1992 CLADE III gathering in Quito, Ecuador, a definitive statement of Latin American theology of mission was drafted and given the descriptive title, "The Whole Gospel from Latin America for All Peoples."[34]

Missão Integral Defined

Given this historical development in which Brazilians and Latin Americans have labored to forge their own theology of mission, let us now move toward a definition of *missão integral*, which will be presented rather thickly as a tapestry of thought from Brazilian and Latin American thinkers. Padilla defines the whole gospel as "a real integration of the vertical and horizontal dimensions of mission."[35] He adds, "The salvation that the gospel proclaims is not limited to man's reconciliation to God. It involves the remaking of man in all the dimensions of his existence. It has to do with

30. Cited in Steuernagel, "The Theology of Mission in Its Relation to Social Responsibility," 169, 213; and Kirk, *What is Mission?*, 62–64.

31. See Steuernagel, "The Theology of Mission in Its Relation to Social Responsibility," 227.

32. See Van der Meer, "The Scriptures, the Church, and Humanity," 154.

33. See Steuernagel, "The Theology of Mission in Its Relation to Social Responsibility," 227.

34. The statement has been published in English in Scherer and Bevans, *New Directions in Mission and Evangelization II*, 191–98.

35. See Padilla, "Holistic Mission," 157.

the recovery of the whole man according to God's original purpose for his creation."[36] Commenting with more color on these aspects of the gospel, Van der Meer adds, "Mission is the fruit of the love of God, who so loved the world that he gave his only Son in order to redeem human beings from their blindness, oppression, captivity, and poverty, so that they can experience a new life of fullness given by his grace."[37] Discussing *missão integral* on a more practical level, Steuernagel writes, "What is the whole gospel? It's putting ourselves aside and listening to the needs of the people who are crying for help. It's following Jesus's example."[38] He adds that "mission and *diakonia* are inseparable on both theological and practical levels" and that "the mission of the church is expressed in *diakonia*."[39] Illustrating the integral nature of the gospel, Padilla concludes rather bluntly that "there is no place for statistics on 'how many souls die without Christ every minute' if they do not take into account how many of those who die are dying of hunger."[40] Finally, asserting that the whole gospel leads to the spiritual and physical transformation of communities, Steuernagel states, "[I] want to understand the mission of the church as intentional as possible and as broad as possible in order that Christ is recognized and affirmed, for life to be promoted, for community to be developed, and for justice to flow in God's river as a sign of God's eternal obsession with *shalom*."[41]

Theological Foundations of Missão Integral

In light of this working definition, what are the theological underpinnings of *missão integral*? First, the whole gospel is founded on the integrated nature of the Triune God. Steuernagel writes, "The gospel is complete in

36. See Padilla, *Mission Between the Times*, 22, 179; Heaney, *Contextual Theology for Latin America*, 225–26; and Costas, *Christ Outside the Gate*, 37–38.

37. See Van der Meer, "The Scriptures, the Church, and Humanity," 153.

38. See Steuernagel, "O Evangelho Integral," 184. English translation by Barbara Hubbard.

39. See Steuernagel, "The Theology of Mission in Its Relation to Social Responsibility," 35; see also Bevans and Schroeder, *New Directions in Mission and Evangelization II*, 394.

40. See Padilla, *Mission Between the Times*, 25; also Heaney, *Contextual Theology for Latin America*, 225.

41. See Steuernagel, "To Seek to Transform Unjust Structures," 64. Commenting further on *shalom* as a motif in mission, Kirk (*What is Mission?*, 63) writes, "The root meaning of the original [*shalom*] is 'completeness,' in the sense of possessing a fullness of welfare and health (Ps 38:3; Isa 38:16–17), prosperity for the whole community (Job 15:21; Pss 72:7, 37:11, 122:6), and security (Job 5:24)."

itself just as God is. God has not finished his work in us and the gospel continues to call us to being complete."[42] Second, Padilla asserts that the Holy Spirit, having brought diverse people together in caring community at Pentecost, continues to work powerfully and in a holistic manner.[43]

Third, arguably the most foundational aspect of *missão integral* is its Christology. That is, the whole gospel stems from the life, person, and work of the God-Man Jesus Christ.[44] Escobar and other Latin American thinkers have expressed concern that, in failing to reflect on Christ's concrete acts in history and focusing more on the eternal benefits of Christ's work, North American evangelical theologians have actually presented a docetic Christ.[45] Emilio Núñez writes, "We were presented with a divine-human Christ in the theological formula; but in practice, he was far removed from the stage of the world, aloof to our social problems."[46] Yet, as Jesus's life included feeding, showing compassion, confronting, proclaiming the kingdom of God, and suffering among other acts, his divinity and humanity come to bear in his mission.[47] Ultimately, the whole gospel acknowledges that Jesus is Savior and Lord of the universe.[48]

As Christ established the "definition of what it means to love God above all things and to love one's neighbor as oneself,"[49] His approach to mission serves as a model for all Christians and for the church. Because of Christ, the church is to proclaim salvation, identify with the poor, confront social injustices, as well as suffer.[50] Steuernagel summarizes:

---

42. See Steuernagel, "O Evangelho Integral," 184.

43. See Padilla, "Holistic Mission," 160.

44. For a helpful summary of Latin American Christology, see Heaney, *Contextual Theology for Latin America*, 170–82.

45. Docetism is the ancient heresy that denied that Jesus had a physical body but only appeared (*dokeō*) to have.

46. Cited in Heaney, *Contextual Theology for Latin America*, 172; see also Escobar, "Latin American Theology," 206; Escobar, *Changing Tides*, 118–20; Steuernagel, "The Theology of Mission in Its Relation to Social Responsibility," 257; Costas, *Christ Outside the Gate*, 5–16; and Boff, *New Evangelization*, 16.

47. See Escobar, *The New Global Mission*, 106–111, 143–45; also Escobar, *Changing Tides*, 124; Steuernagel, "To Seek to Transform Unjust Structures," 67–68; and Boff, *New Evangelization*, 75.

48. See Padilla, *Mission Between the Times*, 9–11.

49. See Padilla, "Holistic Mission," 159.

50. See Steuernagel, "The Theology of Mission in Its Relation to Social Responsibility," 130, 161; Padilla, *Mission Between the Times*, 177–78; Padilla, "Holistic Mission," 159; and Heaney, *Contextual Theology for Latin America*, 223.

The whole gospel is to re-encounter Jesus. The mission of today's churches lies in the authority and inspiration of the life of Jesus. Jesus sent out the disciples as God sent him. Jesus went with them and taught them what to do. It is necessary to align our lives and our concept of missions to the strategies within the gospels. It's necessary to bring it all to Jesus and ask if our strategies, concepts and practices correspond to God's methodology; if they correspond to God's heart and his way of communicating with us and establishing his churches; if they correspond to the incarnational model of Jesus. If not, we are getting away from discipleship.[51]

A fourth theological foundation for *missão integral* is anthropology. That is, the whole gospel is necessary because human beings have spiritual and physical needs. Padilla writes that holistic mission "takes into account that people are spiritual, social and bodily beings, made to live in relationship with God, with their neighbors, and with God's creation" and it is concerned with "meeting . . . basic human needs, including the need of God, but also the need of food, love, housing, clothes, physical and mental health, and a sense of human dignity."[52]

Steuernagel and other FTL theologians have particularly reflected on how the gospel should confront human poverty and social injustice. After describing conditions in Northeast Brazil where World Vision has begun some humanitarian work, Steuernagel wrote, "The challenge of the church, and even of an organization such as World Vision, is that it cannot rob itself of contributing with her drop of hope in the ocean of poverty and human suffering. Moreover, this drop has to have the face of Jesus and a call to meet this same Jesus who calls the poor and sinners to be part of his family."[53] Others have affirmed this and argued that the global church must actively confront corrupt economic structures that oppress the poor. At the same time, the church should come alongside the poor to aid them in realizing economic transformation and to find solutions for problems such as clean water, hunger, community health, and sustainable agriculture.[54]

---

51. See Steuernagel, "O Evangelho Integral," 184; also Bosch, *Transforming Mission*, 399.

52. See Padilla, "Holistic Mission," 158; also Heaney, *Contextual Theology for Latin America*, 129–30, 239.

53. See Steuernagel, "O Menino Nu Na Rampa do Lixo," 612.

54. See Campbell, "Holistic Mission," 24–39; also Heaney, *Contextual Theology for Latin America*, 234–35.

Regarding the human need for justice, Steuernagel argues that though evangelicals have historically focused their energies on ministries of compassion, the significant biblical motif of justice requires that the church become more engaged in confronting institutional and social sins.[55] Defining justice as "liberating the oppressed from the yoke of the oppressors and giving them the promise and the vision of a new land and a new life,"[56] Steuernagel asserts that justice is "a fundamental expression of God's search for transformation."[57] Arguing that confronting injustice should receive more emphasis in a holistic evangelical missiology, he concludes: "In our missionary journey, we need to listen, especially to those who are crying, who are suffering, and who are lonely. We must respond to their cry and go to those places where God is already present—places of the orphan, the widow, and the stranger . . . the abused children, the single mothers, and the refugees."[58]

A fifth theological foundation for the whole gospel is the kingdom of God. This theological motif, which has figured prominently in the work of many theologians, has been especially meaningful to the FTL thinkers and has provided a hermeneutical framework for reading Scripture that has resulted in *missão integral*.[59] For Padilla, the New Testament emphasis on the kingdom of God and the mission of Jesus is much more present than it is future, thus the gospel is "God's good news in Jesus Christ; it is good news of the reign he proclaimed and embodies; of God's mission of love to restore the world to wholeness through the cross of Christ and him alone; of his victory over the demonic powers of destruction and death; of his Lordship over the entire universe; it is good news of a new creation, a new humanity, a new birth through his by his life-giving Spirit."[60] He adds that, by implication, the gospel is "good news of liberation, of restoration, of

---

55. See Steuernagel, "The Theology of Mission in Its Relation to Social Responsibility," 242–44; also Steuernagel, "To Seek to Transform Unjust Structures," 62–76; Steuernagel, "Learning from Escobar," 131; Heaney, *Contextual Theology for Latin America*, 133–35; and Costas, *Christ Outside the Gate*, 21–26.

56. See Steuernagel, "The Theology of Mission in Its Relation to Social Responsibility," 243–44.

57. See Steuernagel, "To Seek to Transform Unjust Structures," 64

58. Ibid., 71.

59. See Steuernagel, "The Theology of Mission in Its Relation to Social Responsibility," 260; also Kirk, *What is Mission?*, 64–65; Smith, "The Essentials of Missiology," 31–32, 104–108; and Campos, "Premillenial Tensions and Holistic Missiology," 159–69.

60. See Padilla, *The New Face of Evangelicalism*, 93; also Heaney, *Contextual Theology for Latin America*, 174.

wholeness, and of salvation that is personal, social, global, and cosmic."[61] In light of this view of the kingdom, Padilla makes social action an equal partner with proclamation. He writes, "Good works are not, therefore, a mere addendum to mission, rather they are an integral part of the present manifestation of the kingdom: they point back to the kingdom that has already come and forward to the kingdom that is yet to come."[62] Reflecting practically, Padilla concludes: "In actual practice, the question of whether evangelism or social action should come first is irrelevant. In every concrete situation, the needs themselves provide the guidelines for the definition of priorities."[63]

Finally, the whole gospel is supported by and proclaimed by a missional church. While Padilla asserts that "the mission of the church . . . can be understood only in light of the kingdom of God,"[64] Steuernagel goes farther and describes the church as the "display window" of the kingdom.[65] Both Padilla and Steuernagel assert that a missional ecclesiology, in contrast to Western individualism that pervades the church, must be characterized by authentic and transformational community. Steuernagel writes, "To speak of the whole gospel is to speak of the need we have to be corrected by the gospel and by our interdependence. We need one another as we need to take in the gospel in totality and integrality."[66] While the local church experiences transformation from within as a true community, it is also an agent of holistic mission in which every member plays a role.[67] This vision of a missional church at work in kingdom mission is helpfully summarized by the "Micah Declaration on Integral Mission" which states: "God by his grace has given local churches the task of integral mission [proclaiming and demonstrating the gospel]. The future of integral mission is in planting and enabling local churches to transform

---

61. See Padilla, *The New Face of Evangelicalism*, 93.

62. See Padilla, *Mission Between the Times*, 192–93; also Heaney, *Contextual Theology for Latin America*, 179.

63. See Padilla, *Mission Between the Times*, 198.

64. Ibid., 186.

65. See Steuernagel, "The Theology of Mission in Its Relation to Social Responsibility," 263–64.

66. See Steuernagel, "O Evangelho Integral," 184; also Padilla, "Holistic Mission," 161.

67. See Steuernagel, "The Theology of Mission in Its Relation to Social Responsibility," 130–31; also Heaney, *Contextual Theology for Latin America*, 205–7.

the communities of which they are part. Churches as caring and inclusive communities are at the heart of what it means to be integral mission."[68]

Missão Integral Applied

In light of the historical development and theological foundations of *missão integral* in the Brazilian and Latin American contexts, how has this theology affected the work of Brazilian missions in the Arab-Muslim world? Let us first examine how some Brazilian missions organizations regard holistic ministry and then consider how Brazilian missionaries are applying this missiology in their contexts.

It seems that *missão integral* is becoming increasingly central to the vision of Missão Antioquia, Brazil's first indigenous mission, which has a growing presence in the Arab-Muslim world. In 2006, after doing some strategic planning and reflecting on its vision and mission, the organization articulated the following: "Our vision then would be to bring about transformation through the gospel [in unreached areas] with the Word and good deeds. That certainly results in glory to God here and now. In practice, we didn't even consider the possibility of doing only good deeds. For us it is essential that the proclamation of the gospel and good deeds go together. First and foremost, we believe that Jesus is the only one who can bring about transformation in this world."[69] Following this statement in the same document, the Antioquia leadership expressed encouragement that more doors were being opened for sports ministry and community development—ministries that would be a partner and support to church planting.[70] Hence, with a great sense of humility and dependency on the Lord, the organization has communicated a clear strategy of holistic mission.

As Missão Antioquia personnel are increasingly entering fields in the Muslim world that are closed to conventional missions, Antioquia director Silas Tostes is convinced that each missionary should have a professional skill in order to gain employment and residency. On one hand, this approach gives the worker credibility in the eyes of those in the host culture—including neighbors and government officials—and it alleviates the worker's frustration and discouragement when their identity is questioned. On the other hand, such work is also an opportunity to testify

---

68. Cited in Padilla, "Holistic Mission," 160.
69. See "Missão Antioquia." English translation by Cristina Boersma.
70. Ibid.

to the gospel through tangible deeds. For this reason, Tostes encourages Antioquia personnel to develop skills and find work that corresponds with their gifts, abilities, and passions so that they can perform their job with joy. Indeed, Tostes's thoughts reveal a theology of work that regards labor as a viable act of worship—a winsome partner and support to kergymatic proclamation. However, Tostes warns that social ministry alone is inadequate and that it must be deliberately integrated with a verbal witness and a plan for church planting.[71]

Missão integral is also evident in the work of PMI, the first Latin mission to focus on the Muslim world. Daniel Calze, the present director of PMI Brasil, is quick to assert that one's platform or tentmaking job is not merely a "cover" that allows a PMI worker an excuse to preach the gospel. Rather, he argues that a nurse, for instance, must truly be a nurse and that he or she glorifies God and testifies to the gospel in part through a job well done. When asked if the whole gospel was especially strategic in the Arab-Muslim context where resistance to the gospel is common, Calze admitted that while this approach did promote trust and helped relationships with Muslims, he asserted that they would pursue *missão integral* in any context because this was simply the ministry model of Jesus.[72] Similar perspectives were captured by Steven Downey in his interview with Marcos Amado, the former director of PMI:

> "A good example is a PMI worker, an engineer by trade, who designs water purification systems for needy communities," Amado says. "This puts him in contact with people of various social levels, principally the needy, and gives him a chance to share his faith." PMI recognizes that to do ministry in poorer countries, one must engage in holistic witness. But Amado says, "We are not involved in community development projects only because they give us the opportunity to go into Muslim countries. We are involved in them because we believe that it is part of our mission as Christians. At the same time, we speak about Christ."[73]

Calze added that while PMI workers certainly needed to be discerning about communicating their faith during the course of a work day, it was not unusual for Muslims to expect to discuss faith issues at work. Hence,

---

71. Related to me in personal conversation, July 23, 2009.
72. Ibid., July 21, 2009.
73. See Downey, "Ibero-Americans Reaching Arab-Muslims."

a holistic approach in the Arab-Muslim world is important because Muslims tend not to compartmentalize faith from other parts of their lives.[74]

Finally, like Tostes, Calze affirmed that humanitarian work was not the end of holistic mission. The goal of their mission was not to train good soccer players or small business owners who would then die without knowing Christ in a saving way. He added that pursuing *missão integral* meant that they were deliberate about every aspect of ministry—ministering to human needs, evangelism, and church planting.[75]

In addition to Missão Antioquia and PMI, other Brazilian missions organizations have also demonstrated a conviction for holistic mission. As noted, the Junta de Missões Mundiais (global missions board) of the Brazilian Baptist Convention has developed ministries around the skills of educational specialists, health professionals (doctors, dentists, and nurses), and humanitarian aid workers—especially those trained to work with women and children. It has also developed a soccer school strategy that integrates teaching soccer skills while communicating the gospel message.[76] In addition, Interserve, with its stated vision "to proclaim by word and action, that Jesus Christ is the Savior of all humanity," has *missão integral* as a central focus. While offering formal training in holistic ministry through its partner mission school, the Centro Evangélico de Missões, Interserve Brasil has built its mission around Christians with medical, technical, and community development training who are able to care for real human needs and verbally proclaim the gospel.[77]

How have Brazilian transcultural workers demonstrated a commitment to *missão integral* in their field ministry in the Arab-Muslim world? First, as shown, nearly half of the forty-five Brazilian workers surveyed indicated that they were involved in some form of humanitarian work through existing NGOs or through ones that they have established. This has been a clear strength of the Brazilian missions movement among Arabs. Brazilian missionaries have cared for the physical needs of the handicapped, women, and refugees in a variety of Arab contexts. While these efforts have dignified the poor and marginalized in society and brought measurable improvements to their lives, they have also offered Brazilians the opportunity to share the reason for their service. As one Brazilian

---

74. Related to me in conversation, July 23, 2009.
75. Related to me in personal conversation, July 21, 2009.
76. See "JMM."
77. See "Centro Evangélico de Missões."

worker related, "God has opened doors to work with refugees and we have seen people healed and desiring to follow God."

Second, Brazilians are also proclaiming the whole gospel through medical work. One nurse recounted the great freedom that she had to pray for patients and communicate the gospel as she visited patients and dispensed medicine. She shared that her medical work allowed her to be a tangible witness for Christ. Other Brazilians are beginning to adopt the Community Health Evangelism (CHE) strategy in order to integrate more into their community and minister in word and deed.

Third, Brazilian missionaries who have accessed the Arab world through business platforms have also shown a commitment to holistic ministry. As noted, one worker's carpet export business enabled him to build a rich network of relationships in which it was quite natural to verbalize his faith. Another Brazilian, pursuing a Business as Mission (BAM) strategy, has endeavored to run his business according to biblical principles, to create jobs, and bring economic and spiritual transformation to his community. While committed to BAM principles, he is also burdened for faithful proclamation—a strategy that includes "good, godly business and sharing the gospel." Finally, another worker has opened a small business development center that offers Christian men training in the Scriptures and in running a business with skill and integrity. The strategy operates on the assumption that a business owner is strategically placed within a community where he can have a viable witness in word and deed and can also plant churches.

Fourth, *missão integral* has also been evident in the work of Brazilians who are ministering through sports. This includes those working as physical trainers, who spend meaningful time working with their clients and, within this environment of trust, are able to communicate the gospel. It is probably most apparent in the ministry of those who coach soccer and organize soccer schools. While soccer is the number one sport in the Arab world and Brazilian players and coaches are quickly welcomed even in otherwise tense areas, the strategy of integrating soccer skills with biblical principles is quite holistic. One coach summarized his enthusiasm for this opportunity by sharing, "I love using sports—something I really enjoy—for ministry."[78]

Fifth, Brazilians have also ministered in a holistic manner through teaching English and Portuguese in Arab contexts. While one worker indicated that she had been able to present Christ during the course of lessons

---

78. All responses were gathered from surveys and interviews. See appendices.

and tutorials, others have seen the work of teaching itself as a ministry. With that, one Brazilian added that an important part of her ministry was simply offering words of encouragement to her students.

Finally, many Brazilians have ministered the whole gospel through offering hospitality. As argued, hospitality is certainly an important shared cultural value for Brazilians and Arabs, which affords Brazilian missionaries a natural opportunity to connect with their host culture. More than that, it is a biblical value in which Christians invite, serve, listen, and ultimately care for their guests. The kerygmatic gospel is certainly not intrusive in this environment. One Brazilian couple offered this winsome description of the holistic ministry of hospitality: "Opening the doors of our home ... seeking to always be available to our friends, spending time with them and helping them in what is needed."

The Missiological Significance of Missão Integral in the Arab World

Given the theological foundations for the whole gospel and how it is being applied currently, what is the missiological significance of a Brazilian *missão integral* for the Arab-Muslim world? First, it is relevant because the Arab world has many social problems and physical needs. Not unlike Latin America, where *missão integral* was nurtured, the Arab nations face poverty, unemployment, political corruption, abandoned children, violations against women, and educational deficiencies among others. Though Brazilian workers must, of course, maintain a posture of respect toward Arab governments and their infrastructures—including departments established to meet social needs that may not be functioning effectively—there remain many open doors for Brazilians to relieve suffering, show compassion, and facilitate development and transformation. In short, teachers, business people, medical professionals, soccer coaches, and humanitarian specialists are still welcomed in the Arab world to carry on this aspect of the earthly ministry of Jesus.

Second, Brazilian *missão integral* is peaceful and disarming in a region that has been resistant to Christian missions. Much of this resistance has come in response to an overly polemical style of proclamation through the history of Christian work among Muslims. As a result, the gospel has come to be regarded by many Arab-Muslims as simply another form of

Western propaganda. While Brazilian evangelicals serving in the Arab world are clearly committed to proclaiming the kerygmatic gospel—a message that will often be met with resistance and even violence—their verbal message receives credibility because of their tangible and useful service.[79] Many Brazilian workers involved in humanitarian work reported that they were often invited by Arab friends to share their motivation for serving, which led to opportunities to communicate their faith.

Third, a Brazilian holistic approach is meaningful in the Arab-Muslim world because it is Brazilian and not North American or European. Though a discussion of "missions from below" is forthcoming, it should simply be noted that the humanitarian efforts of Brazilian workers are received with far less suspicion than that of their Western colleagues, who bring significant historical, political, and cultural "baggage" with them to the field, simply because of their nationality. Reflecting on his experience in North Africa, Marcos Amado recalled sadly that "everything that the Americans attempted [in terms of humanitarian projects] was met with suspicion."[80]

Fourth, *missão integral* is important because Arab-Muslims are integrated peoples. That is, Arabs tend to think and talk about subjects like religion and politics even on the job. Therefore, it is not unusual for Brazilians working in the Arab marketplace to communicate spiritual matters during the course of their day. It also makes sense that a Brazilian nurse, while caring for sick patients, would pray for and even offer a spiritual word of encouragement to them. Though Arab-Muslims have resisted the gospel historically, they would still expect Brazilians to be Christians (of some sort) who talk about their faith.

In summary, Brazilian *missão integral* is relevant in the Arab-Muslim context because it is an authentic expression of incarnational ministry. In following the model of Jesus's ministry, Brazilian holistic mission involves identifying with Arabs, living among them, loving and serving them, and proclaiming the gospel message. Such incarnational ministry is perhaps best summarized by a Brazilian worker who shared, "During the past years, I've come to learn to look at my friends here as people created according to the image of God, people with human value and dignity, and not as 'contacts' or people to whom I'm trying to win for a specific faith.

---

79. Escobar advocates the effectiveness of service in resistant (i.e., Marxist, Muslim) contexts. See Smith, "The Essentials of Missiology," 213.

80. Related to me in conversation, August 4, 2009.

To love my friends who are part of the major [Muslim] religion is the basis for sharing the gospel."[81]

A Church-Centered Missiology

Though a lack of local church support and involvement in Brazilian missions was listed as a challenge for Brazilian missions in the Arab world, the Brazilian missions movement remains committed to the local church as the center, source, and a goal of missions. Even Brazilian missionaries that struggled with their sending church's lack of support still expressed admiration for their congregation, regarding it as a concrete expression of God's kingdom. In order to support this claim, let us explore further this church-centered focus, the role of the local church in missions, and the implications of this missiology for Brazilian work in the Arab world.

As it was argued in the discussion on *missão integral*, the church in Brazil and Latin America, through the influence of the FTL thinkers, has rejected the individualism characterized by North American evangelical missions and has celebrated the church as a place of community and transformation. Commenting on the relationship of the individual to the community, Escobar writes, "A holistic approach recognizes the need for a personal experience of God's saving grace, but at the same time it recovers the biblical vision of the human being [for whom] transformation takes place primarily in the context of a community that is itself an expression of God's reign and proclamation of the new creations. The church is where the personal and community dimensions of salvation are first experienced."[82] As it relates to sending missionaries, Ekström adds that this transformational community continues to play a vital role. He writes, "From a Latin American point of view, the local church plays an important role in the selection and sending process. There is very little real participation in missions apart from the local communities. Even the parachurch agencies understand, after a while, that the basis for the support of their mission work is the local church."[83] As a leader of a missions organization, Daniel Calze affirms this reality in stating, "We also understand that the local church is the main organization in charge of sending missionaries to

---

81. Similar thoughts on incarnational ministry are related in Guzmán and Guzmán, "Nós Como Servos," 738–41.

82. See Escobar, *Changing Tides*, 43.

83. See Ekström, "The Selection Process," 185.

the field."[84] In contrast to the twentieth-century North American missions movement, which experienced a widening gap between mission societies and the local church because of volunteerism and individual initiative, the Brazilian movement has maintained a high regard for the church's role in missions.[85] In fact, this church and mission connection can be observed physically as a number of Brazilian missions organizations actually share the same campus with a local church.[86] While this arrangement is certainly in part due to the need to reduce the costs for facilities and offices, this physical proximity surely fosters a church-centered mission focus. Also, as noted the leadership of COMIBAM, Missão Antioquia, PMI, CCI-Brasil and others strive to maintain a close relationship with the local churches of their personnel.

In light of this church-centered missiology, what are the specific roles of the Brazilian churches in missions sending? First, Ekström asserts that the local church is the place for spiritual nurture for potential missionary candidates.[87] To this point, Steuernagel warns that the Brazilian church must uphold the value of authentic community in order to truly disciple Christians and, of course, prospective missionaries.[88]

Second, Ekström sees the local church as a strategic place for potential missionaries to apprentice in ministry. He adds that, following a season of faithful apprenticeship, the pastor should be able to make an informed recommendation about the potential missionary's suitability for transcultural ministry.[89] Indeed, many of the Brazilians interviewed for this study talked about investing years in their local church before going to their Arab world, while many also continue to serve in their churches while home on furlough. As Brazilian mission candidates have apprenticed in their local churches, they have certainly gained valuable training

---

84. See Smither, "Brazilian Evangelical Missions," 392–407.

85. For more on the North American gap between missions agencies and churches, see Tennent, *Invitation to World Missions*, 438; also Ekström, "The Selection Process," 185.

86. For example, the offices of PMI Brasil are located in a Presbyterian Church in Curitiba, which shares the same property with a theological seminary. Also, in Curitiba, Steuernagel directs a Lutheran seminary that shares facilities with a publishing house and a missions organization. Missão Antioquia's "valley of blessing" property near São Paulo includes a local church, foster care facility, and mission training center. Finally, Interserve shares the same property with its partnering school, the Centro Evangélico de Missões

87. See Ekström, "The Selection Process," 185–86.

88. See Steuernagel, "Learning from Escobar," 130.

89. See Ekström, "The Selection Process," 185–86.

for ministry in the Arab world; however, at the same time, they have also helped to cultivate a vision for global missions in the hearts of their church leaders and members.

Third, Ekström asserts that the local church, the only biblically warranted missions agency, should not merely recommend candidates but should also oversee the selection process.[90] Because of its regard for the local church, Missão Antioquia enters into a covenant with the local church of each of its candidates once their training is completed. This statement of mutual commitment is articulated in a three-page document.[91]

Finally, in the minds of many mission leaders, the local church should act as the primary means of financial support for Brazilian missionaries. While the problems with this view were discussed in the previous chapter, this position still points to the prominent role that the sending church plays in the life of the missionary.

What are the implications of this church-centered missiology for Brazilians serving in the Arab world? First, because Brazilians generally have a high regard for the church as an institution, it follows that they will take that conviction with them to the Arab world and be increasingly instrumental in planting churches. Second, because Brazilians and Arabs have similar values regarding relationships, community, and family—qualities that are important in the establishment of churches—Brazilians should pursue church planting in light of these advantages. Because many Arab-Muslims that embrace Christ will continue to be rejected by their own families, it is important that churches that have been planted and nurtured by Brazilians be prepared to meet these real needs for family and community. Indeed, one Brazilian church planter, perhaps recognizing the strategic relationship between the family and the church, asked for prayer that "[we would] be a blessing to the small Arab church in our city [that] we help lead and disciple [and that we would] be an example of a godly family."[92] Finally, as churches in Brazil, particularly Pentecostals, have integrated peoples from diverse ethnic backgrounds and have successfully overcome racial barriers,[93] Brazilian church planters should also plant transformational churches in the Arab world that will combat racism and other social sins.

---

90. See Ekström, "The Selection Process," 185–86; also Adiwardana, "Formal and Non-Formal Pre-Field Training," 209.

91. Related to me in personal conversation, July 23, 2009.

92. Related in personal correspondence (ministry prayer letter), April 2009.

93. See Heaney, *Contextual Theology for Latin America*, 208–9.

Missions from Below

A third area of Brazilian theology of mission that is significant, especially when considering mission in the Arab-Muslim world, is the idea of "missions from below" or missions from a place of vulnerability. While concepts like "missions" and "theology from below" employ the language of Liberation Theology,[94] it is nevertheless valuable to consider the role that Brazilian missionaries play as they minister from a point of economic and political vulnerability.

Escobar boldly declares, "The poor of the world are the greatest missionary force of the present stage in mission history."[95] Reflecting on missions in light of the southward shift of global Christianity, he adds, "Missionary initiative expressed in numbers of people volunteering for missionary work seems to be passing from North to South at a time when the South is increasingly poor."[96] As noted, Escobar asserts that the majority of twentieth-century Latin American Christian workers actually went to the "mission field" in search of employment. That is, while immigrating abroad and surely struggling to make a living, they also managed to share their faith and even plant churches. Those who were sent out by their churches in an official missionary capacity were forced to live simply because of modest resources.[97]

While Padilla admonishes Western missionaries to pursue simple lifestyles in their contexts of ministry, he also argues that poverty does not excuse a church from being involved in the mission of God.[98] At least one *favela* (shanty) church near Porto Alegre, Brazil agrees with Padilla. After sending a sacrificial gift of $300 to Haiti following the January 2010 earthquake, the church leadership stated, "We are working under the belief that no one has so little that he is unable to share. Moreover, we believe that the field is the world and that our aid will open doors for our missionaries on foreign soil."[99]

How then do Brazilian transcultural workers demonstrate a theology of missions from below and why is this significant in the Arab-Muslim

---

94. See Bosch, *Transforming Mission*, 439.

95. See Escobar, *New Global Mission*, 66.

96. Ibid.; also Escobar, "The Global Scenario," 42; and Walls, *The Cross-Cultural Process*, 81.

97. See Escobar, *Changing Tides*, 163.

98. See Padilla, *Mission Between the Times*, 136–37.

99. Related in correspondence with Patrick Hubbard of Living Bread Ministries working in Porto Alegre, February 23, 2010.

context? As shown in the previous chapter, many Brazilian missionaries are forced to live on modest economic resources and this allows them to identify more effectively with the peoples in their host culture. In some cases, they are indeed the poor reaching the poor. Referring specifically to urban missions, Escobar argues, "The churches of the poor have learned to respond to the urban challenge: they speak the language of the masses."[100] As related previously, Amado testified, "Because of our background of relative poverty and economic crises and inflation, we can identify with [Arab] Muslims," and that "[Arab] people perceive that and it is possible to bond with Arabs in a deep level of friendship." Hence, mutual identification has resulted merely from the reality of the economic position of Brazilian workers—not in their choosing to take a vow of poverty or to live simply. Daniel Calze adds that being able to identify with the poor has also helped Brazilians to be more thoughtful and deliberate in humanitarian efforts, enabling Brazilians to do "excellent work in different areas, such as sports, health, and special needs." Finally, it is interesting to note that in one Brazilian missions organization, which is more Pentecostal in orientation, the majority of the personnel come from the Northeast of Brazil—the poorest part of the country. One worker in the mission marveled at how God was truly raising up Brazil's poor to reach the poor in the Arab world.[101]

Second, Brazilians exemplify missions from below because, in coming from a non-Western country that lacks "power, progress, and prestige,"[102] they minister from a posture of political vulnerability. Padilla lamented that even in the post-colonial period and at the end of the twentieth century that "in many cases, missionary work continues to be done from a position of political and economic power and with the assumption of Western superiority in matters of culture and race."[103] Discussing the outcomes of "missions from above," Leonardo Boff, a Brazilian Catholic theologian and contributor to liberation thought, helpfully asserts: "The link between Christianity and the ideology and practice of Western domination produces a cloud of ambiguity and complicity, enormously tarnishing the brilliance of the evangelical practice and the utterance of Jesus."[104]

---

100. See Escobar, *New Global Mission*, 67.

101. Related to me in personal conversation, January 6, 2010.

102. See Escobar, "Missions from the Margins to the Margin," 88.

103. See Padilla, *Mission Between the Times*, 134.

104. See Boff, *New Evangelization*, 41; see also Bosch, "The Vulnerability of Mission," 83–84.

Toward a Brazilian Theology of Mission

Thus, Padilla has urged Western missionaries, especially those serving in Latin America, to see things from the "underside" and to resist ministering from a posture of power.[105] Escobar adds that one of the realities of the post-colonial and post-Christendom world is that Western missionaries are beginning to lose protection from their governments and that they will need to learn from majority world missionaries on how to serve from a place of vulnerability.[106] Bosch concludes with some conviction, "Only if we turn our backs on false power and false security can there be authentic Christian mission."[107]

One of the advantages that Brazilian workers have in the Arab world is that they do approach their context from a posture of vulnerability. Costas has celebrated this reality and has even proposed a missiological model of "from the peripheries of society to the peripheries," which is based on Jesus beginning his ministry among Galilean fisherman.[108] This missiological posture has perhaps been best summarized by Antônia Van der Meer, a Brazilian missiologist who served as a single woman missionary in Southern Africa. She writes, "It is a great privilege to be a missionary who does not come from a country with a powerful economy, whose country does not represent any threat whatsoever, and who cannot be expected to solve all financial problems that arise . . . thus we are freer to serve as partners, as equals, as it was in the beginning when the apostles went out from the least significant countries of the Roman Empire."[109]

In summary, the missiological implications for Brazilians approaching the Arab world from a missions-from-below posture seem quite evident. As noted, Brazilian workers with modest resources can identify with poor Arabs, while poor Arabs readily open their hearts to struggling Brazilians. Also, Brazilians are more likely to be accepted by Arabs on the basis of friendship alone, rather than for the material benefits that they might provide—a challenge that Western missionaries in the Arab world regularly face. Finally, as Brazilians approach mission from a place of political vulnerability, they can also identify with Arabs who are powerless, marginalized, and living in oppressive contexts. Bosch writes that "victim-missionaries," in identifying with the struggles and vulnerabilities of their

---

105. Cited in Smith, "The Essentials of Missiology," 231.
106. See Escobar, "The Global Scenario," 35.
107. See Bosch, "The Vulnerability of Mission," 85.
108. See Costas, *Liberating News,* 49, 67; also Escobar, "Missions from the Margins to the Margins," 88.
109. See Van der Meer, "The Scriptures, the Church, and Humanity," 154.

host people, are able to "lead people to freedom and community."[110] Also, as Bosch has noted, Brazilians are free to pursue authentic mission apart from the expectation that political leverage would help their work. In this sense, they serve as a model to Western missionaries striving to minister in a post-Christendom world.

Spiritual Awareness

A final notable aspect of Brazilian theology of mission is its awareness of the spiritual world. While this was discussed at length in chapter 3, it should simply be restated that Brazilians and Latin Americans are generally sensitive to and have an explanation for the spiritual world. This includes the reality of the demonic world within the animistic practices of Brazilian Spiritism and Folk Islam. While declarations on spiritual warfare from the 1978 Willowbank Report have been cited, Padilla, a Baptist theologian, also references similar thoughts in the Lausanne Covenant: "We believe that we are engaged in constant spiritual warfare with the principalities and powers of evil, who are seeking to overthrow the church and frustrate its task of world evangelization."[111]

For many of the FTL theologians, an awareness of the spiritual world is a key element of holistic mission. Warning against an individualistic and rather compartmentalized view of salvation, Padilla argues, "We have lost sight of the demonic nature of the whole spiritual environment that conditions man's thought and conduct."[112] Interpreting the Gospels and Acts in a functional manner in light of the present context, Escobar adds, "Today's mission in Latin America also confronts the powers of darkness and needs the same empowering that made possible the mission of Jesus."[113] As shown, Brazilian missionaries have brought their spiritually aware backgrounds with them to the Arab world and have integrated kerygmatic proclamation with power encounters in mission.

While Brazilians from the historic, non-Pentecostal churches have shown much sensitivity to the spiritual realities in Folk Muslim contexts, it seems that Brazilian Pentecostals have a special role to play in the Arab-Muslim world on account of their spiritual worldview. Citing the general continuity that exists between animistic worldviews—including those that

110. See Bosch, "The Vulnerability of Mission," 81.
111. Cited in Padilla, *Mission Between the Times*, 45.
112. Ibid., 7.
113. See Escobar, *Changing Tides*, 144.

Toward a Brazilian Theology of Mission

undergird Folk Islam—and a Pentecostal worldview, Miller and Yamamori conclude: "The major difference between Pentecostals and people in animistic cultures is that the former affirm that there is only *one* Spirit, the Holy Spirit."[114] Brazilian Pentecostals serving among Arabs are not unlike historic Pentecostal missionaries who also preached a whole gospel. Anderson writes, "Pentecostal missionaries proclaimed a pragmatic gospel that sought to address practical issues like sickness, poverty, unemployment, loneliness, evil spirits, witchcraft and sorcery" and that "healing, guidance, protection from evil, and success were some of the practical benefits offered." Hence, while the gospel is proclaimed verbally, attention is also given to other real needs, including deliverance from spiritual oppression.[115]

In summary, the spiritual worldview of Brazilian transcultural workers serving among Arab-Muslims is quite relevant to the context. As the great majority of Arab-Muslims are adherents to Folk Islam, which seems to produce spiritual conflicts, the sensitivity of Brazilian workers toward these spiritual issues is important. While the majority of Brazilian missionaries are currently not from the Pentecostal tradition, it seems that as Brazilian Pentecostal missions involvement develops, that the Pentecostal worldview will also prove helpful in the Arab-Muslim context.

Summary

In this chapter, four aspects of Brazilian theology of mission have been discussed. Understood in light of the history of Brazilian missions sending, the cultural experiences of Brazilians in the Arab world, as well Brazilian approaches to mission among Arabs, these elements seem to build upon the general characteristics of Brazilian evangelicalism presented in chapter 1.

In terms of methodology, I have followed Steuernagel in recognizing that there is still much continuity between Brazilian and Latin American theology of mission and that the Brazilian church has gleaned much from the Latin American Theological Fellowship, which, of course, has included Brazilian voices from its earliest days. Also, while these four areas of missiology have been supported by works of articulated theology, it has also proven beneficial to observe them directly in the work of Brazilians

---

114. See Miller and Yamamori, *Global Pentecostalism*, 25.

115. See Anderson, *Spreading Fires*, 240; also Anderson, "Towards a Pentecostal Missiology," 33–35; and Peterson, *Not By Might, Nor By Power*, 98–102, 225–26.

serving among Arabs. Finally, it should be noted that as the Brazilian missions movement is a young one, its theology of mission is still in development. Yet, as the Brazilian missions movement grows, we expect that the literary output from Brazilian missiologists will only increase in the years to come.

The most prevalent aspect of theology presented in the chapter was *missão integral*—the whole gospel or holistic mission. Because of its significance, it was important to discuss the historical development of *missão integral*, the key FTL theologians who helped articulate it, the essence of the theology itself, how *missão integral* has been reflected upon and applied in Arab contexts, and its missiological relevance for the Arab-Muslim world. While for the most part, *missão integral* has been discussed in isolation, it could be argued that the church-centered and spiritually aware aspects of Brazilian missiology actually flow from *missão integral*.

Second, it was shown that despite the shortcomings of the Brazilian local churches in global mission, Brazilian transcultural workers continue to be committed to their churches. In addition, it was shown that the local church was cherished as the focal point for missions sending and that Brazilian evangelicalism has not experienced the gap between the local church and the mission agency that was observed in North America in the nineteenth and twentieth centuries. By implication, it seems that this Brazilian conviction for the local church will result in more transformational churches being planted in the Arab world.

Third, I have argued that missions from below is an important theological motif for Brazilians serving among Arabs. Contrary to nineteenth and twentieth centuries Western missions, which originated from wealthy and powerful countries and moved to poorer and weaker ones, Brazilians have gone to the Arab world from a place of vulnerability. For some Brazilians, this means that they have pursued mission with very modest financial resources and have struggled. Yet, for all Brazilians, it means that their passport does not have the currency of a Western one, and that they do not benefit from the political protection enjoyed by many Westerners. In short, it has been argued that ministering from a place of economic and political vulnerability has enabled Brazilians to identify with their host peoples and to pursue authentic ministry.

Finally, I asserted that Brazilian theology of mission includes a strong awareness of the spiritual world. Building largely on arguments made in chapter 3, it has been shown that Brazilian transcultural workers have an explanation for and response to the spiritual issues encountered in the

Muslim world. While Brazilians from the Pentecostal tradition seem especially equipped for spiritual warfare ministry, non-Pentecostals are also quite in tune to the spiritual world of Muslims and have also responded appropriately to such needs.

Conclusion

IN THIS WORK, I have endeavored to tell part of the story of the emerging Brazilian evangelical missions movement, specifically focusing on Brazilian work in the countries of the Arab-Muslim world since 1976. This has been accomplished first by recounting how Brazil was evangelized largely by North American missionaries in the nineteenth and twentieth centuries. From this narrative, it has become clear that while the Brazilian evangelical church does share common characteristics with North American and global evangelicalism, it has also begun to forge its own evangelical identity. An important part of this identity is its concrete participation in global mission efforts. Indeed, Brazil has gone from being a mission field to being a missions sender.

In considering Brazilian mission efforts in the Arab-Muslim world, it has been valuable to reflect upon how Brazilians have adapted culturally by focusing on eight aspects of culture that have clear missiological implications. They include race, economics, time, communication, family, relationships, hospitality, and spiritual worldview, and have been discussed in both the Arab and Brazilian contexts. While a study of the relevant literature has been foundational, the theme analysis has been founded on the descriptions of Brazilian transcultural workers and mission leaders at work in the Arab-Muslim world. It has become evident that there are some definite differences in Arab and Brazilian culture—most notably in the areas of conflict resolution, personal hygiene as it relates to food and hospitality, and the role of women. On the other hand, some aspects of Arab and Brazilian culture are rather similar. The strongest areas seem to be hospitality, relationship building, and a general spiritual worldview that acknowledges the role of demons and spirits. It has also become apparent that transcultural workers from the Northeast of Brazil seem be closest to the Arabs culturally. This was especially evident when considering the cultural aspects of economics, time, family, and relationships. In short, as Brazilians have described their experiences, it seems that there is some favorable continuity between the cultures of Brazilian evangelical workers and the Arab contexts in which they serve. Coupled with the reality that Brazilians seem to adapt well in other cultures, it seems that the contribution of Brazilian transcultural missionaries is important in the Arab world. It also appears that Brazilians, generally speaking, adapt better to ministry in the Arab-Muslim world than their North American and European colleagues.

It has also been profitable to offer a practical summary of Brazilian evangelical approaches to mission in the Arab-Muslim world. This included some prominent historic mission strategies (evangelism, discipleship, and church planting) as well as a summary of integrated support ministries, including humanitarian work, medical work, sports ministry, and Business as Mission among others. In addition, the work and core values of six Brazilian missions organizations that work in the Arab world were considered. These included two groups that are indigenous to Brazil (Missão Antioquia, Missão Kairos), one that is indigenous to Latin America (PMI), one historic denomination (Junta de Missões Mundiais da Convenção Batista Brasileira), and two international organizations that have opened offices in Brazil (CCI-Brasil, Interserve).

Based on this survey of Brazilian mission strategies in the Arab world, the apparent strengths (as described by Brazilians) were discussed. It was argued that Brazilian missionaries seem to be doing well at building relationships, adapting to culture, communicating the gospel, planting churches, and offering humanitarian aid. It was further observed that Brazilian workers and missions organizations tend to measure their success in terms of their ability to persevere and to build relationships. Finally, the chapter concluded by exploring the four most apparent challenges facing Brazilian evangelical missionaries in the Arab world—church support, language acquisition, financial support, and women's issues. In each case, an effort was made to understand and define the problem clearly after which some suggestions—based largely on Brazilian reflections—were offered toward resolving the problem. In short, this chapter has demonstrated that after a few decades, Brazilian evangelical missions efforts in the Arab world are focused, innovative, courageous, and still developing.

Finally, building upon the articulated thought of Brazilian and Latin American theologians as well as the observed practice of Brazilian workers in the Arab world, four key elements of Brazilian theology of mission were presented. While the most defining feature of a Brazilian theology of mission is *missão integral* (the whole gospel or holistic mission), other key areas included: a church-centered missiology, missions from below, and a spiritual awareness.

In summary, in this work, I have attempted to tell part of the story of Brazilian evangelical missions—a first generation movement that is still emerging—by focusing on efforts in the Arab world. Yet, amid the tensions and problems in the world, this majority world missions movement seems poised to lead the way in twenty-first century global mission, particularly in the Arab-Muslim world.

In light of this work, what other areas of study should be pursued? First, the issue of member care among Brazilian missionaries needs continual reflection. While a number of Brazilian mission leaders are making this a priority, this remains an important area for study, reflection, and adjustment. Second, it would be valuable to study the global missions efforts of the nearly 1000 Brazilian evangelical congregations in North America. What is their vision and strategy for missions sending and how should the North American congregations relate to churches and missionaries in Brazil? Third, as the Brazilian Pentecostal churches continue to grow, it will be important to study their global mission efforts, including their theology and approaches to mission. Finally, during the course of this study, I met a Mexican missionary who was facilitating teams of Mexican transcultural workers in the Arab world. It would certainly be interesting to pursue a similar study focusing on Mexican missions in the Arab world.

Appendix A
Brazilian Transcultural Workers Survey Pool

Number	Date	Manner Surveyed	Gender/Marital Status	Years Served	Other
1	March 24, 2009	Online (Portuguese)	Single woman	4 years	
2	March 26, 2009	Online (English)	Single woman	Less than 1 year	
3	March 27, 2009	Online (Portuguese)	Married man	More than 20 years	
4	May 4, 2009	Online (Portuguese)	Married/gender unknown	10–15 years	
5	May 8, 2009	Online (Portuguese)	Married man	4 years	
6	May 9, 2009	Online (Portuguese and English)	Single woman	1–2 years	
7	June 1, 2009	Online (Portuguese and English)	Single/gender unknown	3–5 years	
8	July 19, 2009	Interview in English	Married man	3–5 years	Serving among Arabs in both Middle East and Brazil
9	July 19, 2009	Interview through translation	Married man	5–10 years	Serving among Arabs in Brazil

243

Appendix A

Number	Date	Manner Surveyed	Gender/Marital Status	Years Served	Other
10	July 19, 2009	Interview in English	Married woman (wife of n. 9)	5–10 years	Serving among Arabs in Brazil
11	July 20, 2009	Interview through translation	Married man	5–10 years	Serving in both North Africa and Brazil
12	July 20, 2009	Interview through translation	Married woman (wife of n. 10)	5–10 years	Serving in both North Africa and Brazil
13	July 21, 2009	Interview through translation	Married man	10–15 years	Serving among Arabs in Brazil
14	July 24, 2009	Online (Portuguese)	Married (probably woman based on responses)	10–15 years	
15	July 24, 2009	Online (Portuguese)	Married/gender unknown	3–5 years	
16	July 24, 2009	Online (Portuguese)	Married/gender unknown	5–10 years	
17	July 27, 2009	Online (English)	Single woman	8.5 years	
18	July 29, 2009	Interview in English	Single man	5–10 years	Served among Arabs in North Africa, USA, Brazil
19	July 31, 2009	Online (Portuguese)	Single woman	4 months	
20	August 3, 2009	Online (Portuguese)	Married/gender unknown	unknown	
21	August 4, 2009	Interview in English via Skype	Married man	15–20 years	Presently pastor in Brazil
22	August 14, 2009	Online (Portuguese and English)	Married woman	12 years	

Brazilian Transcultural Workers Survey Pool

Number	Date	Manner Surveyed	Gender/ Marital Status	Years Served	Other
23	October 15, 2009	Paper questionnaire filled out in Portuguese, translated to English; focus group discussion	Married woman	3–5 years	
24	October 15, 2009	Paper questionnaire filled out in Portuguese, translated to English; focus group discussion	Single woman	3–5 years	
25	October 15, 2009	Paper questionnaire filled out in Portuguese, translated to English; focus group discussion	Single woman	Less than 1 year	
26	October 15, 2009	Paper questionnaire filled out in Portuguese, translated to English; focus group discussion	Married woman	3–5 years	
27	October 15, 2009	Paper questionnaire filled out in Portuguese, translated to English; focus group discussion	Married woman	1–2 years	
28	October 15, 2009	Paper questionnaire filled out in Portuguese, translated to English; focus group discussion	Married woman	3–5 years	
29	October 15, 2009	Paper questionnaire filled out in Portuguese, translated to English; focus group discussion	Single woman	5–10 years	

Appendix A

Number	Date	Manner Surveyed	Gender/Marital Status	Years Served	Other
30	October 15, 2009	Paper questionnaire filled out in Portuguese, translated to English; focus group discussion	Single woman	Less than 1 year	10 years of prior transcultural experience.
31	October 15, 2009	Paper questionnaire filled out in Portuguese, translated to English; focus group discussion	Married man (husband of n. 28)	3–5 years	
32	October 15, 2009	Paper questionnaire filled out in Portuguese, translated to English; focus group discussion	Married man (husband of n. 27)	1–2 years	
33	October 29, 2009	Interview in English	Single man	2 years	Presently working as a tentmaker/church planter in the USA
34	January 7, 2010	Interview in English	Single woman	5–10 years	
35	January 7, 2010	Interview in English	Married woman	5–10 years	
36	January 7, 2010	Interview in English	Married man	5–10 years	
37	January 7, 2010	Interview in English	Married woman (wife of n. 36)	5–10 years	
38	January 7, 2010	Interview in English	Single man	5–10 years	
39	January 7, 2010	Interview in English	Single woman	4 years	
40	January 7, 2010	Interview in English	Married woman	3–5 years	Spouse is non-Brazilian

Brazilian Transcultural Workers Survey Pool

Number	Date	Manner Surveyed	Gender/Marital Status	Years Served	Other
41	January 7, 2010	Interview through translation	Married man	3–5 years	
42	January 7, 2010	Interview through translation	Married woman (wife of n. 41)	3–5 years	
43	January 8, 2010	Interview through translation	Married woman	3–5 years	Spouse is non-Brazilian
44	January 10, 2010	Interview in English	Married man	10–15 years	Serving in Brazil and the Middle East
45	January 10, 2010	Interview in English	Married woman (wife of n. 44)	10–15 years	Serving in both Brazil and the Middle East

Appendix B
Brazilian Transcultural Workers Survey Questions

1. I understand and agree to participate in the survey.
2. In general, how comfortable do you feel in an Arab-Muslim cultural context? Very comfortable? Comfortable? Uncomfortable? Very Uncomfortable? Comments?
3. What aspects of Arab-Muslim culture do you really enjoy?
4. What aspects of Arab-Muslim culture are difficult for you?

For questions 5-13, in your opinion, is your culture similar to or different from Arab culture in the following areas:

5. View of Time? Very similar? Similar? Different? Very Different? Comments?
6. Tastes in Food? Very similar? Similar? Different? Very Different? Comments?
7. Verbal Communication? Very similar? Similar? Different? Very Different? Comments?
8. Nonverbal Communication? Very similar? Similar? Different? Very Different? Comments?
9. Building relationships? Very similar? Similar? Different? Very Different? Comments?
10. Resolving Conflict? Very similar? Similar? Different? Very Different? Comments?

11. Family Life and Relationships? Very similar? Similar? Different? Very Different? Comments?

12. Hospitality? Very similar? Similar? Different? Very Different? Comments?

13. Views about work? Very similar? Similar? Different? Very Different? Comments?

14. How long have you been serving in cross-cultural ministry in the Arab world? More than 20 years? 15–20 years? 10–15 years? 5–10 years? 3–5 years? 1–2 years? Less than 1 year?

15. How would you rate your preparation for cross-cultural ministry before coming to the Arab world? Very Adequate? Adequate? Inadequate? Very Inadequate? Comments?

16. How would you rate your financial support? Adequate? Adequate? Inadequate? Very Inadequate? Comments?

For questions 17-20, How would you rate your overall health in:

17. Marriage? Very healthy? Healthy? Unhealthy? Very unhealthy? Comments?

18. Family Life (including children)? Very healthy? Healthy? Unhealthy? Very unhealthy? Comments?

19. Physical Health? Very healthy? Healthy? Unhealthy? Very unhealthy? Comments?

20. Spiritual Life? Very healthy? Healthy? Unhealthy? Very unhealthy? Comments?

21. How would you rate the care (encouragement, pastoral care, prayer support) that you receive from your missions agency or sending church? Very Adequate? Adequate? Inadequate? Very Inadequate? Comments?

22. Are there aspects of support, care, or resources that you need for your ministry that are lacking? If so, what are they?

23. How much longer do you hope/intend to stay in the Arab world? Wanting to leave immediately? Less than 1 year? 2–4 years? 5–10 years? More than 10 years? Comments?

24. Describe your relationship with missionaries from other cultures (e.g. North America, Europe, Asia).

Appendix B

25. How well are you doing in language learning? Excellent? Well? Average? Below Average? Poor? Comments?

26. What are your main areas of ministry? Evangelism? Teaching/Discipleship? Church Planting? Spiritual Warfare? Humanitarian Aid? Translation? Media development? Others?

27. How has spiritual warfare prayer and ministry been a part of your ministry?

28. How have you experienced success in your ministry? Please comment.

29. In what areas have you experienced failure? Please comment.

30. What are you most excited about in your present and future ministry?

31. Please feel free to comment on anything else relevant to your cross-cultural ministry experience in the Arab world.

Appendix C
Brazilian Mission Leaders Survey Pool

Number	Date	Manner Surveyed	Gender/Marital Status	Role	Other
1	April 27, 2009	Online (English)	Married man	Theological seminary dean	
2	May 1, 2009	Online (English)	Single woman	Missions instructor	North American
3	May 2, 2009	Online (Portuguese)	Man	Pastor, mission leader	
4 (Silas Tostes)	May 5, 2009	Online (Portuguese)	Married Man	Mission agency leader	I spent a day with the participant, Silas Tostes, at the Missão Antioquia headquarters near São Paulo
5 (João Mordomo)	July 21, 2009	Interview in English	Married Man	Mission agency leader	North American; I spent 3 days with him at the CCI mission headquarters and at a training event
6 (Daniel Calze)	July 21, 2009	Online (Portuguese)	Married Man	Mission agency leader	I spent part of a day with him at the PMI Brasil headquarters in Curitiba.

Appendix C

Number	Date	Manner Surveyed	Gender/Marital Status	Role	Other
7 (Robson Ramos)	July 29, 2009	Interview in English	Single Man	Missiologist, church planter, author	Same as n. 18 in Brazilian workers. I visited his current work in Southern Brazil.
8	August 3, 2009	Online (Portuguese)	Woman (marital status unknown)	Mission agency leader	
9 (Tim Halls)	August 24, 2009	Telephone interview	Married Man	Mission agency leader	North American who spent many years in Brazil; currently mobilizing Latins in the USA to mission
10 (Marcos Amado)	August 27, 2009	Interview in English via skype	Married Man	Mission agency leader, missions pastor	Same as n. 21 in workers survey

Appendix D
Mission Leaders Survey Questions

1. I understand the survey and agree to participate.
2. What is the name of your organization?
3. What is your denominational affiliation?
4. Give a brief history of your organization.
5. What is your specific role in missions preparation and mobilization within your organization?
6. How long have you been serving in your present role?
7. Describe in as much detail as you would like the vision of your organization toward global missions.
8. What is the vision of your organization toward mobilizing Brazilians for mission work in the Arab-Muslim world?
9. Approximately, how many Brazilian missionaries have been sent by your organization to minister in the Arab-Muslim world since 1976?
10. What are the major areas of ministry encouraged by your organization in the Arab-Muslim world? Evangelism? Teaching/Discipleship? Church Planting? Spiritual Warfare? Humanitarian Aid? Translation? Media development? Others?
11. Of the areas listed in the last question, what are the 2-3 priorities of your organization in the Arab-Muslim world?
12. How much do you emphasize spiritual warfare prayer and ministry in your training?

Appendix D

13. In your opinion, how have your missionaries been "successful" (please define this by your own criteria) in ministry in the Arab-Muslim world?

14. In your opinion, how have your missionaries experienced failure in ministry in the Arab-Muslim world?

15. Within your specific role, what is your strategy for preparing Brazilian missionaries for the Arab-Muslim world (e.g. missiological, theological, church planting training, tentmaking/business training)?

16. In your opinion, what is the overall quality of pre-field training of Brazilian missionaries from your organization? Why?

17. What do you see as presently lacking in the pre-field training of Brazilian missionaries to the Arab-Muslim world?

18. What is the philosophy of your organization for raising financial support for missionaries?

19. In your opinion, do missionaries from your organization (and other organizations) have adequate financial resources to stay on the field?

20. What are the greatest difficulties and challenges faced by your missionaries serving in the Arab-Muslim world?

21. What percentage of missionaries in your organization have left the mission field in the Arab-Muslim world?

22. What are the main reasons for your missionaries not continuing in ministry in the Arab-Muslim world?

23. In what ways does your organization provide pastoral care (member care) for your missionaries in the Arab-Muslim world?

24. Does your organization have a prayer strategy for missionaries in the Arab-Muslim world? If so, please describe it.

25. Please feel free to comment on anything else that you feel is important about Brazilian missions in the Arab-Muslim world and the preparation, sending, and care of Brazilian missionaries in the Arab Muslim world.

Bibliography

Abdol Masih, Bashir. "The Incarnational Witness to the Muslim Heart." In *The Gospel and Islam: A 1978 Compendium*, edited by Don McCurry, 85–96. Monrovia, CA: MARC, 1979.
Adeney, Miriam. *Kingdom Without Borders: The Untold Story of Global Christianity*. Downers Grove, IL: InterVarsity, 2009.
Adiwardana, Margaretha. "Formal and Non-Formal Pre-Field Training: Perspective of the New Sending Countries." In *Too Valuable to Lose: Exploring the Causes and Cures of Missionary Attrition*, edited by William D. Taylor, 207–15. Pasadena, CA: William Carey Library, 1997.
———. "Treinar Missionários Para Perseverar: Um Preparo Holístico Para Situações de Adversidade." *Capacitando* 9 (2001) 5–15.
Ahlstrom, Sidney E. *A Religious History of the American People*. New Haven: Yale University Press, 2004.
Alvarez, Miguel. "The South and the Latin American Paradigm of the Pentecostal Movement." *Asian Journal of Pentecostal Studies* 5.1 (2002) 135–53.
Amado, Marcos. "A Capacitação Contínua do Obreiro." *Capacitando* 9 (2001) 39–46.
American Presbyterians in Brazil. "151 Years (and counting) of Missionary Involvement." http://www.apib.org
Anderson, Allan. *An Introduction to Pentecostalism: Global Charismatic Christianity*. Cambridge: Cambridge University Press, 2004.
———. *Spreading Fires: The Missionary Nature of Early Pentecostalism*. Maryknoll, NY: Orbis, 2007.
———. "Towards a Pentecostal Missiology for the Majority World." *Asian Journal of Pentecostal Studies* 8.1 (2005) 29–47.
Anderson, Justice. *An Evangelical Saga: Baptists and Their Precursors in Latin America*. Longwood, FL: Xulon, 2005.
Araujo, Alex. "Impressions of III COMIBAM Missionary Congress." *Connections* (2007) 29–34.
Arnold, Frank L. "A Peek in the Baggage of Brazil's Pioneer Missionaries." *Missiology: An International Review* 34.2 (2006) 125–34.
Associação de Missões Transculturais Brasileiras. http://www.amtb.org.br/
Associação de Professores de Missões no Brasil. http://www.apmb.org.br/index.html
Avante: Missão Evangélica Transcultural. http://www.missaoavante.org.br/index3.asp
Azevedo, Fernando de. *Brazilian Culture: An Introduction to the Study of Culture in Brazil*. Translated by William Rex Crawford. New York: Hafner, 1971.

Bibliography

Badr, Habib. "American Protestant Missionary Beginnings in Beirut and Istanbul: Policy, Politics, Practice, and Response." In *New Faith in Ancient Lands: Western Missions in the Nineteenth and Early Twentieth Centuries,* edited by Heleen Murre-van den Berg, 211–39. Leiden: Brill, 2006.

Barakat, Halim Isber. *The Arab World: Society, Culture, and State.* Berkeley: University of California Press, 1993.

Barakat, Robert. "Arabic Gestures." *Journal of Popular Culture* 6 (1973) 749–93.

Barbosa, Lívia. "The Brazilian Jeitinho: An Exercise in National Identity." In *The Brazilian Puzzle: Culture on the Borderlands of the Western World,* edited by David J. Hess et al., 35–48. New York: Columbia University Press, 1995.

———. *O Jeitinho Brasileiro: A Arte de Ser Mais Igual que os Outros.* Rio de Janeiro: Editora Campus, 1992.

Barnett, Mike, and Tom Steffen. *Business as Mission: From Impoverished to Empowered.* Evangelical Missiological Series 14. Pasadena, CA: William Carey Library, 2006.

Barrett, David B. et al., editors. *World Christian Encyclopedia: An Analysis of Six Thousand Contemporary Religious Movements.* Oxford: Oxford University Press, 2001.

Bastian, Jean-Pierre. "The Metamorphosis of Latin American Protestant Groups: A Sociological Perspective." *Latin American Research Review* 28.2 (1993) 33–61.

———. "Protestantism in Latin America." In *The Church in Latin America, 1492–1992,* edited by Enrique Dussel, translated by John Cumming, 313–50. Maryknoll, NY: Orbis, 1992.

BBC News. "Sudan Profile." (2012) http://news.bbc.co.uk/2/hi/middle_east/country_profiles/827425.stm.

Beach, Harlan P. et al. *Protestant Missions in South America.* New York: Student Volunteer Movement for Foreign Missions, 1900.

Bebbington, David William. *Evangelicalism in Modern Britain: A History from the 1730s to the 1980s.* London: Allen & Unwin, 1989.

Berg, Mike, and Paul Pretiz. "Five Waves of Protestant Evangelization." In *New Face of the Church in Latin America: Between Tradition and Change,* edited by Guillermo Cook, 56–67. Maryknoll, NY: Orbis, 1994.

Bertuzzi, Federico. "Internationalization or 'Anglonization' of Missions." *Journal of Frontier Missions* 21.1 (2005) 13–16.

———. *Latinos No Mundo Muçulmano.* São Paulo, Brazil: Sepal, 1993.

Bevans, Stephen B., and Roger P. Schroeder. *Constants in Context: A Theology of Mission for Today.* Maryknoll, NY: Orbis, 2004.

Boff, Leonardo. *New Evangelization: Good News to the Poor.* Translated by Robert R. Barr. Maryknoll, NY: Orbis, 1991.

Bonino, José Míguez. *Faces of Latin American Protestantism: 1993 Carnahan Lectures.* Grand Rapids: Eerdmans, 1995

Bosch, David J. *Transforming Mission.* Maryknoll, NY: Orbis, 1991.

———. "The Vulnerability of Mission." In *New Directions in Mission and Evangelization II: Theological Foundations,* edited by James A. Sherer et al., 73–86. Maryknoll, NY: Orbis, 1994.

Bothelo, David. "The Principles, Practice and Plan of Horizontes Latin America." Online: http://www.ad2000.org/celebrate/bothelo.htm, 2000.

Bradford, Kevin D. et al. *Perspectivas No Movimento Cristão Mundial.* São Paulo: Vida Nova, 2009.

Bibliography

Braga, Erasmo, and Kenneth G. Grubb. *The Republic of Brazil: A Survey of the Religious Situation.* London: World Dominion, 1932.

Brewster, E. Thomas, and Elizabeth S. Brewster. *Language Acquisition Made Practical: Field Methods for Language Learners.* Pasadena, CA: Lingua House, 1982.

Brown, Rick. "Communicating God's Message in an Oral Culture: Communicating Effectively to Non-Readers." *International Journal of Frontier Missions* 21 (Fall) 122–28.

Brown, Rose. *The Land and People of Brazil.* Philadelphia: Lippincott, 1972.

Burns, Barbara. "Brazilian Antioch, Community, Spirituality, and Mission." In *Global Missiology for the Twenty-First Century: The Iguassu Dialogue,* edited by William D. Taylor, 515–17. Grand Rapids: Baker, 2000.

Bush, Luis. "Brazil, a Sleeping Giant Awakens: An AD 2000 Report." *Mission Frontiers* (1994). Online: http://www.missionfrontiers.org/issue/article/brazil-a-sleeping-giant-awakens.

CCI-Brasil. http://www.ccibrasil.org

Campbell, Evvy Hay. "Holistic Mission." Lausanne Occasional Paper 33. Lausanne Committee for World Evangelization. Online: http://www.lausanne.org/documents/2004forum/LOP33_IG4.pdf, 2005.

Campos, Oscar A. "Premillennial Tensions and Holistic Missiology: Latin American Evangelicalism." In *A Case for Historic Premillennialism: An Alternative to "Left Behind" Theology,* edited by Craig A. Blomberg et al., 147–69. Grand Rapids: Baker Academic, 2009.

Carrasco, Pedro. "Training Latins for the Muslim World." *International Journal of Frontier Missions* 11.1 (1994) 1–4.

Carilló, Pablo. "Struggles of Latin Americans in Frontier Missions." Translated by Kelly O'Donnell. *International Journal of Frontier Missions* 12.4 (1995) 195–98.

Carmichael, Joel. *The Shaping of the Arabs: A Study in Ethnic Identity.* New York: Macmillan, 1967.

Cascudo, Luís da Câmara. *História dos Nossos Gestos: Uma Peguisa na Mímica do Brasil.* São Paulo: Melhoramentos, 1976.

Central Intelligence Agency. "World Fact Book: Brazil." https://www.cia.gov/library/publications/the-world-factbook/geos/br.html

———. "World Fact Book: Economy, Brazil." Online: https://www.cia.gov/library/publications/the-world-factbook/geos/br.html.

Centro Evangélico de Missões. http://www.cem.org.br/site/interserve/

Chaney, Charles L. *The Birth of Missions in America.* Pasadena, CA: William Carey Library, 1976.

Chestnut, R. Andrew. *Born Again in Brazil: The Pentecostal Boom and the Pathogens of Poverty.* Rutgers: Rutgers University Press, 1997.

Comblin, José. "Brazil: Base Communities in the Northeast." In *New Face of the Church in Latin America: Between Tradition and Change,* edited by Guillermo Cook, 202–5. Maryknoll, NY: Orbis, 1994.

COMIBAM Internacional Cooperación Misionera Iberoamericana. http://www.comibam.org

Cook, Guillermo. "Introduction: The Changing Face of the Church in Latin America." In *New Face of the Church in Latin America: Between Tradition and Change,* edited by Guillermo Cook, ix–xiv. Maryknoll, NY: Orbis, 1994.

Bibliography

———. *New Face of the Church in Latin America: Between Tradition and Change*. Maryknoll, NY: Orbis, 1994.

———. "Protestant Mission and Evangelization." In *New Face of the Church in Latin America: Between Tradition and Change*, edited by Guillermo Cook, 41–55. Maryknoll, NY: Orbis, 1994.

———. "The Many Faces of the Latin American Church." In *New Face of the Church in Latin America: Between Tradition and Change*, edited by Guillermo Cook, 268–76. Maryknoll, NY: Orbis, 1994.

Corrie, John. *Dictionary of Mission Theology: Evangelical Foundations*. Downers Grove, IL: InterVarsity, 2007.

Costas, Orlando. *Christ Outside the Gate: Mission Beyond Christendom*. Maryknoll, NY: Orbis, 1982.

———. *Liberating News: A Theology of Contextual Evangelization*. Grand Rapids: Eerdmans, 1989.

Cox, Harvey Gallagher. *Fire from Heaven: The Rise of Pentecostal Spirituality and the Reshaping of Religion in the Twenty-First Century*. New York: Addison-Wesley, 1995.

Creswell, John W. *Qualitative Inquiry & Research Design: Choosing Among Five Approaches*. Thousand Oaks, CA: SAGE, 2007.

DaMatta, Roberto A. "For an Anthropology of the Brazilian Tradition; or 'A Virtude está no Meio.'" In *The Brazilian Puzzle: Culture on the Borderlands of the Western World*, edited by David J. Hess et al., 270–91. New York: Columbia University Press, 1995.

DeCarvalho, Levi. "COMIBAM III: Research Project—Phase I." *Connections* (2007) 20–24.

Decker, Murray, and Ryan Keating. "Mission Mobilization: The Radical Project." *Evangelical Missions Quarterly* 39.3 (2003) 312–321.

Dias, Zwinglio. "Brazilian Churches in Mission: Editorial." *International Review of Mission* 85.338 (1996) 347–53.

Dillman, Don A. et al. "Principles for Constructing Web Surveys." Unpublished paper. Online: http://survey.sesrc.wsu.edu/dillman/papers/websurveyppr.pdf.

Douglass, J. D., editor. "Brazil National Strategy Group Report." In *Let the Earth Hear His Voice: International Congress on World Evangelization Lausanne, Switzerland*, 1344–1346. Minneapolis: World Wide Publications, 1974.

———. Editor. *Let the Earth Hear His Voice: International Congress on World Evangelization, Lausanne, Switzerland*. Minneapolis: World Wide Publications, 1974.

Downey, Steven. "Ibero-Americans Reaching Arab-Muslims." *Lausanne World Pulse* (2003). Online: http://www.lausanneworldpulse.com/worldpulse/325.

Dussel, Enrique, editor. *The Church in Latin America, 1492–1992*. Maryknoll, NY: Orbis, 1992.

Ekström, Bertil. "Brazilian Sending." In *Perspectives on the World Christian Movement: A Reader*. 4th ed. Edited by Ralph Winter et al., 371–72. Pasadena, CA: William Carey Library, 2009.

———. *Espiritu de Comibam*. Brazil: Comibam, 2006.

———. "Missões a Partir do Brasil." In *Perspectivas No Movimento Cristão Mundial*, edited by Kevin D. Bradford et al., 367–69. São Paulo: Vida Nova, 2009.

———. "Missões e Cia." In *Perspectivas No Movimento Cristão Mundial*, edited by Kevin D. Bradford et al., 778–81, São Paulo: Vida Nova, 2009.

———. *Modelos Missionários Brasileiros Para ó XXI*. Brazil: AMTB, 1998.

———. "The Selection Process and the Issue of Attrition: Perspective of the New Sending Countries." In *Too Valuable to Lose: Exploring the Causes and Cures of Missionary Attrition*, edited by William D. Taylor, 183–93. Pasadena, CA: William Carey Library, 1997.

———. "Uma Análise Histórica dos Objetivos da Associação de Missões Transculturais Brasilerias e o seu Cumprimento." MTh thesis, Faculdade Teológica Batista de São Paulo, 1998.

Ekström, Bertil, and Ted Limpic. "Signs of Improvement in the Brazilian Mission Movement." *Connections* (2005) 31–32.

Elmer, Duane. *Cross-Cultural Conflict: Building Relationships for Effective Ministry*. Downers Grove, IL: InterVarsity, 1993.

———. *Cross-Cultural Connections: Stepping Out and Fitting In Around the World*. Downers Grove, IL: InterVarsity, 2002.

Escobar, Samuel. *Changing Tides: Latin America and World Mission Today*. Maryknoll, NY: Orbis, 2002.

———. "Latin American Theology." In *Dictionary of Mission Theology: Evangelical Foundations*, edited by John Corrie, 203–7. Downers Grove, IL: InterVarsity, 2007.

———. "Missions from the Margins to the Margins: Two Case Studies from Latin America." *Missiology: An International Review* 26.1 (1998) 87–95.

———. "Missions New World Order." *Christianity Today* (1994) 48–52.

———. "The Church in Latin America after Five Hundred Years: An Evangelical Missiological Perspective." In *New Face of the Church in Latin America: Between Tradition and Change*, edited by Guillermo Cook, 21–37. Maryknoll, NY: Orbis, 1994.

———. "The Global Scenario at the Turn of the Century." In *Global Missiology for the Twenty-First Century: The Iguassu Dialogue*, edited by William D. Taylor, 25–46. Grand Rapids: Baker, 2000.

———. *The New Global Mission: The Gospel from Everywhere to Everyone*. Downers Grove, IL: InterVarsity, 2003.

Finley, Donald K. "Contextualized Training for Missionaries: A Brazilian Model." PhD diss., Asbury Theological Seminary, 2005.

Fleischmann, Ellen. "Evangelization or Education: American Protestant Missionaries, the American Board, and the Girls and Women of Syria (1830–1910)." In *New Faith in Ancient Lands: Western Missions in the Nineteenth and Early Twentieth Centuries*, edited by Heleen Murre-van den Berg, 263–80. Leiden: Brill, 2006.

Fletcher, James C., and Daniel P. Kidder. *Brazil and the Brazilians: Portrayed in Historical and Descriptive Sketches*. Boston: Little, Brown, and Co., 1866.

Freston, Paul. "Brazil: Church Growth, Parachurch Agencies, and Politics." In *New Face of the Church in Latin America: Between Tradition and Change*, edited by Guillermo Cook, 226–42. Maryknoll, NY: Orbis, 1994.

———. "Contours in Latin American Pentecostalism." In *Christianity Reborn: The Global Expansion of Evangelicalism in the Twentieth Century*, edited by Donald M. Lewis, 221–70. Grand Rapids: Eerdmans, 2004.

———. "The Universal Church of the Kingdom of God: A Brazilian Church Finds Success in Southern Africa." *Journal of Religion in Africa* 35.1 (2005) 33–65.

Bibliography

"General Report of the III Iberoamerican Missions Congress, November 13–17, 2006, Granada Spain." Unpublished paper.

George, Sherron K. "Brazil: An 'Evangelized' Giant Calling for Liberating Evangelism." *International Bulletin of Missionary Research* (2002) 104–9.

———. "Presbyterian Seeds Bear Fruit in Brazil as Doors to Partnership Open and Close." *Missiology: An International Review* 34.2 (2006) 135–49.

George, Timothy. "Evangelical Revival and the Missionary Awakening." In *The Great Commission: Evangelicals and the History of World Missions*, edited by Martin I. Klauber et al., 44–63. Nashville: B & H Academic, 2008.

Global CHE Network. http://chenetwork.org/index.php

González, Justo L., and Ondina E. González. *Christianity in Latin America: A History*. Cambridge: Cambridge University Press, 2007.

Greenham, Anthony. "Muslim Conversions to Christ: An Investigation of Palestinian Converts Living in the Holy Land." PhD diss., Southeastern Baptist Theological Seminary, 2004.

Guarneri, Julio. "COMIBAM: Calling Latin Americans to the Global Challenge." Unpublished paper, Evangelical Missiological Society Annual Meeting, Denver, CO, September 27, 2008.

Guthrie, Stan. *Missions in the Third Millennium: 21 Key Trends for the Twenty-First Century*. Waynesboro, GA: Paternoster, 2000.

Guzmán, Andrés, and Angelica Guzmán. "Nós Como Servos: Os Obreiros Latino-Americanos no Oriente Médio." In *Perspectivas No Movimento Cristão Mundial*, edited by Kevin D. Bradford et al., 738–41, São Paulo: Vida Nova, 2009.

Hall, Edward T. *Beyond Culture*. New York: Doubleday, 1981.

———. *The Silent Language*. Westport, CT: Greenwood, 1980.

Hall, Timothy D. "The Protestant Atlantic Awakening and the Origins of an Evangelical Missionary Sensibility." Unpublished paper, Conference on Awakenings and Revivals in American History, Liberty University, Lynchburg, VA, April 16, 2009.

Hankins, Barry. *The Second Great Awakening and the Transcendentalists*. Westport, CT: Greenwood, 2004.

Harrison, Phyllis A. *Behaving Brazilian: A Comparison of Brazilian and North American Social Behavior*. Cambridge: Newbury House, 1983.

Haykin, Michael, and Kenneth J. Stewart. *The Advent of Evangelicalism: Exploring Historical Continuities*. Nashville: B & H Academic, 2008.

Heaney, Sharon E. *Contextual Theology for Latin America: Liberation Themes in Evangelical Perspective*. Colorado Springs, CO: Paternoster, 2008.

Heikes, Laura. "Una Perspectiva Diferente: Latin Americans and the Global Missions Movement." *Missiology: An International Review* 31.1 (2003) 69–85.

Hess, David J., and Roberto A. DaMatta. *The Brazilian Puzzle: Culture on the Borderlands of the Western World*. New York: Columbia University Press, 1995.

Hess, David J. "Hierarchy, Heterodoxy, and the Construction of Brazilian Religious Therapies." In *The Brazilian Puzzle: Culture on the Borderlands of the Western World*, edited by David J. Hess et al., 180–208. New York: Columbia University Press, 1995.

Hesselgrave, David J. *Communicating Christ Cross-Culturally: An Introduction to Missionary Communication*. 2nd ed. Grand Rapids: Zondervan, 1991.

Hesselgrave, David J., and Edward Rommen. *Contextualization: Meanings, Methods, and Models*. Grand Rapids: Baker, 1989.

Hiebert, Paul. *Cultural Anthropology*. Grand Rapids: Baker, 1976.

———. "Cultural Differences and the Communication of the Gospel." In *Perspectives on the World Christian Movement: A Reader*. 3rd ed. Edited by Ralph D. Winter et al., 373–83. Pasadena, CA: William Carey Library, 1999.

———. "Power Encounter and Folk Islam." In *Muslims and Christians on the Emmaus Road*, edited by J. Dudley Woodberry, 45–61. Monrovia, CA: MARC, 1989.

———. *Transforming Worldviews: An Anthropological Understanding of How People Change*. Grand Rapids: Baker Academic, 2008.

Hoornaert, Edouardo. "The Church in Brazil." In *The Church in Latin America, 1492–1992*, edited by Enrique Dussel, translated by Francis McDonagh, 185–200. Maryknoll, NY: Orbis, 1992.

———. *The Memory of the Christian People*. Maryknoll, NY: Orbis, 1988.

Horner, Norman. *Cross and Crucifix in Mission: A Comparison of Protestant-Roman Catholic Missionary Strategy*. Nashville: Abingdon, 1965.

Hourani, Albert. *A History of the Arab Peoples*. London: Faber & Faber, 2002.

Huneycutt, Yvonne Wood. "New Pioneers Leading the Way in the Final Era." In *Perspectives on the World Christian Movement: A Reader*. 4th ed. Edited by Ralph D. Winter et al., 377–81. Pasadena, CA: William Carey Library, 2009.

Idir: Le Site Officiel. http://www.idir-officiel.fr.

Igreja Universal de do Reino de Deus. http://www.arcauniversal.com/iurd/

International Orality Network. http://ion2008.ning.com/.

Interserve International. http://www.interserve.org.

Itiokia, Neuza. "O Desafio Da Umbanda A Communidade Evangélica O Baixo Espiritismo Brasileiro Implicações Teolóligicas e Pastorais." DMiss diss., Fuller Theological Seminary, 1986.

———. "Third World Missionary Training: Two Brazilian Models." In *Internationalizing Missionary Training*, edited by William D. Taylor, 111–20. Grand Rapids: Baker, 1991.

Iulianelli, Jorge Atililio Silva. "Brazilian Peoples, Brazilian History: Reading Between the Lines." *International Review of Mission* 85.338 (1996) 353–65.

JMM: Missões Mundiais. http://www.jmm.org.br/

Jarrad, Jeffrey. "The Brazilianization of Alcoholics Anonymous." In *The Brazilian Puzzle: Culture on the Borderlands of the Western World*, edited by David J. Hess et al., 209–36. New York: Columbia University Press, 1995.

Jenkins, Philip. *The New Faces of Christianity: Believing the Bible in the Global South*. Oxford: Oxford University Press, 2006.

———. *The Next Christendom: The Coming of Global Christianity*. Oxford: Oxford University Press, 2007.

Johnson, C. Neal. *Business as Mission: A Comprehensive Guide to Theory and Practice*. Downers Grove, IL: InterVarsity, 2010.

Johnson, Neal, and Steve Rundle. "Distinctives and Challenges of Business as Mission." In *Business as Mission: From Impoverished to Empowered*. Evangelical Missiological Series 14. Edited by Mike Barnett et al., 19–36. Pasadena, CA: William Carey Library, 2006.

Johnson, Todd. "World Christian Trends, Update 2007." *Lausanne World Pulse* (2007). Online: http://www.lausanneworldpulse.com/766/08-2007?pg=all.

Bibliography

Johnson, Todd, and Sandra S. K. Lee. "From Western Christianity to Global Christianity." In *Perspectives on the World Christian Movement: A Reader.* 4th ed. Edited by Ralph D. Winter et al., 387–92. Pasadena, CA: William Carey Library, 2009.

Johnstone, Patrick. "Expecting a Harvest." In *Perspectives on the World Christian Movement: A Reader.* 4th ed. Edited by Ralph D. Winter et al., 382–86. Pasadena, CA: William Carey Library, 2009.

———. "Look at the Fields: Survey of the Task." In *From Seed to Fruit: Global Trends, Fruitful Practices, and Emerging Issues Among Muslims,* edited by J. Dudley Woodberry, 3–20. Pasadena, CA: William Carey Library, 2008.

Johnstone, Patrick, and Jason Mandryk. *Operation World: Twenty-First Century Edition.* Waynesboro, GA: Authentic, 2005.

Joshua Project. "Brazil." http://www.joshuaproject.net/countries.php?rog3=BR

Journal of World Christianity. http://www.journalofworldchristianity.org.

Jovens Com Uma Missão. http://www.jocum.org.br/

Kane, J. Herbert. *A Concise History of the Christian World Mission: A Panoramic View of Missions from Pentecost to the Present.* Grand Rapids: Baker, 1982.

Karam, John Tofik. "Distinguishing Arabesques: The Politics and Pleasures of Being Arab in NeoLiberal Brazil." PhD diss., Syracuse University, 2003.

Keyes, Lawrence E. *The Last Age of Missions: A Study of Third World Missionary Societies.* Pasadena, CA: William Carey Library, 1983.

Keyes, Lawrence E., and Larry D. Pate. "Two-Thirds World Missions: The Next 100 years." *Missiology: An International Review* 21.2 (1993) 188–206.

Kidd, Thomas. *American Christians and Islam: Evangelical Culture and Muslims from the Colonial Period to the Age of Terrorism.* Princeton: Princeton University Press, 2009.

———. "Prayer for a Saving Issue." In *The Advent of Evangelicalism: Exploring Historical Continuities,* edited by Michael Haykin et al., 129–45, Nashville: B & H Academic, 2008.

Kirk, J. Andrew. *What is Mission? Theological Explorations.* Minneapolis: Fortress, 2000.

Kottak, Conrad Phillip. "Swimming in Cross-Cultural Currents." In *The Brazilian Puzzle: Culture on the Borderlands of the Western World,* edited by David J. Hess et al., 49–58. New York: Columbia University Press, 1995.

Kraft, Charles. *Anthropology for Christian Witness.* Maryknoll, NY: Orbis, 1996.

———. *Worldview for Christian Witness.* Pasadena, CA: William Carey Library, 2008.

Kraft, Larry W., and Stephanie K. Kraft. "Evangelical Revival vs. Social Reformation: An Analysis of the Growth of the Evangelical Church in Brazil from 1905 to the Present." Unpublished paper, 1995.

———. "Spiritual Warfare in Brazil: A Study Concerning the Interaction Between Culture, the Church, and Evil Supernaturalism in Brazil." Unpublished paper, 1993.

Kumar, Beram. "Majority World Sending." In *Perspectives on the World Christian Movement: A Reader.* 4th ed., Ralph D. Winter and Stephen C. Hawthorne, eds., 369–76. Pasadena, CA: William Carey Library, 2009.

———. "No Longer Emerging." In *Perspectives on the World Christian Movement: A Reader.* 4th ed. Edited by Ralph D. Winter et al., 369–70. Pasadena, CA: William Carey Library, 2009.

L.C. "Mais Missionários Brasileiros Para O Mundo Muçulmano." *Perspectivas No Movimento Cristão Mundial*, edited by Kevin D. Bradford et al., 470–71. São Paulo: Vida Nova, 2009.

Laing, Mark. "The Changing Face of Mission: Implications for the Southern Shift in Christianity." *Missiology: An International Review* 34.2 (2006) 165–77.

Latourette, Kenneth S. *A History of the Expansion of Christianity, Vol. 1–7*. New York: Harper Brothers, 1937–1945.

Le Printemps de Tous Ses Espoirs. http://www.tamazgha.fr

León, Mario A. Rodríguez. "Invasion and Evangelization in the Sixteenth Century." In *The Church in Latin America, 1492–1992*, edited by Enrique Dussel, translated by Paul Burns, 43–54. Maryknoll, NY: Orbis, 1992.

Levine, Robert M., and John J. Crocitti, editors. *The Brazil Reader: History, Culture, Politics*. Durham, NC: Duke University Press, 1999.

Lewis, Bernard. *The Middle East: A Brief History of the Last 2,000 Years*. New York: Scribner, 1995.

Lewis, Donald M. *Christianity Reborn: The Global Expansion of Evangelicalism in the Twentieth Century*. Grand Rapids: Eerdmans, 2004.

Lewis, Jonathan. "Designing the ReMap Project." In *Too Valuable to Lose: Exploring the Causes and Cures of Missionary Attrition*, edited by William D. Taylor, 77–83. Pasadena, CA: William Carey Library, 1997.

Lidório, Ronaldo. *Indígenas do Brasil*. Viçosa, Brazil: Editora Ultimato, 2006.

Limpic, Ted. "As Tribos Indígenas Brasileiras." (2005). Online: http://www.comibam.org/transpar/_menus/por/08jogo-tr.htm

———. "Brazilian Missionaries: How Long Are They Staying?" In *Too Valuable to Lose: Exploring the Causes and Cures of Missionary Attrition*, edited by William D. Taylor, 143–54. Pasadena, CA: William Carey Library, 1997.

———. *Catálago de las Organizaciones Misioneras de Iberoamérica*. Guatemala: COMIBAM Internacional, 2002.

———. "O Movimento Missionário Brasilerio (2005)." (2002). Online: http://www.comibam.org/transpar/_menus/por/09jogo-mb.htm

———. "The Challenge of Brazil's Unreached Peoples." *Global Prayer Digest* (2000). Online: http://www.global-prayer-digest.org/monthdetails/2000/md-March-2000.asp

Lingenfelter, Sherwood, and Marvin K. Mayers. *Ministering Cross-Culturally: An Incarnational Model for Personal Relationships*. Grand Rapids: Baker Academic, 2003.

Liverman, Jeff. "Unplowed Ground: Engaging the Unreached." In *From Seed to Fruit: Global Trends, Fruitful Practices, and Emerging Issues Among Muslims*, edited by J. Dudley Woodberry, 21–22. Pasadena, CA: William Carey Library, 2008.

Livingstone, Greg. "Laborers from the Global South." In *From Seed to Fruit: Global Trends, Fruitful Practices, and Emerging Issues Among Muslims*, edited by J. Dudley Woodberry, 51–66. Pasadena, CA: William Carey Library, 2008.

Londoño, Jesus. "General Report of the III Iberoamerican Missions Congress." *Connections* (2007) 11–13.

Love, Rick. *Muslims, Magic, and the Kingdom of God: Church Planting among Folk Muslims*. Pasadena, CA: William Carey Library, 2000.

———. "Power Encounter among Folk Muslims." In *Encountering the World of Islam*, edited by Keith D. Swartley, 209–15. Waynesboro, GA: Authentic, 2005.

Bibliography

Makdisi, Ussama. *Artillery of Heaven: American Missionaries and the Failed Conversion of the Middle East*. Ithaca, NY: Cornell University Press, 2008.

Mansfield, Peter. *The Arabs*. New York: Penguin, 1978.

Mariz, Cecília. "Religion and Poverty in Brazil." In *New Face of the Church in Latin America: Between Tradition and Change*, edited by Guillermo Cook, 75–81. Maryknoll, NY: Orbis, 1994.

Martin, David. *Tongues of Fire: The Explosion of Protestantism in Latin America*. Oxford: Wiley-Blackwell, 1990.

Matheny, Tim. *Reaching the Arabs: A Felt Need Approach*. Pasadena, CA: William Carey Library, 1981.

McCurry, Don. *The Gospel and Islam: A 1978 Compendium*. Monrovia, CA: MARC, 1979.

McLeod, Karina. "Transformando Atitudes Raciais e Sociais Através do Preparo Missionário." *Capacitando* 8 (1999) 3–23.

Mendonça, Antonio G. "A History of Christianity in Brazil: An Interpretive Essay." *International Review of Mission* 85.338 (1996) 367–87.

Miller, David L. "Mission-Minded Latinos No Longer Staying Home." *Christianity Today* (1997) 70–71.

Miller Donald E., and Tetsunao Yamamori. *Global Pentecostalism: The New Face of Christian Social Engagement*. Berkeley: University of California Press, 2007.

Missão Antioquia. http://www.missaoantioquia.com.

Missão Horizontes. http://www.mhorizontes.org.br/

Moll, Rob. "Missions Incredible." *Christianity Today* (2006). Online: http://www.christianitytoday.com/ct/2006/march/16.28.html.

Mordomo, João. "Bossa Nova, the 'Beautiful Game,' and Business as Mission." *Connections* (2009) 20–21.

———. "The 10/40 Window Moves West." (2000). Online: http://www.strategicnetwork.org/index.php?loc=kb&view=v&id=3428&fby=3c6df0dea370e2e9d9fdeb94b56b8613&

———. "The Brazilian Way: A Brief Study of Brazil and Its People." Unpublished paper, 2005.

———. "Unleashing the Brazilian Missionary Force." In *Business as Mission: From Impoverished to Empowered*. Evangelical Missiological Series 14. Edited by Mike Barnett et al., 219–39. Pasadena, CA: William Carey Library, 2006.

Moreau, A. Scott et al. *Introducing World Missions: A Biblical, Historical, and Practical Survey*. Grand Rapids: Baker Academic, 2004.

Murphy, Isabel. "Etnocentrismo e Racismo no Campo Missionário." *Capacitando* 8 (1999) 41–50.

Murre-van den Berg, Heleen. *New Faith in Ancient Lands: Western Missions in the Nineteenth and Early Twentieth Centuries*. Leiden: Brill, 2006.

Musk, Bill. *Touching the Soul of Islam: Sharing the Gospel in Muslim Cultures*. Oxford: Monarch Books, 1995.

———. *The Unseen Face of Islam: Sharing the Gospel with Ordinary Muslims at Street Level*. Oxford: Monarch Books, 1989.

Naja, Ben. *Releasing Workers of the Eleventh Hour: The Global South and the Remaining Task*. Pasadena, CA: William Carey Library, 2007.

Neill, Stephen. *A History of Christian Missions*. London: Penguin, 1990.

Nida, Eugene. *Customs and Cultures: Anthropology for Christian Missions.* Pasadena, CA: William Carey Library, 1954.
Niebuhr, H. Richard. *Christ and Culture.* New York: Harper & Row, 1951.
Noll, Mark A. *A History of Christianity in the United States and Canada.* Grand Rapids: Eerdmans, 1992.
———. "Evangelical Identity, Power, and Culture in the 'Great' Nineteenth Century." In *Christianity Reborn: the Global Expansion of Evangelicalism in the Twentieth Century,* edited by Donald M. Lewis, 31–51. Grand Rapids: Eerdmans, 2004.
———. *The New Shape of World Christianity: How American Experience Reflects Global Faith.* Downers Grove, IL: InterVarsity, 2009.
Nydell, Margaret K. *Understanding Arabs: A Guide for Modern Times.* 4th ed. Boston: Intercultural, 2006.
OneStory Partnership. http://www.onestory.org.
Oxbrow, Mark. "Recovering Mission: Majority World Mission—A Return to Mission for the Majority." *Lausanne World Pulse* (2009). Online: http://www.lausanneworldpulse.com/themedarticles.php/1071?pg=all.
Padilla, René. "Holistic Mission." In *Dictionary of Mission Theology: Evangelical Foundations,* edited by John Corrie, 157–62. Downers Grove, IL: InterVarsity, 2007.
———. *Mission Between the Times: Essays.* Grand Rapids: Eerdmans, 1985.
———. "New Actors on the Political Scene." In *New Face of the Church in Latin America: Between Tradition and Change,* edited by Guillermo Cook, 82–95. Maryknoll, NY: Orbis, 1994.
———. *The New Face of Evangelicalism: An International Symposium on the Lausanne Covenant.* Downers Grove, IL: InterVarsity, 1976.
Page, Joseph A. *The Brazilians.* Cambridge: Da Capo, 1995.
Parker, Michael. *The Kingdom of Character: The Student Volunteer Movement for Foreign Missions (1886–1926).* Lanham, MD: University Press of America, 1998.
Parshall, Phil, and Julie Parshall. *Lifting the Veil: The World of Muslim Women.* Waynesboro, GA: Gabriel, 2002.
Patai, Raphael. *The Arab Mind.* Rev. ed. New York: Hatherleigh, 2002.
Pate, Larry. *From Every People: A Handbook of Two-Thirds World Missions with Directory/Histories/Analysis.* Monrovia, CA: Marc, 1989.
Pate, Larry D., and Lawrence E. Keyes. "Emerging Missions in a Global Church." *International Bulletin of Missionary Research* 10.4 (1986) 156–61.
Penyak, Lee M., and Walter J. Petry. *Religion in Latin America: A Documentary History.* Maryknoll, NY: Orbis, 2006.
Peterson, Douglas. "A Moral Imagination: Pentecostal Theology—and Praxis—of Social Concern in Latin America." Unpublished paper. Online: http://www.agts.edu/faculty/faculty_publications/klaus/dmiss/moral_imagination.pdf
———. *Not by Might, nor by Power: A Pentecostal Theology of Social Concern in Latin America.* Oxford: Regnum, 1996.
PMI Brasil: Latinos ao Mundo Muçulmano. "Pursued Faith, Proved and Approved." http://www.pmibrasil.org.br/.
PMI USA. http://www.pmi-usa.org.
Prado, Oswaldo. "A New Way of Sending Missionaries: Lessons from Brazil." *Missiology: An International Review* 33.1 (2005) 48–60.

Bibliography

———. "The Brazil Model." (2000). Online: http://www.ad2000.org/gcowe95/prado.html.

Prado, Rosane. "Small Town, Brazil: Heaven and Hell of Personalism." In *The Brazilian Puzzle: Culture on the Borderlands of the Western World*, edited by David J. Hess et al., 59–82. New York: Columbia University Press, 1995.

Ramos, Ariovaldo. "A Bíblia e as Questões Raciais e Sociais." In *Perspectivas no movimento Cristão Mundial*, edited by Kevin D. Bradford et al., 174–80. São Paulo: Vida Nova, 2009.

Ramos, Robson. "Tentmaking and Missions: Reflections on the Brazilian Case." *International Journal of Frontier Missions* 15.1 (1998) 47–52.

Read, William R., and Frank A. Ineson. *Brazil 1980: The Protestant Handbook: The Dynamics of Church Growth in the 1950s and 60s, and the Tremendous Potential for the 70s*. Monrovia, CA: MARC, 1973.

Rembao, Alberto. "The Presence of Protestantism in Latin America." *International Review of Mission* 37.1 (1948) 51–70.

Ribeiro, Darcy. *The Brazilian People: The Formation and Meaning of Brazil*. Translated by Gregory Rabassa. Gainesville, FL: University of Florida Press, 2000.

Robert, Dana L. "Shifting Southward: Global Christianity Since 1945." *International Bulletin of Missionary Research* 24.2 (2000) 50–58.

———. "The Origin of the Student Volunteer Watchword: 'The Evangelization of the World in this Generation.'" *International Bulletin of Missionary Research* 10.4 (1986) 146–49.

Rodriques, José Honório. *The Brazilians: Their Character and Aspirations*. Translated by Ralph Edward Dimmick. Austin: University of Texas Press, 1967.

Rundle, Steven L., and Tom Steffen. *Great Commission Companies: The Emerging Role of Business in Missions*. Downers Grove: InterVarsity, 2003.

Ruiz, David. "COMIBAM as a Process Leading to a Congress." *Connections* (2007) 8–10.

———. "The Two-Thirds World Church." Lausanne Occasional Paper 44. Lausanne Committee for World Evangelization, 2005. Online: http://www.lausanne.org/documents/2004forum/LOP44_IG15.pdf.

Ryad, Umar. "Muslim Response to Missionary Activities in Egypt: With a Special Reference to the Al-Azhar High Corps of 'Ulama' (1925–1935)." In *New Faith in Ancient Lands: Western Missions in the Nineteenth and Early Twentieth Centuries*, edited by Heleen Murre-van den Berg, 287–98. Leiden: Brill, 2006.

Salinas, J. Daniel. "The Great Commission in Latin America." In *The Great Commission: Evangelicals and the History of World Missions*, edited by Martin I. Klauber et al., 134–48. Nashville: B & H Academic, 2008.

Sanneh, Lamin. *Disciples of all Nations: Pillars of World Christianity*. Oxford: Oxford University Press, 2008.

———. *The Changing Face of Christianity: Africa, the West, and the World*. New York: Oxford University Press, 2005.

———. *Whose Religion is Christianity? The Gospel Beyond the West*. Grand Rapids: Eerdmans, 2003.

Saracco, Norberto. "Mission and Missiology from Latin America." In *Global Missiology for the Twenty-First Century: The Iguassu Dialogue*, edited by William D. Taylor, 357–66. Grand Rapids: Baker, 2000.

Sarti, Cynthia A. "Morality and Transgression Among Poor Families." In *The Brazilian Puzzle: Culture on the Borderlands of the Western World*, edited by David J. Hess et al., 114–33. New York: Columbia University Press, 1995.

Scherer, James A., and Stephen B. Bevans, editors. *New Directions in Mission and Evangelization II: Theological Foundations*. Maryknoll, NY: Orbis, 1994.

Schneider, Ronald M. *Brazil: Culture and Politics in a New Industrial Powerhouse*. Boulder: Westview, 1966.

Scott, Carlos. "Latin American Sending." In *Perspectives on the World Christian Movement: A Reader*. 4th ed. Edited by Ralph D. Winter et al., 375. Pasadena, CA: William Carey Library, 2009.

———. "Projections and Challenges for the Ibero American Mission Movement." *Connections* (2007) 17–19.

Scott, Carlos, and Jesus Londoño. "Where is COMIBAM International Heading? Strategic Focal Points." Online: http://www.comibam.org/docs/whereiscomibamheading.pdf.

SEPAL: Servindo aos Pastores e líderes. http://www.lideranca.org/cgi-bin/index.cgi.

Serving in Mission (SIM): New Initiatives in Mission. http://www.sim.org/index.php/category/new-initiatives-in-missions.

Sepúlveda, Juan. "The Pentecostal Movement in Latin America." In *New Face of the Church in Latin America: Between Tradition and Change*, edited by Guillermo Cook, 68–74. Maryknoll, NY: Orbis, 1994.

Sharkey, Heather J. *American Evangelicals in Egypt: Missionary Encounters in an Age of Empire*. Princeton: Princeton University Press, 2008.

Shaw, Perry W. H. "Westerners and Middle Easterners Serving Together: Potential Sources of Misunderstanding." *Evangelical Missions Quarterly* 46.1 (2010) 14–20.

Shenk, Wilbert R. *North American Foreign Missions, 1810–1914: Theology, Theory, and Policy*. Grand Rapids: Eerdmans, 2004.

Silverstein, Leni M. "The Celebration of Our Lord of the Good End: Changing State, Church, and Afro-Brazilian Relations in Bahia." In *The Brazilian Puzzle: Culture on the Borderlands of the Western World*, edited by David J. Hess et al., 134–51. New York: Columbia University Press, 1995.

Sinclair, John H. "Research on Protestantism in Latin America: A Bibliographic Essay." *International Bulletin of Missionary Research* (2002) 110–17.

Smith, Anthony Christopher. "The Essentials of Missiology From the Evangelical Perspective of the 'Fraternidad Teológica Latinoamerica.'" PhD diss., The Southern Baptist Theological Seminary, 1983.

Smith, W. Douglas. "COMIBAM: Takeoff Toward AD 2007." *International Journal of Frontier Missions* 15.1 (1998) 53–55.

Smither, Edward L. "Brazilian Evangelical Missions in the Arab World: History, Culture, Practice, and Theology." PhD diss., University of Pretoria, 2010. Online: http://upetd.up.ac.za/thesis/available/etd-06132011-114730/unrestricted/00front.pdf.

———. "Bridging the 'Excluded Middle': The Relevance of the Spiritual Worldview of Brazilian Missionaries Serving Among Folk Muslims." *Global Missiology* 2.8 (2011). Online: http://ojs.globalmissiology.org/index.php/english/article/view/454.

———. "Missão Integral Applied: Brazilian Models of Holistic Mission in the Arab-Muslim World." Unpublished paper, Evangelical Theological Society national meeting, Atlanta, GA, November 17, 2010.

Bibliography

———. "The Impact of Evangelical Revivals on Global Mission: The Case of North American Evangelicals in Brazil in the Nineteenth and Twentieth Centuries." *Verbum et Ecclesia* (2010). Online: http://www.ve.org.za/index.php/VE/article/view/340/pdf_19.

Souza, Isaac. *De Todas as Tribos*. Viçosa, Brazil: Editora Ultimato, 2003.

Souza, Isaac, and Ronaldo Lidório. *A Questão Indígena: Uma Luta Desigual*. Viçosa, Brazil: Editora Ultimato, 2008.

Speer, Robert E. et al. *Christian Work in South America: Official Report of the Congress on Christian Work in South America at Montevideo, Uruguay, April 1925*. 2 vols. New York: Revell, 1925.

———. *South American Problems*. New York: Student Volunteer Movement for Volunteer Missions, 1912.

Spickard, Paul R., and Kevin M. Cragg. *A Global History of Christians: How Everyday Believers Experienced their World*. Grand Rapids: Baker Academic, 1994.

Stark, Rodney. "Efforts to Christianize Europe, 400–2000." *Journal of Contemporary Religion* 16.1 (2001) 105–23.

Steuernagel, Valdir R. "Learning from Escobar . . . and Beyond." In *Global Missiology for the Twenty-First Century: The Iguassu Dialogue*, edited by William D. Taylor, 123–32. Grand Rapids: Baker, 2000.

———. *Missionary Obedience and Historical Practice: In Search for Models*. São Paulo: ABU Editoria, 1993.

———. "O Evangelho Integral." In *Perspectivas No Movimento Cristão Mundial*, edited by Kevin D. Bradford et al., 184–89. São Paulo: Vida Nova, 2009.

———. "O Menino Nu Na Rampa do Lixo." In *Perspectivas No Movimento Cristão Mundial*, edited by Kevin D. Bradford et al., 611–13. São Paulo: Vida Nova, 2009.

———. "Social Concern and Evangelization: The Journey of the Lausanne Movement." *International Bulletin of Missionary Research* 15.2 (1991) 53–56.

———. "The Theology of Mission in Its Relation to Social Responsibility within the Lausanne Movement." ThD diss., Chicago Lutheran School of Theology, 1988.

———. "To Seek to Transform Unjust Structures of Society." In *Mission in the Twenty-First Century: Exploring the Five Marks of Global Mission*, edited by Andrew F. Walls et al., 62–76. Maryknoll, NY: Orbis, 2008.

Stoll, David. *Is Latin America Turning Protestant? The Politics of Evangelical Growth*. Berkeley: University of California Press, 1991.

Stott, John R. W. "Evangelism and Social Responsibility: An Evangelical Commitment." Lausanne Occasional Paper 21. Lausanne Committee for World Evangelization, 1982. Online: http://www.lausanne.org/all-documents/lop-21.html

Swartley, Keith D., editor. *Encountering the World of Islam*. Waynesboro, GA: Authentic Media, 2005.

Taylor, William D., editor. *Global Missiology for the Twenty-First Century: The Iguassu Dialogue*. Grand Rapids: Baker, 2000.

———. "Global Partnership: Now is the Time." In *Perspectives on the World Christian Movement: A Reader*. 4th ed. Edited by Ralph D. Winter and Stephen C. Hawthorne, 376. Pasadena, CA: William Carey Library, 2009.

———. *Internationalizing Missionary Training: A Global Perspective*. Grand Rapids: Baker, 1991.

———. Editor. *Too Valuable to Lose: Exploring the Causes and Cures of Missionary Attrition*. Pasadena, CA: William Carey Library, 1997.

Tennent, Timothy. *Invitation to World Missions: A Trinitarian Missiology for the Twenty-First Century*. Invitation to Theological Studies Series. Grand Rapids: Kregel, 2010.
"The Iguassu Affirmation." In *Global Missiology for the Twenty-First Century: The Iguassu Dialogue*, edited by William D. Taylor, 15–21. Grand Rapids: Baker, 2000.
The Lausanne Covenant. http://www.lausanne.org/covenant.
"The Whole Gospel from Latin America for All Peoples." In *New Directions in Mission and Evangelization II: Theological Foundations*, edited by James A. Sherer et al., 191–98. Maryknoll, NY: Orbis, 1994.
"The Willowbank Report: Consultation on Gospel and Culture." Lausanne Occasional Paper 2. Lausanne Committee for World Evangelization, 1978. Online: http://www.lausanne.org/all-documents/lop-2.html#1.
Tizon, Al. *Transformation After Lausanne: Radical Evangelical Mission in Global-Local Perspective*. Eugene, OR: Wipf & Stock, 2008.
Tostes, Silas. *Brilhe a Sua Luz Num Mundo em Trevas*. Londrina, Brazil: Editora Descoberta, 2008.
———. *Jihad et o Reino de Deus*. Brazil: Agape Editores, 2002.
———. *O Islamiso e a Cruz de Cristo*. Brazil: ICP Editora, 2001.
———. *O Islamiso e a Trinidade*. Brazil: Agape Editores, 2001.
Tucker, Hugh Clarence. *The Bible in Brazil: Colporteur Experiences*. New York: Revell, 1902.
Tucker, Ruth A. *From Jerusalem to Irian Jaya: A Biographical History of Christian Missions*. Grand Rapids: Zondervan, 2004.
Tunehag, Mats. "A Global Overview of the Business as Mission Movement: Needs and Gaps." *Lausanne World Pulse* (2009). Online: http://www.lausanneworldpulse.com/perspectives.php/1074?pg=all
———. "The Mission of Business: CSR+." *Connections* (2009) 9–12.
———. et al. "Business as Mission." Lausanne Occasional Paper 59. Lausanne Committee for World Evangelization, 2005. Online: http://www.lausanne.org/documents/2004forum/LOP59_IG30.pdf
Ubabolo eAfrica. http://www.ubabalo2010.com/.
Van der Meer, Antônia Leonora. "A Vida dos Missionários que Servem em Situação de Risco." *Capacitando* 9 (2001) 27–37.
———. "O Preparo Social do Missionário para a Realidade do Campo: A Influência Destrutiva dos Preconceitos Sociais e Racias." *Capacitando* 8 (1999) 53–67.
———. "The Scriptures, the Church, and Humanity." In *Global Missiology for the Twenty-First Century: The Iguassu Dialogue*, edited by William D. Taylor, 149–61. Grand Rapids: Baker, 2000.
Van Manen, Max. *Research Lived Experience: Human Science for an Action Sensitive Pedagogy*. Albany: State University of New York Press, 1990.
Vincent, Jon S. *Culture and Customs of Brazil*. Westport, CT: Greenwood, 2003.
Walls, Andrew F. *The Cross-Cultural Process in Christian History: Studies in the Transmission and Appropriation of Faith*. Maryknoll, NY: Orbis, 2002.
———. *The Missionary Movement in Christian History: Studies in Transmission of Faith*. Maryknoll, NY: Orbis, 1996.
Walls, Andrew F., and Cathy Ross. *Mission in the Twenty-First Century: Exploring the Five Marks of Global Mission*. Maryknoll, NY: Orbis, 2008.

Bibliography

Wan, Enoch, and Michael Pocock. *Missions from the Majority World: Progress, Challenges, and Case Studies.* Evangelical Missiological Series 17. Pasadena, CA: William Carey Library, 2009.

Wiebe, James P. "Persistence of Spiritism in Brazil." DMiss diss., Fuller Theological Seminary, 1979.

Willems, Emilio. *Followers of the New Faith: Culture Change and the Rise of Protestantism in Brazil and Chile.* Nashville: Vanderbilt University Press, 1967.

Willis, Avery et al. *Making Disciples of Oral Learners.* Bangalore, India: Sudhindra, 2005.

Winfried Every-Clayton, Joyce. "The Legacy of Robert Reid Kalley." *International Bulletin of Missionary Research* 26.3 (2002) 123–27.

Winter, Ralph D. "Are We Ready for Tomorrow's Kingdom?" In *Perspectives on the World Christian Movement: A Reader.* 4th ed. Edited by Ralph D. Winter and Stephen C. Hawthorne, 393. Pasadena, CA: William Carey Library, 2009.

Winter, Ralph D., and Stephen C. Hawthorne. *Perspectives on the World Christian Movement: A Reader.* 3rd ed. Pasadena, CA: William Carey Library, 1999.

———. *Perspectives on the World Christian Movement: A Reader.* 4th ed. Pasadena, CA: William Carey Library, 2009.

Woodberry, J. Dudley, editor. *From Seed to Fruit: Global Trends, Fruitful Practices, and Emerging Issues Among Muslims.* Pasadena, CA: William Carey Library, 2008.

———. Editor. *Muslims and Christians on the Emmaus Road.* Monrovia, CA: MARC, 1989.

Yale University: Genocide Studies Program. "Sudan." (2010). http://www.yale.edu/gsp/sudan/index.html.

Yin, R. K. *Case Study Research: Design and Method.* Thousand Oaks, CA: SAGE, 2003.

VI Congresso Brasileiro de Missões. http://www.congressobrasileirodemissoes.com/

Index

American Bible Society, 23, 38
Assemblies of God, 31, 50
Baptists (missionaries), 8, 23, 27–29, 32, 36, 40, 50
Baptists (Brazilian), xi, 52, 54–55, 157–58, 160, 170, 179, 184–85, 226
Braga, Erasmo, 24, 39, 41–42, 47, 50, 55
Business as Mission (BAM), 8, 166, 175, 188, 204–5, 210, 227, 241
CCI-Brasil (Crossover Communications International, Brazil), x-xi, 179, 186–89, 204–5, 207, 210, 231, 241, 257
Catholicism; Roman Catholic Church (Brazilian), 20–21, 24–26, 28, 37–39, 42, 44, 48, 52, 78, 117, 140, 146–49, 151–53, 160, 214, 234
Church planting, 2, 13, 23, 27–28, 53, 56, 111, 122–23, 133, 140, 166, 170–71, 175, 184–85, 187–88, 191, 193, 206, 210, 224–26, 232, 241
COMIBAM (Ibero-American Missionary Congress), ix, xi, 1, 6–7, 13, 57–60, 63, 231
Communication (Arab), 96–101
Communication (Brazilian), 101–9
Economics (Arab), 83–86
Economics (Brazilian), 86–90, 164
Evangelicalism (Brazilian), 2, 16, 34–36, 41–52, 60, 63, 81, 191, 212

Evangelical revivals, 35–37, 41, 43, 46, 49, 51, 63
Evangelism, 2, 17, 27, 37, 43, 47, 49, 53, 56, 60, 86, 111, 133–34, 140, 155, 166–77, 181, 184–85, 187–88, 190, 193, 198, 206, 210, 213, 216–17, 223, 226–27, 241
Family (Arab), 110–15
Family (Brazilian), 115–123
Hospitality (Arab), 134–36
Hospitality (Brazilian), 136–40
Humanitarian work, 17, 27, 166, 171–74, 184–86, 188, 191, 199, 210, 221, 226, 228–29, 234, 241
Global South, 1, 5–6, 42, 88, 154
Interserve, 179, 185–86, 205, 210, 226, 241, 261
Islam; Muslims, 1–3, 6–7, 9–10, 12–14, 17, 19, 47, 59, 61–62, 65–66, 69, 71, 74, 77, 80, 81, 84, 86, 90, 92, 100–01, 106–8, 118, 122, 129, 131, 133–34, 139–47, 157–59, 163–70, 173, 177, 179–84, 187–90, 192–95, 205, 208–210, 212, 224–26, 228–30, 232–34, 238–39
Islam (Folk Islam), 142–46, 149, 153–56, 160, 236–37
Jeito; Jeitinho Brasileiro, 128, 150, 161–64, 204
Kalley, Robert Reid, 25–26, 41, 46, 51
Latin American Theological Fellowship (FTL), xi, 6–7, 34, 47, 52, 60, 211, 213–17, 221–22, 230, 236–38

271

Index

Lausanne Movement, 5-7, 32, 34, 55-57, 64, 211, 216-18, 236

Methodists, 22-25, 29, 32, 36, 40, 50, 52

Missão Antioquia (Antioch Mission), 13, 55-56, 155, 179-82, 184, 189, 191-92, 195, 205, 210, 224-26, 231-32, 241, 251, 264

Missão Horizontes (World Horizons), 61-62, 200, 264

missão integral (holistic mission), 17, 47, 166, 186, 212-15, 218-22, 224-30, 238, 242

Pentecostals, 29, 32-34, 48, 53, 63, 140, 156-57, 160, 232, 236-37, 239

PM International, PMI (Muslim Peoples International), x-xi, 13, 61, 178-79, 182-84, 189-90, 195-96, 209-10, 225-26, 231, 241, 251

Presbyterians, 22-23, 26-27, 29, 32, 36, 40, 44, 50, 52, 54-55

Race (Arabs), 74-78

Race (Brazilians), 78-83

Relationships (Arab), 123-26

Relationships (Brazilian), 126-134

Spiritism, 128, 140, 148-62, 236

Sports ministry, 12, 56, 166, 176-78, 181, 184-85, 188, 210, 224, 227, 234, 241

Time (Arab views), 90-92

Time (Brazilians views), 93-96

Women in missions (Brazilian), 81, 108, 121, 139, 172-73, 176, 206-10

www.ingramcontent.com/pod-product-compliance
Lightning Source LLC
Chambersburg PA
CBHW071242230426
43668CB00011B/1553